BISON
BOOKS

Upton Sinclair

California Socialist, Celebrity Intellectual

LAUREN COODLEY

UNIVERSITY OF NEBRASKA PRESS

LINCOLN AND LONDON

"For America," by Jackson Browne
© 1986 Swallow Turn Music.
Used with permission.

Publication of this volume was assisted
by a grant from the Friends of the
University of Nebraska Press.

Library of Congress
Cataloging-in-Publication Data
Coodley, Lauren.
Upton Sinclair: California socialist,
celebrity intellectual / Lauren Coodley.
pages cm
Includes bibliographical references
and index.
ISBN 978-0-8032-4382-8 (cloth: alk. paper)
1. Sinclair, Upton, 1878–1968. 2. Social
reformers—California—Biography.
3. Novelists, American—20th century—
Biography. 4. Social change—United
States—History—20th century.
5. Investigative reporting—United
States—Biography. I. Title.
PS3537.I85Z59 2013
813'.52—dc23   [B]   2013004489

Set in Sabon Next by Laura Wellington.
Designed by Nathan Putens.

The kid I was when I first left home
Was looking for his freedom and a life of his own
But the freedom that he found wasn't quite as sweet
When the truth was known
I have prayed for America
I was made for America
I can't let go till she comes around
Until the land of the free
Is awake and can see
And until her conscience has been found

JACKSON BROWNE, "For America"

6770

Contents

Illustrations

Preface

Upton Sinclair both disrupted and documented his era. The impact of his most famous work, *The Jungle*, would merit him a place in American history had he never written another book. Yet he wrote nearly eighty more, publishing most of them himself. What Sinclair did was both simple and profound: he committed his life to helping people of his era understand how society was run, by whom and for whom. His aim was nothing less than to "bury capitalism under a barrage of facts," as Howard Zinn describes it.[1]

Upton Sinclair introduced himself to American readers in 1906 with the publication of *The Jungle*, his exposé of the meatpacking industry. He was only twenty-five years old. For the next six decades, he would remain an unconventional, often controversial, and always innovative character in American life. He was also a filmmaker, a labor activist, a women's rights advocate, and a health pioneer on the grandest scale—a lifetime surprisingly relevant for twenty-first-century Americans.

A hundred years ago, investigative journalism was just being conceived, and Sinclair's undercover reporting on the conditions in a meatpacking plant may have been its birthing moment. Filmmaking was beginning to change the way stories were told and how people gained access to information. His friends were experimenting with sexual freedom and birth control, but the shadow of alcoholism was beginning to take its toll in the radical community, and Sinclair would record his own assessment of the dangers of alcohol in his novel—and later film—*The Wet Parade*.

Sinclair critiqued institutions ranging from organized religion to journalism to education. These analyses remain surprisingly relevant. The problems with education and with media concentration, which Sinclair identified so presciently in 1920, have become impossible to ignore.

In the first decades of the twentieth century, organized labor was struggling with the question of how to cope with the emergent hegemony of large-scale corporate capitalism. Sinclair responded by organizing a daily picket of Rockefeller headquarters in New York City to show support for embattled coal miners in Colorado. That same year he wrote a science fiction novel, *The Millennium*, which predicted what life would be like in 2013 with startling accuracy.

His activism was as attuned to his time—and as contemporary—as the Occupy Wall Street movement is today. Sinclair demonstrated not only how a writer attempts to change history through literature but also lends his or her personality to the political struggles of the times. A conscious creator of popular history, Sinclair himself starred in one of the first prolabor films, *The Jungle*, in 1914. He wrote *Boston* to document the Sacco-Vanzetti trial; *Oil!* exposed the depredations of the oil industry in California; *Singing Jailbirds* in 1924 recorded the imprisonment of Wobblies in Los Angeles.

In his sixties, Sinclair wrote a series of antifascist spy novels, the World's End series. The series was, as Dieter Herms has noted, "antifascist propaganda entertainingly packaged in the wrappers of popular literature."[2] The books garnered him best-seller status again, and in 1942 he became the oldest author to receive a Pulitzer Prize. This biography incorporates the many lives changed by Upton Sinclair—intellectuals, union leaders, and common citizens, who were impacted by not only the World's End series but by his other novels, his plays, and by his EPIC Campaign for governor of California.

For Sinclair, his books were significant only to the degree that they exerted social influence, as the concluding pages of his autobiography reveal. He asks himself, "Just what do you think you have accomplished in your long lifetime?" and then provides ten answers.[3] All involve social change in which his books were instrumental. Nowhere in this list of accomplishments is there a judgment that any of his novels represent an exclusively literary achievement. Yet, oddly enough, it has been left to literary critics to assess his reputation.

Part of Sinclair's political analysis was that a healthy and sober personal life would make him a more effective agent of change—an early understanding of what would become a radical injunction that the personal is political. Sinclair, writes critic William Bloodworth, made "an unusually vigorous attempt to combine questions of food with political propaganda."[4] As the adult child of an alcoholic, Sinclair was almost alone among his radical colleagues in abstaining from alcohol for political reasons, and his embrace of temperance is one of the many aspects by which contemporary historians might reevaluate him. Temperance crusader Frances Willard's argument that the welfare of women and children suffered from the effects of male alcoholism animated Sinclair's crusade. He was not afraid of identifying with what many at the time considered a women's issue. His mother's temperance beliefs and his father's alcoholism made him a lifelong crusader both for Prohibition and for temperance.

Indeed, Upton Sinclair was a man who challenged conventional masculinity. In that sense, he was ahead of his own time and vitally relevant to ours. He was a radical much influenced by women. His interest in communal living and communal childcare is quite unusual.[5] His reading of Charlotte Perkins Gilman's theories on domestic labor and public life inspired his founding of the utopian colony Helicon Hall in 1906, created to allow both men and women full lives as artists and activists.[6] Yet until now, the available Sinclair criticism has omitted discussion of Sinclair's feminism.

This book includes, for the first time, some of the extraordinary correspondence that Upton Sinclair maintained with many of the leading women activists of the twentieth century. Sinclair exemplifies an alternative identity for male radicals in the first half of the twentieth century; the connections between Sinclair's personal and political decisions can help us make sense of his story. This work will add to the scholarship produced by the two fine biographies published in 2006; I will be citing important insights from Anthony Arthur and Kevin Mattson. All chapter titles in my book are based on works written by Upton Sinclair.

Upton Sinclair's activism spanned half a century, and he wrote book after book in an effort to draw others to his causes. As his son, David, recalled, "My father used to say, I don't know if anyone will care to examine my heart after I die. But if they do, they will find two words there: social justice."[7] Because Sinclair was so passionately engaged in the world around him, his story is inextricably linked to the major struggles that gave his life meaning. It is my hope that this work will offer a fresh understanding of the life and times of Upton Sinclair.

Acknowledgments

Over the past fifteen years, I became acquainted with a fascinating group of Sinclair scholars, who generously shared their work with me. I am profoundly grateful to Ron Gottesman, John Ahouse, and to Robert Hahn for their enthusiasm, their kindness, and their tremendous body of knowledge.

Along the way to this biography, I was able to edit a collection of Sinclair's writings in and about California. I thank Malcolm Margolin for bringing *Land of Orange Groves and Jails* to fruition, and the Mesa Writers Refuge for offering me the opportunity to begin my book there. I thank the Lilly Library for the Everett Helm Fellowship, which allowed me to spend time in the archives, and library staff Cherry Williams and Zach Downey for their generous assistance in this project. For their constant encouragement, I thank Harvey Schwartz, Lisa Rubens, Cita Cook, Nils McCune, Gregg Coodley, Anita Catlin, Stephanie Grohs, and Cathy Mathews.

My deepest appreciation to Karen Brown, Paula Amen Judah, Caitlin Vega, and Steve Hiatt, who each provided brilliant editorial insights. Lauren Ellsworth aided mightily as a research assistant. She, and later Hillary Schwartz, handled all technical aspects of production with grace and humor. I offer a most fervent thanks to Matt Bokovoy and the University of Nebraska Press for their interest in my work. To all of you who kept faith with me in the

Sinclair project over these many years: here it is. This book is dedicated to the two Sinclair biographers, Dieter Herms and Sachiko Nakada, whose work remains to be translated into English, and to the "common reader" whose devotion paved the way for the Sinclair scholarship of today, Edward Allatt.

Danke
Arigatō
Thank you

UPTON SINCLAIR

CHAPTER ONE

Southern Gentleman Drank
[1878–1892]

Whiskey in its multiple forms—mint juleps, toddies, hot Scotches, eggnogs, punch—was the most conspicuous single fact in my boyhood. I saw it and smelled it and heard it everywhere I turned, but I never tasted it.

UPTON SINCLAIR, 1962

In 1838 twenty-year-old Frederick Douglass quietly slipped away from the shipyards of Baltimore toward a life of freedom.[1] His autobiographical account of his youth as a slave in Maryland electrified the abolitionist movement of the Northern states. Douglass developed an original and devastating style as an orator, and his fervent calls for racial justice challenged and molded the nation's conscience. In the century to follow, another famous son of this once slave-owning city, Upton Sinclair—with his fierce commitment to truth telling—would set out to educate and provoke the American people, and later, his international readers, to defend these ideals of equality. Baltimore's rich history, poised between North and south throughout the tumultuous period of the Civil War and its aftermath, inspired the passions of both Douglass and Sinclair to seek justice across lines of gender, class, and race.

Maryland had been a slave state, but its proximity to the District of Columbia prevented it from ever joining the Confederacy, despite substantial support for the South among its white citizens. In the presidential election of 1860, Abraham Lincoln received just over one thousand votes, out of thirty thousand cast. Southern Rights Democrats controlled the state legislature, and only the refusal of Maryland's pro-Union governor Thomas Hicks to call the legislature into session prevented them from forming an alliance with the Confederacy. Baltimore's mayor barely supported the Union, and its police chief was a Confederate sympathizer. Countless buildings and homes boldly flew the Confederate flag, when the Sixth Massachusetts Regiment—the first fully equipped unit to respond to Lincoln's call for troops—entered Baltimore on its way to Washington on April 19, 1861.

There was no rail line through Baltimore, so the troops had to cross the city on foot to board a train for the capital. A mob surrounded the soldiers and attacked the rear companies of the regiment with bricks, paving stones, and pistols. A few soldiers opened fire. Four soldiers and twelve citizens of Baltimore died in the skirmish, the first combat deaths of more than seven hundred thousand during the next four years.

Within four weeks of the clash, President Lincoln had established martial law in Maryland, suspended habeas corpus, and sent troops to occupy the city, ending any chance that the state would join the Confederacy. Yet support for the Confederacy remained high among the white population. In 1862 the *Savannah Republican* reported that high-society ladies of Baltimore appeared daily in the streets in secession colors of red and white. Despite Maryland's uncertain support for the Union, Baltimore seemed poised to become an important economic center as the Civil War wound to a close.

In September 1865 Frederick Douglass made a return to Baltimore, despite warnings that he could be assassinated. There he delivered the inaugural speech of the Douglass Institute, which would go on to become the political heart of the city's African American community for the next twenty-five years. In his speech Douglass evoked a better America, telling his audience that "the establishment of an institute bearing my name by the colored people in the city of my boyhood, so soon after the act of emancipation in the state, looms before me as a first grand indication of progress."[2]

Reconstruction brought industrial power and its consequences to Maryland. Baltimore became known as the New York of the South, a destination for both European immigrants and freed slaves. Chesapeake Bay tobacco was made into cigars and exported to Europe by H. L. Mencken's grandfather and other German immigrants. The Baltimore and Ohio Railroad, one of the country's first railroads, linked the city with western Maryland and the states beyond. City mills, powered by rivers and streams known as "falls," produced flour and meal, while clothing, cotton goods, leather, machinery, footwear, canned oysters, pork, beef, lumber, furniture, and liquors flowed from its factories.

Rural families driven out by the rising power of banks and railroads were drawn to Baltimore's diverse economy. Its neighborhoods were compact, with red brick rows lining an irregular street pattern. Poor families crowded into cellars and basements, where water was often contaminated and air circulation was poor. As capitalist development changed the landscape, Baltimore's contradictory growth became plain. It had the "attractive dirt of a fishing town, the nightmare horizons of a great industrial town," as Christina Stead put it.[3] Raw sewage ran through hot streets, and infectious diseases killed increasing numbers of poor children in Baltimore.[4]

Within a decade, the contradictions of Reconstruction had brought class conflict to a head. The economic crash of 1873 began what was known at the time as the "Great Depression." Unemployment skyrocketed as construction came to a standstill across the nation. In 1878 railroad workers called a strike in a dozen cities, including at the Baltimore and Ohio Railroad. The strike began with wage cuts on the railroads, where brakemen were making $1.76 for a twelve-hour day, and where loss of hands, feet, and fingers was routine.

In Baltimore, thousands of strike sympathizers surrounded the armory of the National Guard. The crowd hurled rocks, and the soldiers came out, firing. At one point fifteen thousand people surrounded the depot, setting fire to three passenger cars and a locomotive. President Hayes sent federal troops to smash the strike. When the strikes were over, a hundred people had died, a thousand people were in jail, and one hundred thousand workers experienced their first labor action.

On September 20, 1878, exactly forty years after Frederick Douglass escaped from Baltimore, a Southern railroad baron's daughter, Priscilla Harden Sinclair, gave birth in the row house where she lived with her husband at 417 North Charles Street. The child, a boy, was named for his father, Upton Sinclair, a whiskey wholesaler. Within twenty-five years, this young man would change the course of American history.

The Sinclair family of Virginia had served in the navy since the country began. Great-grandfather Arthur Sinclair served as a midshipman on the U.S. frigate *Constellation* in 1798.[5] He commanded the U.S. frigate *Argus* during the War of 1812, fought not only to expel the British but also to expand America's borders into Florida, Canada, and Indian territories. Upton Sinclair's grandfather, Arthur Sinclair II, was also a career officer in the navy and commanded one of the vessels in Admiral Perry's fleet that opened up Japan.[6]

Grandfather Sinclair had been a Confederate blockade runner, one of the most romanticized figures of the war, who would slip past fleets of heavily armed Union ships at night to bring food and armaments to Southern cities. It was a risky business, and a London newspaper reported his death after the *Leila* sailed from London in 1865 with seven hundred tons of coal and iron. In a raging storm, the boat apparently sank.[7] Nearly five months later, a fisherman found Commander Sinclair's body ten miles out to sea wrapped in his nets. The *Fleetwood Chronicle* reported that "his skeletal remains were still clothed, even to his cravat held in place by a gold and agate pin. His overcoat was still buttoned up and he had retained his watch in his breast pocket."[8] The pocket watch was stopped at 4:10—approximately the time the *Leila* sank, which led to the identification of the body.[9]

Upton Sinclair's father was born in the 1850s in Norfolk, Virginia, and his parents had named him for the Episcopal minister Upton Beall. The once prominent Sinclair family emerged destitute from the Civil War, and Sinclair's father abandoned the family's naval tradition in favor of a business career. The liquor trade thrived in the ruined South, so Upton Beall Sinclair entered the wholesale liquor business, and drinking became a key element of the Sinclair family legacy. Upton Beall Sinclair's sales trips took him to Baltimore, a city where newly impoverished Southerners often traveled, looking for a new start in life.

Here Upton Beall Sinclair met and courted Priscilla Harden, who was born into privilege as the daughter of John S. Harden, the secretary and treasurer of the Western Maryland Railroad. The Harden family emerged from the Civil War with its fortune intact, in stark contrast to the Sinclairs. Upton Beall Sinclair married Priscilla Harden shortly before the birth of their son.

Floyd Dell, an early biographer, wrote that Upton Beall Sinclair "worshipped his only son." Although he was unable to provide for his family, "he could at least teach his son to be a kind and chivalrous Southern gentleman."[10] Upton Sinclair often described his father in fascinated detail, a reminder that an absent or unavailable parent is often the more intriguing one to a child. His father was proud of his clothing and interested in food. "What was the size and flavor of Blue Point oysters as compared to Lynnhaven Bays? Why was it impossible to obtain properly cooked food north of Baltimore? Would the straw hats of next season have high or low brims?"[11] Sinclair remembered these kinds of preoccupations.

Well-dressed or not, Sinclair recalled, "everywhere he went he had to have a drink before the deal was made and then they celebrated by another drink after the deal was made."[12] His father's drinking was responsible for the dismal living conditions of the family: "I remember boarding-house and lodging-house rooms. We never had but one room at a time, and I slept on a sofa or crossways at the foot of my parent's bed."[13]

Wendy Gamber's research on American boardinghouses reveals that after the Civil War, "home" represented far more than merely a household. It was characterized as a refuge from the world, a site where relations between the sexes were regulated, and a location of moral guidance. Gamber notes that, in contrast, "in boarding-houses women washed, cleaned, and cooked for money, services that elsewhere they presumably provided out of love."[14] Thus the boardinghouse, a place where strangers of both sexes might meet, represented the very antithesis of a respectable home.

Rather than engaging in naval battles, as paternal family tradition expected, Upton Sinclair would launch a different kind of battle against the inequities of capitalism. As a child, the first injustices he noticed were in the boardinghouse. Wendy Gamber writes that boardinghouse food—"immortalized in innumerable stories, jokes, and even songs—inspired a colorful folklore and equally color-ful vocabulary: 'hirsute butter,' 'damaged coffee,' 'ancient bread,' 'azure milk,' 'antediluvian pies.'"[15] Fortunately for Priscilla Harden Sinclair, she could find solace in the temperance movement and the company of other wives and daughters of alcoholics, women who could neither vote nor earn a living in America at the turn of the century.

Scholars who are rethinking the caricature of temperance advo-cates acknowledge how these women—and men—transformed personal tragedies into a vibrant political movement.[16] After the Civil War, temperance—not suffrage—became the most powerful women's social movement, rising from the desperation to protect family members from the poverty and frequent abuse that was perceived to be caused by alcohol. Lack of clean water meant that weak beer was a healthy alternative for much of the population. Men bonded over beer; masculinity was constructed through a status ritual based on European customs of hospitality.[17] Beyond that, since the sixteenth century, men had engaged in a wave of overindulgence in distilled spirits.

Just prior to her marriage, Priscilla would have heard of the Temperance Crusade of 1873–74. The Crusaders marched from one saloon and bar to the other; they prayed, sang, argued, and begged liquor dealers to abandon their business. Suffragists such as Miriam M. Cole noted with approval the Crusaders' unconventionality: "A woman knocking out the head of a whiskey barrel with an axe, to the tune of *Old Hundred*, is not the ideal woman sitting on the sofa, dining on strawberries and cream."[18] The Crusade, which brought thousands of new women to activism, was the first large-scale temperance movement created specifically by and for women.[19]

The Crusade's successor organization, the Women's Christian Temperance Union (WCTU), solidified women's leadership in the temperance movement. WCTU president Frances Willard envisioned temperance as a movement that would treat women's personal problems seriously and develop a public and political solution for them. By enlisting thousands of women into temperance activity, Willard would also educate them about the urgency of prison reform, child labor laws, and woman suffrage.[20] We know that Priscilla Harden Sinclair marched for temperance, and that she brought her young son to march alongside her. Mrs. Sinclair represented the heart of the temperance army: white, Protestant, born into a family of industrialists.[21] Mrs. Sinclair may have spoken to her son about the many concerns of the WCTU, causes he would come to champion and fight for once grown. Sinclair said, "I gave my word of honor to my mother that I would never touch a drop of liquor in my life."[22] Like other Southern women who had seen the ravages of alcohol among their men, Priscilla had brought up her son to hate liquor. She also abstained from tea and coffee.

Sinclair recounts a typical scene in his home when "Father would hide the money when he came in late, and then in the morning he would forget where he had hidden it, and there would be searching under mattresses and carpets, and inside the lining of his clothing."[23] Wendy Gamber explains that "visiting" other relatives was a necessary economic strategy for boarders who were unable to pay rent on a regular basis, as well as "a necessity for keeping up appearances."[24] When the Sinclairs had no money to pay rent, mother and son sought refuge in the home of her father. Unlike other families where the daughter marries down and the family quietly provides a sinecure for her husband, Priscilla's family must have actively disapproved the marriage and doubted her ability to retain any funds they might give her; indeed, she was a constant victim of the economic chaos created by her husband's alcoholism.

Grandfather Harden, who by the 1880s had become president of the Western Maryland Railroad, was thus a source of stability in their lives. As a deacon of the Methodist Church, he did not drink or serve alcohol. Harden and his wife, Emma, lived at 2010 Maryland Avenue in a four-story brick house with white marble steps rising to the front door. A one-horse streetcar would roll by the front door every morning, taking Grandfather to his office and bringing him home for lunch each day. Upton was given a set of blocks with pictures and letters on them: "I taught myself to read, little by little, to pick out words from those blocks." He adds, "After that I didn't want to do anything but read."[25] He especially loved *Gulliver's Travels* and *Hans Brinker and the Silver Skates*.

Christina Hardyment has studied childrearing culture in English and American middle-class homes during this period. Parents like Priscilla Sinclair embraced fairy tales for their children, images believed to be rooted in ancient European culture. Hardyment observed that "walks in all weathers were the rule, and the windows of the nursery were to be kept open as much as possible."[26] Upton was shaped by these new ideas about child rearing. Fairy tales, with their moral clarity, would set the tone for many of his novels, and his love of outdoor life was undoubtedly made possible by the flinging open of the nursery windows—although his nursery was also his parents' bedroom.

The boy would often choose a book from his grandfather's library and set out for Druid Hill Park to read under the trees. The park, built in 1860, held a zoo, botanical gardens, and a lake for boating. Druid Hill Park's conservatory, where Upton could enjoy exotic plants, was designed by George Frederick, architect of Baltimore City Hall. Henry Adams's memoir describes Baltimore as the child Upton Sinclair may have experienced it: "The brooding heat of the profligate vegetation; the cool charm of the running water; the terrific splendor of the June thunder-gust in the deep and solitary woods, were all sensual, animal, elemental."[27]

The freedom to be alone in nature was one of the salvations of Sinclair's childhood. Books were clearly the other: "While arguments between my father and my mother were going on, I was with Gulliver in Lilliput, or on my way to the Celestial City with Christian, or in the shop with the little tailor who killed 'seven at one blow.'"[28] Writing followed reading, and Upton Sinclair composed his first story at age five, called "The Story of a Pin." "This pin fell into the garbage, and I remember I caused great glee because I spelled it 'gobbage.' The garbage was fed to a pig and the pig was made into sausage, and the pin appeared in the sausage." Decades later, his interviewer, Ron Gottesman, suggested to him, "Kind of anticipating *The Jungle* in that first story?" Surprised, Sinclair answered that he "hadn't thought of that aspect of it."[29]

Back at his grandfather's house on Maryland Avenue, Upton remembered watching the terrapins lumber into the backyard, where a servant would spear them through the heads with a fork and decapitate them with a butcher knife.[30] He described his grandfather "carving unending quantities of chickens, ducks, turkeys, and hams," but could not recall a single word he spoke.[31] He did remember the warmth of his Irish grandmother who "made delightful ginger cookies, played on the piano, and sang little tunes to which I danced."[32]

But the boy absorbed more than the rich food and the music. One night when he was three years old, his mother's brother, Uncle

1. Upton Sinclair at eight years old, in 1886. Upton Sinclair was born on September 20, 1878, in Baltimore, Maryland, where he grew up in a series of boardinghouses. Courtesy of the Lilly Library, Indiana University, Bloomington.

Harry, was drinking and his grandfather was trying to keep him from going out. They had a violent argument. Sinclair comments: "Uncle Harry had been an athlete, handsome, gay, with a hardy laugh. Then at the age of forty, Uncle Harry bought himself a pistol, sat on a bench in Central Park, and put a bullet through his head."[33] Thus his mother suffered the alcoholism not only of her husband, but of her brother as well. Although Sinclair's lifelong dedication to temperance has puzzled and amused his biographers, it makes perfect sense in light of his formative childhood experiences with alcoholism and temperance.

Upton Sinclair grew up as an only child, and there would be no other children in the Sinclair family. Abstinence was the common method used by women of Priscilla Sinclair's class to prevent pregnancy and avoid childbirth, which were often life-threatening. In the nineteenth century, as in all previous centuries, many husbands would outlive two, three, or four wives when women died in childbirth. Certainly, the Sinclairs were also constrained in their intimate life by the presence of a child in the bedroom.

The theories of Darwin, as articulated in the women's magazines she read, may have influenced Priscilla to have only one child.[34] In the work of Sir Frances Galton, a Social Darwinist, Mrs. Sinclair would have read about the importance of preventing "inferior specimens of humanity from transmitting their vices or diseases, their intellectual or physical weaknesses."[35] Knowing the propensity for alcoholism on both sides of the family, she surely had reason to fear this genetic inheritance.

Pricilla Sinclair found comfort in her faith; she took Upton with her to church every Sunday, grooming her precocious child to become a bishop. The boy's father dreamed a different future for his son. Upton Beall Sinclair thought that his son resembled his own father, Arthur Sinclair II, and hoped the boy would grow up to pursue a successful naval career. Floyd Dell imagined him as "a slight, straight, grizzled captain, something of a martinet, unquestionably brave, not very popular, a little aloof, doing his duty, carrying on the family traditions."[36] While trying to earn enough money for a room apart from that of his parents, Sinclair would incorporate his father's fascination with the navy into his first published stories.

In the summers, Upton and his mother lodged in various dilapidated old hot springs in the South; he grew up surrounded by what Kevin Mattson aptly describes as "the bizarre and fantastic side of southern culture."[37] He recalled a place called Jett's, which they traveled to in a bumpy stagecoach: "The members of that household were pale ghosts, and we discovered that they were users of drugs. There was an idiot boy who worked in the yard, and gobbled his food out of a tin plate, like a dog."[38] Later he told Floyd Dell that he could write a Dickensian novel about it "if I thought the old South was worth muckraking."[39] His only novel about the South would be a Civil War novel, *Manassas*, set just before his birth.

At times, rather than going to Grandfather Harden's, Upton and his mother sheltered at her sister's opulent home. Pricilla Harden's sister, Maria, married John Randolph Bland, one of the richest men in Baltimore, who became the president of the powerful United States Fidelity and Guarantee Company. The family business was housed in a seven-story building occupying a quarter of a city block in Baltimore.

During his childhood and adolescence, Upton returned again and again to this home on Howard Street. There was a bay window in one of the parlors, with a sofa in front of it. He would climb into the window, hide behind the sofa, and read picture books. He also looked at the *Christian Herald*, with its pictures of young men wasted by addiction. There in Uncle Bland's brick house, the child watched adults at countless dances and parties. Biographer Anthony Arthur suggests that the Bland world was like the one Edith Wharton describes in *The House of Mirth*, published in 1905, a year before *The Jungle*. Sinclair recalled, "I breathed that atmosphere of pride and scorn, of values based on material possessions. . . . I do not know why I came to hate it, but I know I did hate it from my earliest days."[40]

Arthur notes that Sinclair's moral vision was very similar to that of Wharton, but that "unlike her he would conclude that societal flaws were economic in origin, and therefore curable."[41] Thorstein Veblen wrote *The Theory of the Leisure Class* (published in 1889) based on his experiences in Baltimore. While in graduate school at John Hopkins University, Veblen had boarded with a family of impoverished aristocrats who labored to maintain the style of their antebellum past. "Their servants came cheap, but wine and show did not. That host family spent far more on style at table than they ever collected in board money."[42]

Staying with his cousins offered Upton Sinclair opportunities to explore late nineteenth-century urban life. When both were older, Sinclair wrote to his cousin Howard Bland, reminiscing about their childhood journeys to dime museums. For many children who did not attend school, the dime museums, established by P. T. Barnum, were an important source of information about the social issues of the second half of the nineteenth century.[43] These museums taught about temperance and evolution, using lively exhibits such as Barnum's "half-man-half-monkey" displays. Walking out of the dime museum, his head whirling with these images, the child Upton Sinclair would also have observed European immigrants, like those he would profile in *The Jungle*, men, women, and children who worked in the new Baltimore factories turning out canned tomatoes, pianos, straw hats, and umbrellas.

When Upton was ten, the Sinclairs decided to move to New York City, where his father would try to sell hats instead of whiskey. They gave their son the option of staying behind with his wealthy relatives. Loyal to his parents, Upton went with them to New York, a decision that would change the course of his life. Had his family stayed in Baltimore, Sinclair would never have been introduced to the publishers, the periodicals, or the disruption of the fixed social hierarchy of the South.

Gotham's Expanding Horizons

What a time to be in New York City! In 1886 the Statue of Liberty was unveiled. In 1887 electric streetcars began to carry passengers across the city. By 1890 New York's mass transit system, with both elevated and subterranean railroads, boasted a greater total mileage than London's. In 1888 New York hosted its first tickertape parade, witnessed by new arrival Upton Sinclair. In 1892 Ellis Island was constructed as the entry point for hundreds of thousands of European immigrants each year. In 1895, when Sinclair was seventeen, New York public libraries opened for the first time, allowing him to revel in books not found at home.

But New York's dynamism had a price. By the time the family arrived, ten thousand abandoned or orphaned children lived on the streets of New York. Death from starvation or preventable diseases was routine—penicillin, antibiotics, and sulfa had not been discovered. Many of these children begged. Others, singly or in gangs, stole to stay alive. During the 1890s, the most notorious gang in New York City was the Five Points Gang, named for its home turf in the Five Points (Bowery) section of Lower Manhattan, close to where the Sinclairs lived.[44] Jack Finney describes the streets, full of "carriages of black, maroon, green, brown, some shabby, some elegant and glinting with glass and polish," which "trotted, lumbered, or rattled over the stones."[45] Delivery wagons, loaded with barrels, crates, and sacks, were pulled by teams of enormous steam-breathing dray horses.

The Sinclair family moved frequently, usually living in boarding houses, on West Sixty-Fifth, West Ninety-Sixth, and West 126th Streets, among others. As New York City's population expanded, more and more establishments offered room and board to rural migrants, European newcomers, and assorted people who could not or would not live in "homes." Wendy Gamber's survey of newspaper advertisements reveal that "there was indeed a boardinghouse for everyone: Swedenborgians, tailors, amateur musicians, 'respectable

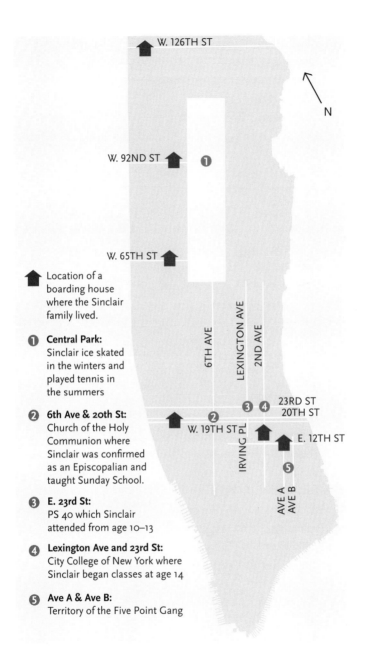

W. 126TH ST

N

W. 92ND ST ① ①

W. 65TH ST

6TH AVE

LEXINGTON AVE

2ND AVE

↑ Location of a
boarding house
where the Sinclair
family lived.

① **Central Park:**
Sinclair ice skated
in the winters and
played tennis in
the summers

② **6th Ave & 20th St:**
Church of the Holy
Communion where
Sinclair was confirmed
as an Episcopalian and
taught Sunday School.

③ **E. 23rd St:**
PS 40 which Sinclair
attended from age 10–13

④ **Lexington Ave and 23rd St:**
City College of New York where
Sinclair began classes at age 14

⑤ **Ave A & Ave B:**
Territory of the Five Point Gang

③ ④ 23RD ST
20TH ST

② W. 19TH ST

IRVING PL

E. 12TH ST

⑤

AVE A
AVE B

2. Upton Sinclair's Manhattan. Courtesy of Molly Roy.

colored people,' Southerners, teetotalers, and disciples of the food reformer Sylvester Graham."[46] Roughly between a third and a half of nineteenth-century urban residents either took in boarders or were boarders themselves.

The Sinclair family lived longest at the Hotel Weisiger on West Nineteenth Street, a rundown establishment where Colonel Weisiger hosted a rag-tag assortment of destitute Confederate sympathizers. Sinclair remembered how he and other boys killed flies on the bald heads of the men, coaxed tea cake from the kitchen, and pulled the pigtails of the little girls playing dolls in the parlor. He comments wryly, "One of these little girls, with whom I quarreled most of the time, was destined to grow up and become my first wife; and our married life resembled our childhood."[47] In *Love's Pilgrimage*, Sinclair's autobiographical novel, he describes a summer that their two families spent together in the country, where he tried to impress little Meta by killing squirrels and chipmunks with a slingshot. Next he began raising young robins and crows, in order to keep her busy feeding them the fish that he caught.[48]

Sinclair remembered the Weisiger house as a treasure trove of "comedies and tragedies, jealousies and greeds, and spites."[49] Some evenings, residents played card games like Patience, or they read aloud from *Frank Leslie's Illustrated Newspaper*. The publication provided illustrations—first using woodcuts and daguerreotypes, then more advanced forms of photography—of conflicts ranging from John Brown's raid at Harpers Ferry through the Spanish-American War. Its cover featured pictures of manly soldiers and epic battles. In the evenings, someone played the organ and the residents sang songs like "Maryland, My Maryland!" or "The Southrons' Chaunt of Defiance." These former Confederate officers continued to celebrate the military pageantry and heroism of the Civil War, teaching the children that theirs had been a sacred cause.[50] And always, the old men drank.

In New York, Sinclair was often sent to hunt down his father in saloons. In *Love's Pilgrimage*, he paints the scene: "It was the Highway of Lost Men ... their faces ... gaunt with misery, or bloated with disease.... The boy sprang forward with a cry: 'Father!' And a man ... fell upon his shoulder, sobbing, 'My son!'"[51] From such experiences, Sinclair, like other children of alcoholics, grew up hating saloons, bars, and all they represented. Sinclair's friend, poet and socialist politician Sam DeWitt, described his own childhood in a New York tenement that contained a bordello. At the age of five, he had played "brothel" with the neighbor children, "as other children play hide and seek, and quarreling over whose turn it was to be the madam."[52]

Sinclair, steeped in naval history and fairy tales in Baltimore, met children like DeWitt when he finally attended a public school in 1888: "Second Avenue was especially thrilling because the 'gangs' came out from Avenue A and Avenue B like Sioux or Pawnees in war paint, and well-dressed little boys had to fly for their lives."[53] The New York neighborhoods presented a startling contrast to the sleepy streets of Baltimore, but Priscilla Sinclair still had grand hopes to preserve gentility in her son. She took him to a church with a wealthy congregation, the Episcopal Church of Holy Communion, on Sixth Avenue and Twentieth Street. This church, like the newly completed Central Park, was within walking distance of the family's various homes.

Central Park had been designed by Calvert Vaux and Frederick Law Olmstead to connect rich and poor, Irish immigrants and Episcopalian aristocrats. In the park, Upton Sinclair played tennis in summer. He ice-skated in the winter on homemade skates, blades attached to wood platforms fitted with leather straps. With friends from the neighborhood, he biked all over the city: down Broadway, across the Brooklyn Bridge, through Prospect Park, and all the way out to Coney Island.

On the streets of New York City, Upton Sinclair's education in politics began. He recalled the election when Harrison defeated Cleveland; "our torch light paraders, who had been hoping to celebrate a Democratic triumph, had to change their marching slogan at the last minute . . . the year was 1888 and my age was ten."[54] The boy sped through eight grammar-school grades in two years. Although academically qualified to start high school when he was twelve, he was not allowed to enroll because he was too young. So at thirteen, he attended a second year of eighth grade. Here he began to learn American history from a new perspective. Floyd Dell notes: "His hatred of the sham aristocracy of the South had made him thrill to the lessons of democracy."[55] Sinclair would always be a fervent believer in civic participation and in mass education.

During his father's many absences, or the times when they were evicted from a boardinghouse, the boy was often sent back to the comforts of Baltimore. At fourteen, he wrote his mother: "I will spend my money for ball & torpedoes & firecrackers. . . . Uncle B. took Howard & me to a Turkish bath. We all went into the plunge . . . had lots of fun."[56] When visiting Baltimore, Upton discovered sets of Milton and Shakespeare in his uncle's library. He found in Hamlet a figure to shine in his imagination alongside that of Jesus. In 1892 he was confirmed in the Episcopal Church, surely strengthening Mrs. Sinclair's hope that he would indeed become a bishop.

When Upton Sinclair graduated, he donated his collection of several hundred books to the school, which became its library. During his final year of high school, a friend named Simon Stern, from his neighborhood, wrote a story that was printed in a monthly magazine published by a Hebrew orphanage. Sinclair decided to try his own hand. He used his hobby of hand-raising young birds: "I put one of these birds into an adventure, making it serve to prove the innocence of a colored boy accused of arson."[57] Just before turning fourteen, Upton Sinclair sold the story for twenty-five dollars to the *Argosy*, the most popular men's adventure magazine at the time. It was the beginning of his life as a writer.

CHAPTER TWO

Making Real Men of Our Boys

[1893–1904]

When he uttered disrespectful opinions concerning Vanderbilts and respectability in general, he passed out of the range of parental comprehension.

FLOYD DELL, 1930

By the 1890s the Sinclairs had managed to rent a tiny apartment on West Sixty-Fifth Street where they could cook their own meals. On a typical day Upton might stop at the neighborhood market on the way home. He would hand a grocery boy a pencil-written order, along with a nickel tip. The meat was wrapped, laid on top of a box of ice, and delivered to his family by sled the next day. Now that they were out of the boardinghouse, he hoped to recover from the stomach ailments that had bothered him since childhood. Although they were still poor, his family's temporary stability in their own apartment must have been a great comfort. Demonstrating his happiness when the family seemed to be thriving, he wrote that "Mother did the cooking and Father would put an apron over his little paunch and wash the dishes; there was much family laughter and father kissed the cook."[1]

Learning Manhood

Although he was technically too young at fourteen, Upton Sinclair had managed to gain entrance to the College of the City of New York (CCNY) in 1892. In those years when private colleges were restricted by race and religion, thousands of brilliant individuals attended City College because they had no other option, although until 1929 City College was an all-male institution. Its academic excellence and its reputation as a school for the working class earned it the reputation of the poor man's Harvard.[2] Students attended classes in the old brick building at Twenty-Third Street and Lexington Avenue. Later Sinclair described the college as "not very good, but convenient for the son of a straw-hat salesman addicted to 'sprees'... we trooped from one classroom to another and learned by rote what our bored instructors laid out for us."[3] College curriculum in 1900 was not designed to be relevant to young people's lives.[4] Certainly for Upton Sinclair, his college classes did nothing to explain his father's alcoholism or what he called the "Cinderella-like" quality of his upbringing.

The teachers at CCNY were all appointed by the Tammany political machine that controlled city government, and thus were all Catholic. In the late nineteenth century, Tammany became a central locus of Irish politics in New York City. In a time before the existence of social welfare programs, Tammany politicians provided aid to the indigent. Irish Catholic immigrants in particular were intensely loyal to Tammany. Sinclair recalled: "It was the first time I had ever met Catholics, and I found them kindly but set in dogma, and as much given to propaganda as I myself was destined to become."[5] When Sinclair found that a course didn't interest him, he dropped it. About his history class, he writes ironically that he could not understand why he had to memorize "the names of so many kings and dukes and generals, and the dates when they had slaughtered so many human beings."[6] In his own novels, the question of why such slaughters occurred, rather than their dates, would be explored.

Upton Sinclair found most of his inspiration on his own, outside of the classroom. When he picked up a volume of Emerson's *Essays*, he found "in this shrewd and practical nobility" what he was looking for.[7] During this period, he also sought guidance from the Reverend William Wilmerding Moir from the Church of Holy Communion. Moir mentored a group of young men, who met at Reverend Moir's home once or twice a month, with a particular attention to the importance of chastity. If they were poor, Moir helped them find a job; if they were tempted sexually, they would go to see him. Sinclair wrote later that he regretted not getting from someone else "advice and aid in the task of finding a girl with whom I might have lived wisely and joyfully."[8] The minister's abstinence education had eliminated any discussion of intimacy.

Historian Anthony Rotundo has noted that "like any human creation, manhood can be shaped and reshaped by the human imagination; that is, manhood has a history."[9] Upton Sinclair came of age in the late nineteenth century, and manhood as an ideal and as a process would fascinate him throughout his life. Like other young men of his generation, he experienced what Rotundo describes as a new passionate manhood, in which the body "became a vital component of manhood: strength, appearance, and athletic skill mattered more than in previous centuries."[10] Upton Sinclair's own athleticism found its outlet in tennis. He lived within a mile or two of the tennis courts in Central Park, where he would go play tennis after school and on Saturdays. "Tennis playing became a religion with me," he explained later.[11]

At the same time, Sinclair was rapidly losing faith in his church. Although he was dutifully teaching Sunday school, he writes: "I was beginning to use my brains on the Episcopalian map of the universe, and a chill was creeping over my fervor. Could it possibly be the things I had been taught were merely the Hebrew mythology instead of the Greek or the German?"[12] Reverend Moir thought this crisis of faith was temporary. His family was indifferent to his theological qualms, but Floyd Dell explains that "his refusal to go to church was a different matter. That made his mother very unhappy. And it shattered, moreover, her dream of seeing him a bishop."[13]

In his senior year, while reading Percy Shelley's "To a Skylark" in class, Sinclair experienced an epiphany that college was a "ghastly farce."[14] He was beginning to argue with his father about the latter's beloved Democratic Party. He could not happily continue to live with his parents under these conditions, and in 1896 he moved into an eight-by-ten-foot room in the top story of a lodging house across the street from the college, which cost him $1.25 a week.[15] He wrote in a letter to Dell: "Twenty-five cents a week for clean collars and cuffs, and newspapers. I wore the cuffs up high to keep them from showing too much and getting soiled too fast. I did not have to buy any clothes—my cousin [Howard]—used to send me his cast off clothes."[16] In that room, Sinclair began to write, first jokes, then stories, to pay his rent.

As Americans began attending public schools and becoming literate, their appetite for books was growing. New Yorkers were especially fond of short readable stories that they could bring onto the trains that carried them through the city. The development of mass transportation within cities like New York, with a population of two million in 1890, meant that thousands of people spent hours every day traveling between their neighborhoods and their jobs. Historian Tony Judt notes that "the idea of time, of time as something that organizes us, rather than we organizing it—these were all railway creations."[17] In 1890 most Americans had at least a sixth-grade education, so they were able to understand the stories Sinclair and others produced.[18] The publishing industry was still small and accessible, so an unknown eighteen-year-old could personally deliver his manuscripts and earn a regular income as long as he continued to churn out stories. Upton Sinclair was in a unique historical situation to be able to support his family by writing while he was still a teenager.

Sinclair describes visiting the office of *The Argosy*. He was led "through two or three rooms full of bookkeepers and office girls stamping envelopes."[19] It seemed like a factory, not a location of artistry; Sinclair realized that he was now officially a "hack writer."[20] But he didn't have to be one. If he had been interested, his mother's relatives had extended other possibilities. Uncle Bland had offered him a job in the family banking business, which he turned down, as he had previously turned down a commission to the Annapolis Naval Academy. When he was about seventeen, he wrote to his mother that he did not want his cousin Howard Bland's "wealth, bicycle & fine house & clothes. . . . I do not envy his easy going lazy gentleman of leisure habits." Instead, he hoped for "health, and fame, and knowledge & respect & love & happiness & Heaven . . . besides which wealth is child's play."[21]

Upton Sinclair received his Bachelor of Arts degree in 1897 from ccny and enrolled in Columbia University that same year at the age of nineteen. He still planned to become a lawyer, but first he wanted to experience a year of literature and philosophy at Columbia: "'If you do that, you'll never be a lawyer,' said some shrewd person to me—and he was right."[22]

He found his professors at Columbia to be distinctly influenced by the university's wealthy and conservative trustees. In contrast, he realized that his teachers at the publicly funded City College had been, despite their Tammany affiliations, more progressive and at least were not under the censorious eye of a corporate board of trustees. Sinclair and his friends were resentful they were not learning what they needed to tackle the problems of the world. Jane Addams, whom he would later meet, had the same response at Rockford Female Seminary, describing her education as "lumbering our minds with literature that only served to cloud the really vital situation spread before our eyes."[23]

Sinclair discovered that as long as he hadn't completed his required courses, he could drop in and out of as many fields as he wanted: "I said, 'My God, I'm going to learn everything at Columbia University. I'm going to take all their courses, one after another.'"[24]

Out of twenty courses he started, he completed just five. Despite the limits of the curriculum, he was determined to learn foreign languages. Every day he copied in his notebook a new group of words, studying them while shaving, eating, walking. He spent a year on each language, teaching himself German, French, and Italian.

At Columbia, Sinclair did meet the teacher who would change his life: Edward McDowell, head of the music department. Sinclair describes him as the only authentic genius he met at the university.[25] Sinclair took several courses from McDowell, with fewer than a dozen students in each class; "such was the amount of interest in genius at Columbia," he commented later.[26] In class, at Sinclair's suggestion, McDowell performed compositions for his students. Edward McDowell was one of the few professors who encouraged Upton Sinclair not to give up on becoming a serious writer. He became a mentor to Sinclair and they shared ideas on artistic creation.

At McDowell's suggestion, Sinclair taught himself to play violin during his last year at Columbia. In one of a number of letters to his first girlfriend, Laura Stedman, he wrote: "Music is time made beautiful, the means whereby many people could organize and make harmonious the process of their souls."[27] His love of poetry, begun in childhood, intensified through his exposure to music. He had first known Stedman when they were both children at the Weisiger House. When he was fifteen, he began courting her: "I purchased a new hat of a seductive pearl gray and went walking with Laura in this regalia, so excited that my knees would hardly hold me up."[28] He continued to live separately from his parents in a boardinghouse and found fellowship there with other lodgers. As Wendy Gamber explains, in boardinghouses "communities of strangers might make houses into homes."[29] One resident would play his violin while Sinclair wrote.

Sinclair's stories drew the attention of Street and Smith, one of America's most popular publishers, and editor Henry Harrison Lewis commissioned Sinclair to produce a series of stories about life at West Point Naval Academy. For this project, he ventured out of his little room. He wandered around the academy for days, imbibing its atmosphere and asking cadets about their lives there. Sinclair discovered that he could quickly relax the cadets and could retain in detail all the information they told him, skills that would be essential seven years later when he investigated the Chicago slaughterhouses. He published the West Point series under the pseudonym "Frederick Garrison, USA," earning forty dollars a week—worth about $850 today. He wrote eight thousand words daily, while two full-time stenographers took dictation. Each evening he revised his manuscripts and then took a long walk in order to invent stories for the next day.

When the United States jumped into war with Spain over Cuba and the Philippines, Sinclair sent his fictional heroes into naval battles in Cuba. Mark Twain and other anti-imperialists developed a scorching critique of the war, one that the older Upton Sinclair of 1905 would surely have echoed.[30]

German scholar Dieter Herms thought the West Point stories were worth investigating for themes that would recur in the work of the mature Sinclair.[31] He notes about one of the stories that the character of Sleepy, "even if drawn absurdly and humorously as a self-appointed populist," became "probably the first socialist spokesman in Sinclair's work."[32] Herms points out that Sinclair engages in social analysis at the beginning of the series through his hero, Mark Mallory. Mallory was a precursor of many liberal young men in Sinclair's fiction such as Hal Warner (*The Coal War*), Bunny Ross (*Oil!*), and Lanny Budd (from the World's End series).[33]

After leaving Columbia, Sinclair was torn between the need to earn money to support his parents and his yearning to become a poet. Sinclair published about a dozen verses and satires before 1900, including a verse in the *New Republic* about Frank Lloyd Wright.[34] But he knew he could not support himself, much less his parents, with poetry. So he decided to try writing novels, matching his poetic sensibilities to his narrative skills.

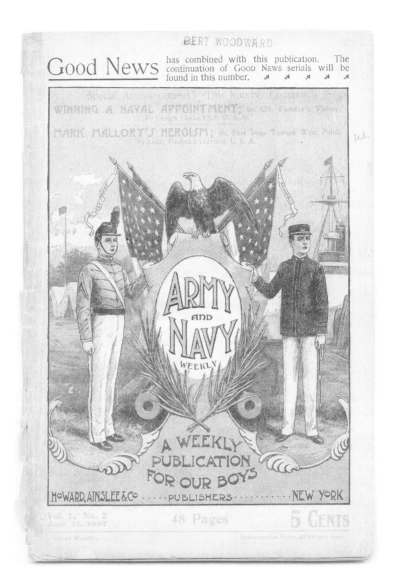

3. Cover of *Army and Navy Weekly*, June 1897. Sinclair's stories about Mark Mallory, a West Point cadet, earned him forty dollars a week at the age of eighteen. Courtesy of the Lilly Library, Indiana University, Bloomington.

It must have been daunting indeed to tell his mother he was going to give up a job that guaranteed a steady income to attempt instead to write the kind of literature that likely would not. Relinquishing his original ambition of being a poet to instead becoming a poetic novelist was a difficult compromise with his sense of duty to the family. By 1900 Sinclair was considered a good-looking young man, with his father's wavy light hair and his mother's regular features and steady gaze. That year he left New York for the solitude of a cabin in Quebec to begin writing his first novel. While he was there, his mother came to visit, bringing her friend Mrs. Fuller. Mrs. Fuller's daughter, Meta, who exuded a dark-eyed youthful sensuality, and whom Sinclair had known at Weisiger House, accompanied her mother.

The women were to stay in lodgings near Sinclair's cabin. He met them at the train station and invited them to dine with him. In *Love's Pilgrimage*, Sinclair describes the evening with romantic nostalgia: "In his old corduroy trousers and his grey flannel shirt, he prepares her supper of rice and raisins, bacon and eggs, and freshly baked bread and butter."[35] After the meal, Meta offered to read the manuscript that Sinclair had just completed (later titled *Springtime and Harvest*). She was convinced (wrongly) that it would be recognized as a great novel. For Sinclair, and for Meta, new ideas about gender meant that, as Anthony Rotundo suggests, "passions formed a vital part of the self. . . . Older forms of virtue—self-restraint, self-denial—became suspect."[36] They fell in love.

Love's Pilgrim

Sinclair recalled the mothers' reactions: "If a bomb had exploded in the midst of their summer vacation, it could not have discommoded them more. A clamor of horrified protest broke out," and Meta was quickly removed.[37] Their parents were disturbed by the intensity of the attraction; they may have assumed the two would outgrow each other. Sinclair naïvely thought Meta was the kind of woman his mother would welcome. As it turned out, "She would not have liked a female angel who had come down to earth and taken away her darling son, until recently destined to become an admiral, or a bishop, or a Supreme Court judge."[38] For her part, Meta's mother had no interest in a suitor who did not have money to support her daughter.

Had the two met a dozen years later, when many sophisticated Bohemians in New York laughed at the idea of marriage and championed "free love," they might have simply had a love affair. But in 1900 Upton and Meta were two inexperienced and sheltered young people with unrealistic ideas about romance, which sent them in a more conventional direction. Sinclair tumbled into the relationship with Meta just when he had given up hack writing and vowed to become a serious novelist. The economic hardship that he now faced compounded the bad timing of the romance.

When the Sinclairs and the Fullers returned to New York City, Upton and Meta spent their time reading Goethe and practicing Mozart sonatas for violin and piano. While downtown waiting for Upton's violin to be repaired, they secretly married on October 18, 1900. The service was performed not by the family friend Reverend Moir but by a Unitarian clergyman, who sympathized with the couple's impatience with formality, and perhaps, says biographer Anthony Arthur, "with their need to consummate an increasingly passionate courtship."[39] The parents were even more appalled by the marriage than by the romance.

The newlyweds first moved to one of the Thousand Islands along the St. Lawrence River. In this lovely setting they built a wooden platform, set up a small tent, and reveled in the beauty around them and within each other. They scooped their drinking water directly out of the river.[40] They found a nest with some orphan sparrows and adopted them, feeding them mosquitoes, flies, and worms. The birds followed Sinclair, refusing to fly away. When he and Meta took them back to the city at the end of the summer, one of them was eaten by a cat. Sinclair almost killed the cat, but didn't because "a cat couldn't help being a cat."[41]

The couple feared pregnancy, so before the marriage Sinclair consulted a doctor about birth control and was instructed to watch the calendar. Although pills and fluid extracts were still available by catalog in 1900, it was illegal for anyone to publish or distribute guides to sexual behavior, including contraceptive techniques. So Meta and Upton were left without reliable information. She immediately became pregnant. In her unpublished autobiography, Meta wrote that Sinclair "was inclined to relegate sex impulses to the limbo of unrestrained human emotions along with drunkenness, wife beating etc." She compared him to a monk "who occasionally threw aside his cassock to try to assume the role of lover for a brief space."[42] Meta and Upton had married too young, with the romantic fantasy that poetry and nature would keep them together. Instead, poverty and a new baby would wear them down and turn them against each other.

Sixty years later Sinclair would comment that the discovery of birth control "is the most important single discovery that the human race has made." He made an impassioned plea for its acceptance: "We have to go to war against the ignorance and superstition that makes it impossible for the masses of the people to use that knowledge."[43] David Sinclair was born on December 1, 1901. Sinclair sat with Meta during her fourteen-hour labor, and soon afterward he put the experience into seven thousand words of prose. One publisher told him that although it was well done, he wouldn't touch it due to the graphic nature of the material. Sinclair chose to include the scene in *Love's Pilgrimage*, published a decade later.

Soon after their son's birth, Upton Sinclair decided that he and Meta must not risk physical intimacy. Decades later he commented: "If we had had another child, I would have been through. I wanted to be a writer, I thought it was my duty to be a writer, and so we were living a celibate life."[44] But celibacy was impossible for Meta, and the marriage was essentially over.[45] By 1902 Meta's parents took her and the baby back to their apartment and her father told Sinclair not to come back until he had a job. Instead, Sinclair chose his commitment to life as a serious writer. Their off-and-on relationship would continue for over a decade.

That autumn, Sinclair moved to a Harlem boardinghouse. At one point, he resorted to playing poker for money. His fellow lodgers included his father, who was drinking continuously, and his mother's brother, Harry, who was nearing the moment of his own suicide in Central Park. Uncle Harry considered it his duty to give "worldly-wise advice to a haggard young author who refused to get a job."[46] Everyone else in the boardinghouse agreed. Despite the barrage of advice, Sinclair kept writing.

One day as he was dropping off an article for consideration at the *Literary Digest*, he began a conversation with Leonard Abbott, an English writer about his age who was a dedicated socialist. In the early twentieth century, the excesses of capitalism and the gaps between rich and poor were becoming more and more acute in industrial urban America. Income inequality in this period was steadily increasing, as wages failed to match increases in corporate gains from increasing industrialization. Lincoln Steffens would shortly publish *The Shame of the Cities*. Socialists advocated nationalizing major industries to insure a more equitable distribution of profits. American socialists believed that the electoral system would bring socialist candidates into office, and in fact these candidates received millions of votes. When Sinclair first heard these ideas in 1902, no country had achieved a successful socialist revolution. The American Socialist Party had been founded in 1901, and Socialist parties were thriving in Europe, evidence of a growing international movement.

Abbott encouraged Sinclair to read some recent pamphlets, including one by a friend of his, George Herron, a former minister and college professor. Sinclair liked Herron's ideas and wrote him a letter of appreciation. Herron replied with an invitation to join him for dinner. Sinclair felt unequal to the challenge of dining out, since his shoes were losing their heels and his cuffs were frayed. But the ideas shared over dinner were what he had longed for. Later he described it as the "falling down of prison walls about my mind; the amazing discovery, after all these years, that I did not have to carry the whole burden of humanity's future! . . . The principal fact the socialists had to teach me was that they themselves existed."[47] Socialist theory helped him make sense of his childhood experiences as a child of both poverty and wealth. Sinclair soon met socialists who had grown up in poverty and often yearned for wealth; he also met socialists who grew up wealthy and could not understand or speak to the poor. Having been both rich and poor gave him a unique double vision.

Sinclair joined the Socialist Party, although he departed from it periodically and disagreed with it profoundly at least once. His sympathies were always with American workers; from the slaughterhouse workers of Chicago to the coal miners of Ludlow to the dock workers of San Pedro, he threw himself into the struggles to organize the unorganized. As a student of class politics all his life, Upton Sinclair was well aware that party politics were dominated by the more privileged sectors of society, while immigrants and workers turned instead to labor organizations such as the United Mine Workers or the Industrial Workers of the World (iww) for immediate relief.

After this political awakening, Sinclair began immediately to plan a new kind of novel, a history of the Civil War that would help him shed the Confederate nostalgia of his upbringing.[48] He had grown up in segregated Baltimore and spent time in his relatives' homes where former slaves were household servants. In his *Autobiography*, Sinclair recalls that as a teenager he had written jokes "about Scotchmen, Irishmen, Negroes, Jews."[49] By the era of the civil rights movement, in the 1960s, he would voice his support, but as a younger man he was complicit in the errors of his time, place, and background. The reconciliationist memory that emphasized what North and South shared in common, particularly the valor of individual soldiers, suppressed understanding of the war's causes. By the end of the century, the forces of reconciliation had supplanted the emancipationist vision."[50]

Yet even in this atmosphere, Sinclair traveled to Boston in order to meet surviving abolitionists like Frank Sanborn and Julia Ward Howe. He stayed with his cousin Howard Bland, who was studying at Harvard. But Sinclair needed funding in order to write. He began by appealing to various philanthropists, who turned him down. Then he asked George Herron, "a socialist, and for the first time found a comrade. . . . How I could have lived and written *Manassas* without that money I am entirely unable to imagine."[51] George Herron offered him about eight hundred dollars, a loan that enabled Sinclair to survive as a writer.

With Herron's loan, in May 1903 Sinclair was able to gather his wife and child and bring them to live on rented land on a farm in Princeton, New Jersey. Sinclair chose Princeton because of its wealth of Civil War archives. He was able to bring some published personal memoirs back to the farm, but the bulk of it—division and regimental histories, abolitionist tracts and Southern responses, recruiting materials, unpublished diaries and letters—could be read only in the library.

The family's home was the same used tent they had bought in the Thousand Islands. As Sinclair described the reunion, "with singing and laughter" they unpacked while the baby crawled about on the tent floor and got into everybody's way. Once the baby was safely asleep, Meta "spread a feast of bread and butter, fresh milk and eggs and a can of fruit, and they sat down to the first meal that they had eaten together in many a long, long month."[52] The couple renewed their love and commitment to each other.

But the tent was by this time musty and mildewed, and conditions only got worse when the rains began. David was already sickly with rickets when they moved to Princeton, and the special diet the doctor advised was expensive and difficult to prepare: hot cereal, poached eggs, oranges, chicken broth, stewed prunes, chopped beef, mashed potato, and canned beets.[53] Sinclair found himself trimming fat and gristle from the meat and pounding it to a pulp. He also needed to peel the skin off the prunes, peaches, and apples, as the doctor had advised. The diet cured the rickets, but led to bouts of diarrhea, requiring frequent trips to the laundry—an exposed flat rock downstream from the spring where they drew their drinking water.

The troubles continued: David suffered from boils, then measles, and then bee stings. Each trip to the doctor was not only costly, but also meant travel by stagecoach along dirt roads to New York City. The first installment of Herron's money was fast running out. By fall 1903 Sinclair must have realized how impossible his living situation was. He worked with local carpenters to build a small cabin. He constructed a concrete cistern, and installed a pump in the kitchen so they finally had running water. The now two-year-old baby had his own room—strikingly unlike Sinclair's own childhood.

Carrie Stout, his landlord's seven-year-old granddaughter, later recalled that Sinclair seemed to like to "saw and hammer and knock things together."[54] Using leftover lumber, Sinclair also constructed an eight-by-ten hut for himself, with his own desk and bed. Carrie Stout often saw Sinclair walking when she delivered buttermilk, cottage cheese, vegetables, and fruits in her homemade wagon. He always walked "with his head down and his hands clasped behind him," so deep in concentration that he often didn't see or hear her.[55] He did bring Carrie candy, along with boxes of nuts for her grandparents, when he came back from his frequent trips to New York.

Sinclair introduced Meta to books by Charlotte Perkins Gilman, the pioneer feminist and sociologist, whose book *Women and Economics* was published in 1898. Gilman's advocacy of communal housework and childcare proved so compelling to Sinclair that he would later found a utopian colony based upon her ideas. Meta responded enthusiastically to Gilman and enjoyed reading the new plays by Henrik Ibsen. But for her, reading was not enough; had they been able to access birth control and resume their physical intimacy, the couple's marriage might have survived.

The couple tried to sleep separately, living as they did in constant terror of another pregnancy, "like people drawing lots for a death sentence."[56] They had less and less to talk about, and the status of the garbage or the diaper pail were constant strains. They had only a wood stove and cotton blankets, and Sinclair wrote that the cold weather "broke down the barriers they had been at such pains to build up between them"; they crawled into the same bed and "so once more the sex factor was introduced into the complications of their lives."[57] Each month they waited "in suspense and dread."[58]

The roles of student and teacher that Meta and Upton assumed in their relationship were manifestly unsuited to the more complicated relationship of married partners. Certainly these unequal roles were contrary to their utopian ideals of equality. Quickly they came to resent each other, she not wanting to be his pupil, he not wanting to be her teacher. As their relationship deteriorated, Meta bought Lydia Pinkham's Vegetable Compound, which was supposed to remedy "female complaints," and did so—through opium.[59]

In March of 1904 the creek flooded and the cabin was surrounded by mud. Meta stopped brushing her hair and left greasy dishes in the sink for days. Sinclair wrote alone in his hut till late at night. One night he awoke to see Meta "sitting in the cold moonlight with a blanket flung about her, her wild hair tossing, and in her hand the revolver with which she had meant to destroy herself."[60] He had given her the gun for protection while he was away.

Meta's suicide attempt was a graphic statement of how this young woman was unsuited for motherhood and celibacy. Equally, Sinclair was unwilling to sacrifice his career for fatherhood. In his biography of Sinclair, Floyd Dell describes sympathetically the mind-numbing effect of the years spent writing the "millions of meaningless and merely saleable words" to explain Sinclair's determination to maintain his artistic goals in the face of domestic chaos.[61] The self-discipline and, perhaps, the self-denial that Sinclair embraced in later years, part of his affinity for Gandhi and the Nearings, can be understood in light of the chaos of this early marriage, the stark demands of celibacy, and the necessity of sacrificing domesticity for poverty and serious craft.

In the midst of their great difficulties, *Manassas* was published in 1904. The novel's protagonist is a young Southerner raised on a plantation. Reading Harriet Beecher Stowe and Fredrick Douglass, he begins to question slavery and eventually enlists in the Massachusetts regiment whose solders were attacked as they marched through Baltimore in 1861. The novel ends with the defeat of the North at Manassas. Floyd Dell describes it not just as a novel, "but as a memorial of a private struggle of his own. . . . He fought the Civil War over again in his imagination. In the person of his hero he had to make war on the South."[62] Despite favorable reviews, *Manassas* sold fewer than two thousand copies. However, the publisher's advance of five hundred dollars was enough. The money he made on *Manassas* freed him up to devote more time to political activism.

Life Makes Literature

That year Sinclair and Jack London formed a national organization, the Intercollegiate Socialist Society (ISS), dedicated to educating young college students about socialism—something Sinclair would have welcomed in his own days as a student: "Since the professors refused to teach the students about modern life, it was up to the students to teach themselves, so I sent a letter to all the college socialists I knew and invited them to organize."[63]

The ISS met in 1905 at Peck's Restaurant in New York and selected Jack London as their president. Sinclair and Meta would sit up until two or three in the morning, "wrapping packages of literature to be mailed to persons who did not always want them and sometimes wrote to say so."[64] The group promoted essay contests and attempted to make socialism more respectable and interesting to young Americans. Sinclair invited London to speak in New York City under the sponsorship of the ISS.[65] He rented Carnegie Hall for the occasion.[66] Jack London traveled from California to Florida by boat, then by train to New York. He arrived just in time to deliver a

4. Upton Sinclair with his son, David, at the Princeton farm where he wrote *The Jungle*, 1906. Courtesy of the Lilly Library, Indiana University, Bloomington.

speech on revolution to an ecstatic, packed crowd from the Lower East Side. Ten years later, London would write the introduction to Sinclair's collection of proletarian literature, *The Cry for Justice*, published in 1915. When London died the following year, Sinclair remembered him as "a delightful companion."[67]

Sinclair's favorite London novel was the largely autobiographical *Martin Eden*, about a working-class young man struggling to succeed as a writer. Another of London's novels, *The People of the Abyss*, introduced realism, the new movement in the arts that fascinated Sinclair. Mathew Brady's collection of stark photographs showing hundreds of corpses lying on the battlefields of the Civil War was a similar project. Sinclair longed to be part of this new movement and found his entry point when he read about a strike in the Chicago stockyards in the socialist weekly *Appeal to Reason*.

In July 1904 the Amalgamated Meat Cutters struck all the meat-packers in Chicago. J. Ogden Armour and the other employers broke the union by hiring thousands of unemployed strikebreakers, an action that provoked a riot involving four thousand union members and their families on August 19, 1904. The strike collapsed in mid-September, but Jane Addams met personally with Armour to secure a contract that helped the union survive.[68] Upton Sinclair sent in a passionate article to the *Appeal to Reason* encouraging the workers not to give up their longer-term struggle. He also sent the *Appeal* a copy of *Manassas*, and the editors responded with an offer that he produce a similar novel about wage slavery for serial publication. Sinclair requested a five-hundred-dollar advance and selected the Chicago stockyards as the setting for his new book. "My error," he would explain, "lay in supposing that it is literature that makes life. Instead it is life that makes literature."[69] He accepted the *Appeal*'s offer with excitement, sent Meta and David to her parents in New York City, and took the train to Chicago.

CHAPTER THREE

Good Health and How We Won It
[1905–1915]

Rise like lions after slumber
In unvanquished number!
Shake your chains to earth like dew
Which in sleep had fallen on you—
Ye are many—they are few.
PERCY BYSSHE SHELLEY, 1832

The years between 1905 and 1916 were rich with possibility for socialists, feminists, and radicals of all kinds in America. Socialism was never again as exciting and persuasive as during these years, before the purges of antiwar activists and immigrant organizers that occurred during World War I. The Republican Progressivism of Theodore Roosevelt opened a space for organizing that flocks of activists surged into, championing causes ranging from passing Prohibition to ending child labor, with food safety and votes for women among the panoply of issues to which women and men dedicated their lives. People still traveled by horse-drawn cart when *The Jungle* was published. Hundreds of magazines and newspapers flourished in every big city, and everyone who could, read them. In this period, Sinclair became both famous and infamous for *The Jungle*, founded a utopian colony, fell in love, divorced and remarried, provided critical assistance to striking coal miners, and starred in a film version of his famous novel.

The *Uncle Tom's Cabin* of the Labor Movement

When the twenty-six-year-old Upton Sinclair stepped off the train at the noisy Chicago Union Station, he spotted the Transit House Hotel, surrounded by horses and hitching posts. The porch was teeming with cowboys, ranchers, and cattle dealers. Carrying a single battered canvas suitcase, he trudged up the steps past the cowboys and cattlemen, who were passing whiskey bottles and clouding the air with the smoke from their cigars. The Union Stockyards sprawled next door, and the odor of cattle and manure mingled with the smell of beef and potatoes from the hotel kitchen.

Sinclair had come from the New Jersey farmland with its maple and dogwood trees, its grassy fields full of milk cows. Nothing about this stockyard crammed with bawling cattle, nor this hotel populated exclusively by men, would have seemed familiar to him. However, to his great relief, he was met and embraced by Ernest Poole, with whom he had been corresponding for the past year. When they met in the lobby of the Transit House, Poole was a publicity agent for the meatpackers union.[1] He later wrote, "In breezed a lad in wide-brimmed hat, with loose-flowing tie and a wonderful warm expansive smile. 'Hello! I'm Upton Sinclair!' he said. 'And I've come here to write the *Uncle Tom's Cabin* of the Labor Movement!'"[2]

In *Manassas* Sinclair had written that critics often derided Stowe's book as being of historical more than literary interest, "but he who can read a hundred pages of it, for the first or the twentieth time, with dry eyes, is not an enviable person."[3] In 1903 *Rebecca of Sunnybrook Farm* was the best-selling novel in America.[4] Inspired by the realistic fiction of Harriet Stowe, Frank Norris, and Jack London, Sinclair wanted to write a novel that would break his readers' hearts and move them to action. He set his novel in Chicago's slaughterhouses because he hoped the focus on food production would appeal to readers' self-interest. Meanwhile, his real subject would be the lives of the workers.[5]

The meatpacking industry was widely regarded as an unqualified success, and it was one of the most financially stable American industries. Behind that force was meat baron Philip Armour, later described as "a sandy-haired, red-whiskered demigod of stock-yards mythology."[6] J. Ogden Armour took over as company president from his father in 1901.[7] Soon afterward sales skyrocketed from $200 million to $1 billion.[8] Sinclair wrote, "It seemed to me I was confronting a veritable fortress of oppression. How to breach those walls, or to scale them, was a military problem."[9] But Chicago was not only the meatpacking center of the United States, it was also the location of Hull House, the settlement project to help immigrant workers that had been founded on the Near West Side by Jane Addams in 1889.

In her own words, Jane Addams wanted to assist "in the solutions of life in a great city, to help our neighbors build responsible, self-sufficient lives for themselves and their families."[10] Addams believed that the privileged young women who wanted to help the poor should live as equal participants in the neighborhood of those they were helping. Hull House was located in the midst of a densely populated urban area peopled by Italian, Irish, German, Greek, Bohemian, and Russian and Polish Jewish immigrants. It provided classes in English, art, and music; meeting places for trade unionists; the Jane Club for single working girls; day care for the children of working mothers; as well as an art gallery, libraries, and a Labor Museum.

Sinclair was a frequent visitor. He remembered meeting Jane Addams at dinner. They immediately plunged into an argument when he told her that "the one useful purpose of settlements was the making of settlement workers into socialists."[11] Jane Addams told a friend that he was a young man who had a great deal to learn. Sinclair wrote, "Both she and I went on diligently learning, so that when we met again we did not have so much to argue over."[12] This simple comment illustrates the equality and respect with which Sinclair regarded his friendship with Jane Addams and the cadre of women activists she created.

Jane Addams was not the only woman who offered guidance to Upton Sinclair during his stay in Chicago. Mary McDowell had directed the University of Chicago Settlement House since 1894, when it opened next to the stockyards. She was called "the Angel of the Stockyards" for her sympathetic devotion to the workers, which extended to vigorous support of their strike in 1904. Sinclair relied on McDowell for information and strategies in navigating Chicago, where he spent seven weeks. He described this pioneering effort as undercover reporting: "I sat at night in the homes of the workers, foreign born and native, and they told me their stories, one after one, and I made notes."[13] Sinclair went to the stockyards in the daytime, where the workers risked their jobs to show him around. He found that by carrying a dinner pail, he could go anywhere.

When the seven weeks were over, Sinclair boarded the train for the bungalow in Princeton, New Jersey, where Meta and David joined him. He began writing *The Jungle* on Christmas Day 1904 and worked on it for the next three months: "I wrote with tears and anguish, pouring into the pages all the pain that life had meant to me. Externally, the story had to do with a family of stockyard workers, but internally it was the story of my own family"—a family that was in crisis.[14] During that winter, David nearly died of pneumonia.

Appeal to Reason published almost all the chapters in serial form, but by November 1905, its editor, Fred Warren, decided not to publish the last two chapters, which described the religious conversion of the protagonist, Jurgis, to socialism. Sinclair expected that Macmillan, which had already published *Manassas*, would be interested in publishing this next book. Warned by their lawyers to expect litigation, Macmillan instead turned it down. Sinclair next approached Doubleday, a publishing house as prestigious as Macmillan.

Doubleday had just hired former reporter Isaac Marcosson, who brought with him the idea that books could be promoted as news stories. He pointed out that Doubleday had "netted a rare bird in

Sinclair: a retiring artist-scholar [who] had proved himself to be a star investigative reporter. . . . Even better: he was a déclassé Southern aristocrat with a boyish charm, but brave enough to take on those fearsome industrial predators, the meatpackers."[15] Marcosson arranged for Sinclair to meet the company attorney and agree to remove potentially libelous material. When Doubleday challenged the title as too provocative, Sinclair refused to change it. He did agree to drop almost all references (other than the title itself) to the world as a jungle.[16]

Senior partner Frank Doubleday was uninterested in the novel; he considered the author a "wild man" and his book both "repellent and doctrinaire."[17] He had already decided to refuse permission to reprint the book in England and elsewhere, for fear of washing "our dirty linen in the capitals of Europe," when he was invited to lunch by Ogden Armour. They met in Armour's private Pullman car in Grand Central Station. Armour offered the publisher a generous advertising contract in return for limiting further publicity and distribution of *The Jungle*. As a sign of good faith, he also offered a large can of preserved meat. Frank Doubleday was enraged and insulted. He told Armour that now "we would give permission to have the book reprinted in Europe. He did not seem to understand why I was so angry. Of all the moral degenerates that I ever saw, he was the first."[18]

The first printing of twenty thousand copies was released in February 1906. Marcosson put together Sinclair's style, his narrative, and the subject of bad meat. He turned *The Jungle* into a celebrity event. The book was reprinted sixty-seven times over the next twenty-six years, and seventeen translations appeared within months of its American publication.

The thirty thousand dollars in royalties that Sinclair earned in one year enabled him to pay back his debts to George Herron and other friends. Both Upton Sinclair and Isaac Marcosson sent copies of the book to President Theodore Roosevelt, who had been getting a hundred letters a day about *The Jungle*. Sinclair remembered that

Roosevelt wrote that he had asked the Department of Agriculture to investigate: "I replied that was like asking a burglar to determine his own guilt."[19] Roosevelt invited Sinclair to the White House for lunch, where the former Rough Rider commented dryly: "Mr. Sinclair, I bear no love for those gentlemen, for I ate the meat they canned for the Army in Cuba."[20]

The president did send his own investigators to confirm the information in the novel, but Sinclair had quickly dispatched his friend Ella Reeve Bloor ahead of them to make sure Roosevelt's men would not be misled by the owners. In 1901 Bloor had worked as a Hearst reporter, writing some of the first exposés of the meatpacking industry; later she worked to expose child labor. Sinclair described her as "a little woman, as tireless as a cat."[21] She telegraphed Sinclair that Roosevelt's investigators didn't want to know the truth, including the fact that her neighbor had heard about a worker who fell into a lard vat and disappeared.

Sinclair tried to reach Roosevelt to warn him of the investigators' whitewash of the industry. Roosevelt rebuked him: "Really, Mr. Sinclair, you must keep your head."[22] Roosevelt then gave a speech in which he coined the word *muckrakers*—and attacked them as meddlers who caused more trouble than they cured. The term was adopted immediately by reporters and corporations. Anthony Arthur notes that with this phrase, Roosevelt "smoothed the path for Sinclair's real enemies—the meatpackers and their minions—who were now redoubling their attacks."[23]

Sinclair battled to get what he felt was the true story out to the public. He knew that he was "pigeon-holed with long-haired violinists from abroad, and painters with fancy-colored vests, and women suffragists with short hair, and religious prophets in purple robes."[24] He wrote articles throughout the spring and summer of 1906, published in *Colliers*, *Everybody's Magazine*, the *Arena*, and the *Independent*. Senator Albert Beveridge introduced a bill on May 22 to begin regulation of the meat industry. Sinclair worried that it would be killed in the House, so he met with the editor of the

New York Times and explained that by publicizing the essence of the investigators' report, he hoped to force Roosevelt to release the entire report. The story appeared on the front page of the paper, with descriptions even more shocking than those in *The Jungle*.[25]

When the official report was released, it was briefer and omitted some of Sinclair's claims. However, the investigators documented what they themselves had observed and that was enough; the only allegation they could not confirm was that workmen had fallen into vats and wound up on the tables of beef-eating Americans. Sinclair knew that the families who had experienced this had been paid off.[26] Congressman Morton, who represented the meatpacking district in Chicago, told the *New York Times* that the entire uproar began with Sinclair's novel and that "I know those packing houses as well as I know the corridors of the Capital. . . . There is not a kitchen of a rich man in this city, or any other, that is any cleaner."[27] He added that the workers were immigrants without intelligence.[28]

However, due to Sinclair's passionate activism and the testimony of the investigators, Congress passed the Pure Food and Drug Act along with the Meat Inspection Amendment, on June 30, 1906—a law that Senator Beveridge hailed proudly as "the most pronounced extension of federal power in every direction ever enacted."[29] President Roosevelt did not acknowledge Sinclair during the signing ceremony, praising Beveridge instead. Neither was there any reference to Upton Sinclair or to *The Jungle* in Teddy's 1913 autobiography.[30]

In 1907, soon after publication of *The Jungle*, Theodore Roosevelt delivered a lecture to Harvard undergraduates, declaring that colleges should not "turn out molly-coddles instead of vigorous men," and warning of the dire consequences of such weakness.[31] Roosevelt asserted his own masculinity through war and exhibited an acceptable obsession with personal and national virility.[32]

The British philosopher Goldsworthy Lowes-Dickinson, touring the United States, capitalized on Roosevelt's damaging remarks in a 1914 essay. He argued that "redbloods" were serious men like soldiers, businessmen, and politicians. The "mollycoddle" only acts by accident, and he is the Crank: "he who accomplishes reforms; who abolished slavery, for example, and revolutionized prisons and lunatic asylums."[33] Given the indictment of men who possess an inner life, champion reform, and are neither businessmen nor soldiers, the pronouncements of these two men could easily be taken as a description of Upton Sinclair. This rhetoric reflects how male activists within reform movements were characterized as defective male specimens in popular discourse.

Sinclair later wrote of *The Jungle*, "I aimed for their hearts but I hit their stomachs."[34] His passionate wish that readers would recognize the brutality that the workers endured under capitalism was not realized. Americans responded to the book instead with outrage about the quality of their food. Jon Yoder notes that Sinclair himself "cared little about meat since he rarely ate it. But he did care deeply about what the meat industry represented."[35] Upton Sinclair continued to press the government for sweeping reforms in the industry. He believed government meat inspection was not enough and argued instead that cities should operate their own slaughterhouses, to be operated for the public interest. He recalled, "Roosevelt sent a message to Frank Doubleday: 'Tell Sinclair to go home and let me run the country for awhile.' I did not accept the advice."[36]

Instead, a determined Sinclair proposed a series of articles to *Everybody's Magazine* exposing the ravages of child labor. He took Ella Reeve Bloor and went first to the glass factories of southern New Jersey, where boys of ten years old labored all night. He describes an "exhausted child staggering home at daybreak, falling asleep on the railroad tracks, and being run over by a train."[37] He traveled next to the Allegheny steel mills, but the editors at *Everybody's Magazine* were so shocked by what he reported that they refused to publish it.

But Sinclair was flush with money from the unexpected success of *The Jungle*. He remembers, "I became drunk, thinking it was going to be like that the rest of my life: and so I could found a colony, or start a magazine, or produce a play, or win a strike—whatever might be necessary to change the world into what it ought to be."[38] Sinclair uncharacteristically used the word "drunk" to indicate the heady excitement he was feeling at his new prosperity. Remarkably, he did go on to found a colony, start a magazine, produce a play, and win a strike, all within the next dozen years. That summer of 1906 he gathered with friends to plan a new venture on which he would spend the rest of the thirty thousand dollars he had earned from *The Jungle*.

New Communities: The Political and the Personal

Sinclair invited a group that included writers, artists, and social reformers to join a community dedicated to pooling resources and childcare responsibilities. Like other founders of utopian colonies, Sinclair was looking for a solution to problems he was experiencing in his own living situation. Sinclair and his wife continued to be overwhelmed by the demands of raising their child alone. As he wrote to Gaylord Wilshire, "Because Meta was almost out of her mind, and I did not know what to do with David, I started Helicon Hall."[39]

A feminist theory provided the framework for Sinclair's intentional community. He based Helicon Hall on Charlotte Perkins Gilman's vision of cooperative housework and childcare. Gilman had advocated childcare operations that would foster a sense of community, while allowing women to pursue "world service" and economic independence.[40] Her suggestions for new kinds of domestic architecture that included public kitchens and community dining rooms resonated with Sinclair. He wrote that it took "a hundred cooks to prepare a hundred meals badly, while twenty cooks could prepare one meal for a hundred families and do it perfectly . . . dragging through life a constantly increasing burden of care or making an intelligent effort and solving the problem once and for all."[41] For this purpose, in November 1906, Sinclair purchased

Helicon Hall, a former boys' boarding school outside Englewood, New Jersey, and moved in immediately with his wife and son.

Twelve other families joined them that first winter. Jo Davidson, who visited Helicon Hall, remembered its "large size palm trees in buckets in front of the enormous fireplace."[42] Conversations would often last until past midnight in front of the fireplace. Eventually more than seventy-five men, women, and children lived at Helicon Hall. Historian Lawrence Kaplan has noted that it was common for families to move to Helicon Hall in order to allow wives or mothers to pursue their careers or artistic project: "moving to a cooperative establishment testified to a husband's willingness to allow both leisure and space for his wife's personal development."[43] A few of the "Colony Customs" give a sense of life at Helicon Hall:

1. The children's department requests assistance in its efforts to treat the children as playmates and equals, rather than as playthings and pets.
2. The billiard-table is in the care of a committee.
3. The grass and ferns in the court are intended to be looked at and not to be walked on.
4. It is thought fair that some of the social rooms of the Hall should not be used by smokers. The parlor, reading room, and dining room have been suggested as such.
5. Private property left in bath-rooms or in other common rooms will be redeemed at the Colony pound at the rate of five cents per article.[44]

Gilman did not suggest that men be involved in childcare. Rather she advocated, and the colony followed, a system where childcare was rotated among mothers. The colony's women enjoyed the arrangements for children very much.[45] One of the Helicon Hall mothers was able to attend medical school in New York. Children at Helicon Hall were encouraged to become self-reliant, dressing and feeding themselves.

This cooperative child rearing, a cornerstone of Gilman's vision, drew the most ridicule from newspaper reporters posing concerns about the "harm" it might cause, but Sinclair believed that the children's program had been the most successful aspect of the project. He described how the children ate in their own dining room with miniature chairs and tables, food designed for their tastes, and "they assembled at a children's parliament and discussed their problems, deciding what was wrong and what right for them."[46]

The experiment was not destined to last even a year. On March 7, 1908, in the middle of the night, Sinclair awoke to a sound like enormous hammers pounding on the walls in the doors of the building. Helicon Hall was on fire—what he heard was hot air blowing out sections of the walls. "We stood in the snow and watched our beautiful utopia flame and roar, until it crashed and died away to a dull glow."[47] A visiting carpenter, who had been drinking the night before, slept through Sinclair's efforts to rouse the community and died. After the fire, Sinclair was forced to defend himself against accusations of arson. The coroner's jury implied that the fire had been deliberately set to collect insurance money; actually, after receiving the proceeds from their fire claim and selling off the land, all stockholders were paid off. Sinclair had also provided for colonists whom the fire had left without resources.[48]

Another blow followed with the death of his father, Upton Beall Sinclair. His son wrote sadly that his father had only lived "until I was thirty, all that time I had him in my thoughts and often in my hands. I did everything I could for him; I took him to church, I made an effort to interest him in reading."[49] Over and over he brought his father to a Catholic hospital in New York and left him, where Upton Sr. would suffer delirium tremens in a cell. He died that way. The heartbreak of caring for, and being unable to help, his alcoholic father, powerfully shaped Sinclair's ideas about abstinence from alcohol and the need to outlaw it, a political resolution that never faltered.

Sinclair must have longed for the mutual support of communal life to ease the troubles between him and Meta and the grief of losing his father: "I took my family to Point Pleasant, New Jersey, rented a little cottage, and went back to the single family mode of life. It was like leaving modern civilization and returning to the dark ages."[50] He recognized that creating community was an important social (and socialist) goal, and he continued to look for new communal possibilities. Leaving Meta and David in New Jersey, he left for California by train to visit Gaylord Wilshire's goldmine in the Sierras.

Gaylord Wilshire was a wealthy young man who had become a socialist. In 1895 he had developed thirty-five acres in Los Angeles for an elite residential subdivision. He donated a strip of land to the city for a boulevard through what was then a barley field, on the conditions that it would be named for him and that railroad lines and commercial or industrial trucking would be banned. He was also publishing his own magazine, *Wilshire's*. Sinclair remembers him as having "a very quiet manner and a delightful, dry sense of humor."[51] Upton had been sending him articles. In Bishop, Wilshire was conducting a socialist experiment in mining, run "on a basis of comradeship, with high wages and plenty of socialist propaganda."[52] But even though Sinclair contributed most of what he had left from *The Jungle*, the mine failed to produce gold that met commercial standards, and its members lost their savings.

Sinclair invited Gaylord and Mary Wilshire along on his next stop, Carmel, where he hoped to set up "an outdoor Helicon Hall beside the Pacific."[53] When they arrived, Carmel was a thriving artist colony, whose decade of greatest vitality was between 1904 and 1914. George Sterling had settled there first, writes historian Kevin Starr, "remaining for ten years as symbolic founder, master of the revels, and a guru-in-chief."[54] Sinclair valued George Sterling deeply as a friend and a poet (in 1936 he would give a speech describing Sterling as one of his closest friends), but Sterling, like his own father, was an alcoholic.[55] Journalist Lincoln Steffens was a regular visitor to Carmel, and novelist Mary Austin was in residence at the time of Sinclair's visit, working on *Santa Lucia*, her novel about the problems of the intellectual woman.

In 1909 Sinclair moved to San Francisco for a four-month visit. There he wrote three short one-act plays. One of them, *Unlikely Confrontations*, was performed by the Sinclair Players in San Francisco that year. It featured John D. Rockefeller debating a character called "the Author" on a Carmel beach.[56] "The Author" convinces Rockefeller to set up cooperatives rather than hoard his wealth, and in an adventurous twist, the audience is asked to act as a judge and jury to the debate.[57] When he wrote to Meta from California he described a horseback ride alone on Seventeen Mile Drive, during which he shouted and sang. He found the coast "enthrallingly beautiful."[58] He also must have reevaluated the problems in his marriage; along with instructions for David's diet, he suggested they obtain a divorce in Reno "with no publicity."[59] However, it would be another three years before the couple was able to obtain a divorce; for American courts, incompatibility alone was not sufficient grounds.

In his essay "Upton Sinclair in Carmel," Franklin Walker comments that the most memorable aspect of Sinclair's visit was his diet: "while others ate mussels and abalones and mountain venison, he munched on big, red, luscious tomatoes."[60] Upton Sinclair's interest in diet and health, so understandable today, has been the subject of constant ridicule from 1909 up through some contemporary biographies. Given his struggles with his own health and his observations of his friends, he had come to believe that poor diet, like alcohol, prevented many activists from fully devoting themselves to movements for social change.

Sinclair identified with the Popular Health Movement, a social struggle for more effective healthcare by feminist and working class reformers.[61] The movement advocated frequent bathing, a healthy diet, and temperance. Prior to the twentieth century, unregulated medical practice flourished in the United States, and medicine during the Progressive Era was a contested arena as the American Medical Association sought control by campaigning to ban what it perceived to be "irregular practices."[62] He wrote: "My college education, which had left out socialism and money and love and marriage, had also left out diet and health."[63] From 1907 to 1908, Sinclair worked with fellow Helicon Hall resident Michael Williams to produce a book about diet and health. *Good Health and How We Won It* begins: "I look about me in the world and nearly everybody I know is sick. I could name one after another a hundred men and women, who are doing vital work for progress and carrying a cruel handicap of physical suffering."[64] Significantly, he wanted his insights about health and diet to be shared with the poor as well as the educated. In his 1908 novel *The Metropolis*, Sinclair satirized the way that the wealthy sampled "rest" and "water" cures. But he himself suffered greatly from insomnia, headaches, and digestive problems.

Although by 1910 the Flexner Commission had officially outlawed alternative medicine, its practitioners continued to thrive. There were countless theorists and theories about better health through diet; Graham (the graham cracker), Fletcher ("Fletcherism"), and Kellogg were probably the most successful.

In 1909, when *Good Health and How We Won It* was published, Upton and Meta visited Kellogg's Battle Creek Sanitarium. T. C. Boyle describes in *The Road to Wellville* how characters as varied as Amelia Earhart, Henry Ford, and Thomas Edison visited the sanitarium; in Boyle's novel, Meta is described as "exotic" and associated with "sun worship and free love."[65] Listening to Dr. John Henry Kellogg, Sinclair initially became a vegetarian. Later he tried raw foods, a milk diet, then a meat diet. Eventually he settled on a simple diet of rice and fruit.

That same summer Mary Craig, a young woman from Mississippi who was working on a biography of Winnie Davis, brought her mother to Battle Creek, and Harry Kemp, a poet whom Sinclair had befriended, came to visit as well. Sinclair had seen one of Kemp's first published poems in 1906 and sent him a congratulatory note. When they met, Kemp described Sinclair as an energetic walker with a decisive chin and a mouth "loose and cruel like mine."[66] Sinclair saw

Kemp as a poet of the common man. Later Sinclair would remember, "The fates wove their webs, unguessed by any of us."[67] Two years later, in 1911, Harry Kemp and Meta would run away together. Four years later, in 1913, Mary Craig and Sinclair would wed.

In her memoir, Mary Craig recalls sitting with her ailing mother at Battle Creek and first seeing Upton Sinclair crossing the lawn in gray flannels and tennis shoes: "His blonde hair was slightly curly, his eyes blue. 'Not quite tall enough,' said Mama, whose husband was six feet two. 'But he looks like a gentleman, in spite of those clothes.'"[68] When they were introduced, he entertained them with a self-deprecating recital of his experiments in diet. Mary Craig recalled: "I doubt if I had ever laughed so much in my life and I surely never expected to see my dignified mother wiping tears from her eyes."[69] During the years between that summer of 1909 and their marriage in 1913, the two kept in touch by correspondence. Mary Craig's parents were neighbors of Winnie Davis's parents at their summer home on the Mississippi Gulf Coast.

In the winter of 1909–10, Sinclair took Meta and David to live at a single-tax colony in Fairhope, Alabama. Single-tax colonies were based on Henry George's 1879 best-seller *Progress and Poverty*. George had proposed a single tax on land, which he believed would produce enough revenue to eliminate poverty. At Fairhope, David attended the colony's experimental Organic School. David slept on a quilt and pillow on the back porch, his father on the front porch. Meta had the bedroom to herself.[70]

At Fairhope, Sinclair began writing *Love's Pilgrimage* because he hoped that a novel "about modern marriage that would show the possibility of a couple agreeing to part, and still remaining friends, would be interesting and useful."[71] This was his dream for his own marriage to Meta; the novel is an account of the problems the couple encountered. Sinclair's ideas about equality in marriage and friendly divorce were in fact part of his larger and evolving feminist ideology, and this period in his late twenties is notable for his enthusiastic support for women activists and writers. As he said of himself, within *Love's Pilgrimage*, "To him woman was an equal." Sinclair suspected that while it was "the world's idea that woman meant vanity and pettiness and frivolity," women liked him for his resistance to this misogyny, "and some men hated him for the same reason."[72]

When he reviewed Susan Glaspell's *The Visioning*, he described it as "the sort of book to give to society girls, if you know any; to kind-hearted ladies who are interested in social reform, in settlement work and charity. It will carry them step by step, never frightening them."[73] It is a book in which Glaspell questions fundamental aspects of American culture: religion, war, class structure, and the double standard of gender roles. Hoping to reach her traditional mother, Glaspell dedicated *The Visioning* to her.[74]

Later in 1910, Sinclair moved the family to another single-tax colony in Arden, Delaware, which labeled itself "a village community holding its land in common, in the spirit of medieval times."[75] Sinclair describes evenings in the colony when everyone "built a campfire in the woodland theatre, sang songs, and recited, and now and then gave Robin Hood or Midsummer's Night's Dream."[76] One anarchist shoemaker was the only person who abused alcohol. When he was locked out of some meetings because he behaved offensively to young women, the shoemaker sought revenge by reporting residents who broke local "Blue Laws." Sinclair had been playing tennis on Sunday, a forbidden activity. The police arrested him and sentenced him to jail, where he served a brief sentence.

Meta, who frequently left on her own, traveled South with David for another trial separation in December of that year. One evening during her absence, Sinclair rode the train to New York to attend a meeting of the Intercollegiate Socialist Society. The novelist Frank Harris remembered Upton Sinclair as having "a fine well balanced face, backed by a direct cordial decisive manner."[77] Sinclair was ushered into the ISS meeting by Inez Milholland, a lawyer who advocated for women's suffrage, abolition of the death penalty, and the rights of working people.

Decades later, Sinclair remembered every detail of their conversation, talking in the lobby until three o'clock in the morning: "What did they not talk about, in the vast range of the socialist and suffrage movements in America and England, where Inez had been to school; the people they knew; the books they had read; the events that the future held behind its veil!"[78] Although Milholland warned him that she was already involved with a married man, Sinclair could not bear to lose her.

Back in Arden, he wrote to her "such mad wild pained distracted letters as would satisfy the most exacting intellectual, the most implacable hater of Puritans!"[79] Inez did not keep the letters, unfortunately for history, but wisely for their reputations. He wrote sadly later: "She was always kind, and straightforward, saying what she meant, as men and women will do in utopia."[80] Inez Milholland was the soul mate that Sinclair never completely found in his other marriages. He had met his intellectual and political equal, but she was not available.

Perhaps Sinclair would not have achieved so much had he married a woman like Inez Milholland, with her own sense of political priorities. Undoubtedly the relationship between Milholland and Sinclair ignited both of them in ways that were enacted in labor and suffrage struggles for the rest of their lives.[81] Sinclair walked in a 1912 suffrage parade in New York, while Inez rode a horse leading the first national suffrage parade in Washington DC in 1915. She collapsed during a speech in Los Angeles and died in November 1916, the only woman to die campaigning for suffrage.

In Delaware, Sinclair constructed his own cabin, the "Jungalow," and played tennis; he was often seen with an axe in his hand, to chop down dead trees to clear the land, and provide wood for furniture.[82] At the beginning of 1911, Meta returned to Arden, and Harry Kemp arrived for a visit. One afternoon, Sinclair discovered his wife and friend making love in his writing cabin. That same day, Harry and Meta packed up and left together. Sinclair filed for divorce in August of 1911, but his petition was initially denied.

He blamed the Catholic judges in New York for this decision. He believed that because he had "failed to beat up his wife, or choke or stab or poison her, or otherwise manifest masculine resentment at her unfaithfulness," the judges did not consider the marriage to be irretrievably broken.[83]

While Sinclair was waiting for the divorce, Mary Craig came to New York looking for a publisher for her book on Winnie Davis. She met Gaylord Wilshire, listened to lectures by John Dewey, and read Henry George. She visited Upton Sinclair, who was staying with his mother. The two went for a walk. Mary Craig claimed that "[i]t might be considered improper" for her to walk with a married man, "but nothing was further from Mr. Sinclair's mind than either romance or impropriety. I got the impression he was slightly bored."[84] He told her the book on Winnie Davis was "terrible." She says she laughed along with him and agreed. Then she asked him to explain socialism. After that, she asked him what had happened to the rest of the money that he had made from *The Jungle*. Thus did their courtship proceed.

A disconsolate Upton Sinclair, unable to get a divorce, took ship to Europe with his son in early 1912, "sick in body and soul, not sure whether he was to live or die, nor caring very much."[85] He was finally able to secure a divorce in the Netherlands, and then he and David stayed with Gaylord Wilshire in England. Mary Craig arrived to visit. In "Craig" (as Upton called her), with her even features and self-confidence as the daughter of Southern gentry, Sinclair found the stable and devoted companion that he needed to continue successfully with his complex life. The two returned from Europe in December 1912, booking passage on separate boats to avoid scandal. Craig, on the *Lusitania*, was thrown violently during a storm, permanently injuring her spine. This injury led to a lifelong battle with pain, and it may be the reason she did not have children.

In 1913 Mary Craig announced her engagement to Upton Sinclair, telling her mother, "Although I haven't chosen the man of your choice, Mama, you will realize in the end that the man of my choice has the spiritual qualities that make him much nearer to you and Papa than any of the others.[86] Sinclair had persuaded Craig's mother that socialism and Christianity had much in common—but her father, Judge Kimbrough, refused to attend the wedding, held at a cousin's home in Virginia. We don't know why Mary Craig chose Upton Sinclair, but late in her life she wrote that it was because of "his hatred of sham and insincerity; he was determined to tell the truth and the whole truth at all costs. And he thought other people would do the same."[87]

After the wedding the Sinclairs traveled to Europe to pick up David from his school in Germany, and then went on to Paris and London. Craig's sister, Dolly, joined them. Like many young American women, Dolly was inspired by the direct action of the fiery suffragists she met in Britain. Like them, Dolly carried a hatchet under her skirt into the National Art Gallery. (British suffragists defaced works of art as a protest against the denial of women's rights.) Craig wrote, "What would Chancellor Kimbrough, President of two banks in Mississippi, have said if a newspaper reporter had called him up and told him that his youngest daughter had been arrested for passing the hatchet?"[88] Because Dolly was not a known suffragist, she was not searched and was never caught.

In London, Sinclair continued to pursue work that examined intimate relationships between men and women. He translated Gene Breaux's play *Damaged Goods* about a man who marries, knowing that he has syphilis, and passes his illness on to his child. In 1914 Margaret Sanger sent Sinclair a letter: "Following are the articles on which I am indicted: prevention of conception, abortion in the U.S. *Can you afford to have a large family? Are preventive means injurious?* If you should care to read them you will be highly amused."[89] Sinclair adapted Breaux's play into his own novel *Sylvia's Marriage*—whose message was that sex education should displace sexual ignorance.

The first part of a collection of previously unpublished stories by

Upton Sinclair, edited by Ruth Engs, is titled "Women's Suffrage and Emancipation." It opens with a quote from *Sylvia's Marriage*: "I believe that women ought to earn their own livings and be independent and free from any man's control."[90] Engs believes that these manuscripts were written mostly during the final years of his first marriage and the beginning years of his second, around 1910 to 1915. In April 1912 Sinclair wrote to Craig that he had met many individuals active in the British movement and had written some "hot stuff" for them.[91]

Engs found two themes in the manuscripts: women who sought independence and defied sexual and social conventions, and men and women looking for dietary cures for their illnesses. Part 2 of her collection begins with a quote from a novel called *Little Algernon*: "'You proposed,' stammered Algernon. 'Of course,' said Lois with a smile. 'When woman is free, she will do most of the proposing. Did you never think of that?'"[92] Engs suggests that the short story "An Experimental Honeymoon" reflects "Sinclair's own internal debate over whether or not he wished to marry again."[93]

In 1914 Sinclair wrote an essay, "To Marry or Not to Marry." His friends John Reed, Louise Bryant, Eugene O'Neil, Jack London, and Isadora Duncan all proclaimed "personal freedom" as a reason to leave, lie to, or abandon their lovers. Sinclair, in perhaps a more radical analysis, considers the costs of these behaviors to personal sanity and social progress and presents his own reasoned approach to marriage, one which was unique, even daring, among Bohemians at the turn of the century.[94] He chose monogamy, the way he chose healthy diet, as a way to be most politically effective.

In London Sinclair was delighted to meet George Bernard Shaw, who was also writing about sexual hypocrisy in works like *Widower's Houses* and *Mrs. Warren's Profession*. The two men would become close friends for the next thirty years. Sinclair described Shaw as "the kindest and sweetest tempered of humans. . . . [H]e had bright blue eyes, the red-gold beard turning gray and the face of a mature angel."[95] In the winter of 1913 the Sinclairs sailed from Europe, leaving David behind. Craig wrote that her husband believed that self-reliance was "his own best gift from adversity. He wanted his own boy to develop it, and had chosen schools in Europe which emphasized this quality."[96] Clearly, the couple wanted to be alone, and that may have been just as powerful a motive.

The honeymooning Sinclairs rented a cottage in Bermuda. Mary Craig recalled those days, writing that her new husband had learned from camping in his early life how to cook steaks, and she had learned how to make coffee: "I learned to get along on Upton's diet of beefsteak, whole wheat bread, green salad, and fruit, with now and then a can of tomato or vegetable soup. Together we were able to prepare a meal quickly."[97] While in Bermuda, Sinclair wrote *The Millennium*, a play set a hundred years in the future, in 2013. With this work, later revised as a novel, John Ahouse believes that "Sinclair earned himself an entry in the bibliographies of American science fiction."[98] Among his prophetic ideas were an airplane that would allow the members of the ruling class to follow the sunset around the world and the invention of an international radio, which in 1913 represented a startling leap of the imagination. Craig writes, "The last act of this fantasy was a picture of a utopia, or perhaps I should say an Uptontopia. These people organized a cooperative colony and went to work to restore the world."[99]

Ludlow and Civil Disobedience

The Sinclairs returned to New York just as the coal miners in Colorado began their strike as part of an organizing drive by the United Mine Workers. At least nine thousand of the eleven thousand miners had gone out, and some were still on the job only because they were forced by armed mine guards to stay. The mine operators began importing scab labor and even turned to the state militia in order to break the strike. The Colorado Guard was called out by the governor, and on April 20, 1913, the Guard attacked mining families living in a tent colony at Ludlow.[100] The strikers stepped out of their tents, hoping to draw fire away from the women and children, but the Guard poured heavy machine gun and rifle fire into the camp. Ludlow burned all night. The next morning, thirteen people were discovered dead in a pit dug underneath a tent—two mothers and eleven children.

Two days later, the strikers retaliated by attacking mine properties. With red bandannas around their heads, shouting "Remember Ludlow," they burned building after building until President Wilson ordered federal troops to Colorado. Over fifty people were killed during the ten days of battle, including the twenty-one known victims who died at Ludlow. A reporter for the *Rocky Mountain News* wrote that "it was a private war, with the wealth of the richest man in the world behind the mine guards."[101] In its official report on the Colorado strike, the newly created United States Commission on Industrial Relations observed that the uprising was possibly "one of the nearest approaches to civil war and revolution ever known in this country in connection with an industrial conflict."[102] Immediately after the massacre at Ludlow, the United Mine Workers sent a group of miners to New York City to publicize what had occurred.

On April 27, Upton Sinclair attended a mass meeting in Madison Square Garden. That night when he and Craig lay in bed talking, Upton suddenly thought of asking a group of sympathizers to put on mourning bands in memory of the murdered of Ludlow and picket the Rockefeller offices. Craig objected: "They will surely arrest you." He answered, "Of course they will; and this is what is needed."[103] Picketing was common in strikes, but as Craig wrote, "So far as we knew it was the first time it had been done on the premises." After the protesters were turned away from the Rockefeller headquarters, they found sympathizers and "more important, a dozen reporters. Now, when the author of *The Jungle* told the story, every reporter was scribbling diligently."[104] As Craig predicted, and he had hoped, Sinclair was arrested for disorderly conduct and booked into a New York jail on April 29. They were taken to the prison known as "the

Tombs," where the women sang "The Marseillaise." Sinclair wrote a poem entitled "The Marseillaise in the Tombs," which allowed him to get published in the New York papers for the first time since *The Jungle*.

Hearing of her son-in-law's arrest, Craig's conservative mother rushed up from Mississippi to support her daughter and "was horrified when I told her of the children burned alive."[105] Craig went to the courthouse, demanded a hearing, and bailed Sinclair out of jail. She rented an office, determined to continue the work: "I had never imagined I would meet lumberjacks, sailors, or garment workers; I had thought of the intellectuals as the 'radicals.' . . . I had once read an essay by John Dewey on 'education by doing' and that was the way I was getting mine."[106] With demonstrations underway in New York City, Sinclair decided to go to Colorado. He planned to personally investigate the conditions in the mines, to create publicity for the miners, and also to gather information for a novel on the coal strike.

At a meeting of the Women's Peace Organization, Sinclair told the audience that he had seen many strikes and knew their symptoms: "I know that period of slow strangling, which is the most heart-breaking and terrifying of all—the more so because it is a silent process, because it happens after the excitement has died down and the country has forgotten."[107] The remainder of Sinclair's stay in Colorado was spent documenting mining conditions. He traveled to the strike zone, visited the embattled camps, and spoke with miners and their families. While Sinclair was in Colorado, Craig carried on the work in New York City. For three weeks she spent every dollar they had.

One evening Craig's mother visited along with Upton's mother. Both women wept. Pricilla Sinclair, Mary Craig remembers, was embarrassed "because her only child—so gifted he might have gone to the top of the business world—had attracted to himself and his new wife the motley crew which was picketing Mr. Rockefeller's own private property!"[108] In the end federal troops crushed the

5. Clement Wood, Mary Craig Sinclair, and George Sterling picketing in front of Rockefeller office, while Upton Sinclair was in "the Tombs" jail, 1914. Courtesy of the Lilly Library, Indiana University, Bloomington.

miners' strike, and the workers were not able to win recognition of their union or any significant improvement in their wages and working conditions. Sixty-six men, women, and children died during the strike, but not a single militiaman or private detective was charged with any crime.

As part of the rage and demoralization that accompanies many strikes, some of the miners built a bomb in New York City. The

Rockefeller compound in Tarrytown had been picketed, and one of the picketers suffered a concussion from being clubbed in the head. He later died in the bombing. Sinclair wrote an open letter to the residents of Tarrytown about the incident. It concluded: "I would die before I would sanction violence." But as a "student of history" he understood why it happened.[109] To his audience in *Appeal to Reason*, he warned that violence must be "resisted at all hazards."[110] Their enemies, he argued, were not men, but systems.

In the summer of 1914, exhausted and looking for a change, the Sinclairs moved to Croton-on-Hudson, where they rented a cottage in the hills. Edgar Selwyn and Margaret Mayo, who wanted to produce a film version of *The Jungle*, lived within bicycling distance. Along with Max Eastman, they also provided tennis partners. Floyd Dell and Robert Minor "constituted a little radical colony, and we could go there and solve all the problems of the world."[111] Craig notes that "Inez Milholland, the suffragist beauty married to a handsome Dutch gentleman, lived on another hill, and Isadora Duncan's sister had established a dance school just down the road."[112] It seems unlikely that Sinclair had ever told her about his relationship with Milholland.

In this early period of film development, production was relatively inexpensive, costing between four hundred and a thousand dollars, so that radicals, reformers, and women's groups, as well as conservative organizations, could produce films to present their cause to a mass public.[113] Nickelodeons were opened, cheap halls where immigrant families could see films for a nickel. Sinclair had watched the lines waiting to enter and saw the potential of film to reach the working class, an opportunity he would welcome twenty years later when Hollywood finally produced a major motion picture based on his work.[114]

But by 1910 antilabor films were so prevalent and damaging that the American Federation of Labor convention endorsed resolutions advising their members to protest to local management whenever these films were shown. Historian Philip Foner noted that none of the films showed the miserable conditions or the exploitation of immigrants: only unions were denounced. Foner describes these films: "Strike leaders were dynamiters, killers, aliens who not only gained nothing for the workers, but left them worse off than before."[115] The American Federation of Labor convention not only suggested its members protest at theaters, but also urged activists to begin the production of their own movies depicting the true lives of workers.[116]

The film *Locked Out* portrayed scenes of starvation in the homes of strikers, police beatings, and the ghosts of martyrs confronting the owner of the factory. The publishers of *Motion Picture World* argued that the National Board of Censorship should have rejected this film and that exhibitors should not "excite the masses by showing them innocent women killed in the act of earning their daily bread."[117] Censorship was not all that radical filmmakers had to cope with. When *Capital vs. Labor* was being filmed in 1911, mounted police were called to the set. The police charged their horses into the actors, injuring many of them.

Trade union activist Elias Strunsky offered Sinclair financing to produce the 1913 film version of *The Jungle*. Selwyn and Mayo formed the All-Star Feature Film Company and produced a six-reel film, the first full-length pro-labor film produced in the United States.[118] Sinclair himself portrayed the socialist labor organizer Eugene Debs. When *The Jungle* was first shown to audiences in theaters in Brooklyn, Newark, and Wilmington, reporters for the *Kinematograph and Lantern Weekly* magazine wrote, "After seeing the picture we begin to have burned into us that Packingtown made enormous profits not simply out of tainted food, but out of the ruined lives of men and women."[119]

But the influential magazine *Variety* warned: "*The Jungle* is not a feature picture of wild animals, just about wild socialists, that's all—and the Lord knows that's enough. . . . The gloom in *The*

6. A poster for the film *The Jungle*, 1914. When the film was screened in 1921, J. D. Cannon (founder of the Labor Film Service) described to Sinclair how the audience came to its feet with a tumultuous standing ovation. Courtesy of the Lilly Library, Indiana University, Bloomington.

Jungle was laid down with a shovel."[120] To a contemporary viewer, the actors, dressed as Lithuanian immigrants during the same period that these immigrants actually came to America, offer a rare glimpse of history through their clothing, houses, and interactions. As an example of early silent film from a proletarian perspective, the scenes inside the slaughterhouse are vivid and enthralling.

Trade journals reported there was intense pressure to keep *The Jungle* out of motion picture houses beyond the big cities.[121] Foner argues that "big business was frightened by the enthusiastic response of the working class and pro-Socialist middle class audiences who, unlike the critic for *Variety*, found the movie a thrilling and educational experience."[122] This pressure was largely successful in limiting distribution of the film. And yet the response by critic Clement Wood, writing in *Appeal to Reason*, the very magazine which had commissioned the book, remains as its legacy: "It isn't usual for moving picture audiences to remain in their seats and applaud five minutes after a film has ended, yet that's what they did. . . . That's what American people are going to do when they see this picture."[123]

The same year *The Jungle* was filmed, news from European correspondents alerted some Americans, including the Sinclairs, to the possibility of armed conflict. Hunter Kimbrough, Craig's younger brother, remembers "they saw World War I coming on."[124] Upton Sinclair's friend, J. G. Phelps Stokes, was known in New York as "the millionaire Socialist." He made arrangements for his butler to bring David back to the States. Sinclair placed David in a North Carolina school run by C. Hanford Henderson, "whose wise and gracious book about education I had read. That left Craig and me free."[125] Craig clearly enjoyed their life without children. When summer approached with David's visit they were faced with the question of what to do with the thirteen-year-old boy. Craig's parents invited them to Mississippi. When they stepped off the train, her teenage brother, Hunter, was waiting, dressed in his gray cadet uniform. He told them, "Sister wrote that she wanted a friend for David."[126]

The couple moved to her family home in Gulfport, Mississippi, joined at last by his son.

Hunter Kimbrough remembered: "When I was twelve years old, I was a cadet at the Gulf Coast Military Academy, and lived with them there for a good many months."[127] The fragile new family was disrupted when Meta arrived in the summer of 1915 to sue for custody of David. It was potentially an ugly confrontation. Meta had recently been involved in another divorce scandal, one reported in the *New York Times* in June 1915. Anthony Arthur comments: "Even Meta's parents acknowledged that she had little real interest in her son."[128] Meta lost her court battle and David stayed in Mississippi. But when Hunter had to return to his military academy, the Sinclairs faced a dilemma: David could go with Hunter, but Upton Sinclair didn't want his son in a military school. They decided that David would live with the Kimbrough family and attend public school with Craig's brothers in Mississippi.

Craig reports, not without some satisfaction, that "Dolly took him home with her and Upton and I were left alone in Ashton Hall."[129] There Upton Sinclair began his novel about the Colorado coal strike, but before he finished it, he and Mary Craig decided to move to California. Sinclair's own public story of the move speaks of tennis and roses and music: "We found ourselves a brown painted two story house on Sunset Avenue, a remote part of the town. It was covered with a huge vine of red roses, and roses were as important to Craig as tennis was to me."[130] Later Sinclair explained that "her mother was still trying to convert her to "the Mississippi brand of religion."[131] But clearly the couple wanted a fresh start. They left her parents—and his son—behind.

After they moved to Pasadena, Frank Harris heard from Sinclair: "He says the wildflowers are tinted like orchids and breathe forth an almost intolerable wealth of perfume. That's the place for this Emersonian. I want him intoxicated with the heady fragrance of love."[132] In the twenties, Sinclair would challenge the reactionary politics of the *Los Angeles Times* and the industrialists of Southern

California. Liberated by his successful second marriage and his hard-won health, Upton Sinclair would be a voice for workers, using his pen to sculpt incendiary prose about political prisoners, the press, organized religion, and finally, the new discovery in Southern California: oil.

CHAPTER FOUR

Singing Jailbirds

[1916–1927]

He is an effeminate young man with a fatuous smile, a weak chin
and a sloping forehead, talking in a false treble. Never before an audience of red-blooded men could Upton Sinclair have voiced his weak,
pernicious, vicious, doctrines. His naïve, fatuous smile alone would
have aroused their ire before he opened his vainglorious mouth. Let
the fact remain that this slim beflanneled example of perverted masculinity could and did get several hundred women to listen to him.
HARRISON OTIS, 1916

The Gabrielino tribe had lived along the Arroyo Seco for thousands
of years before Mexican settlement. After the gold rush, Yankees
evicted Mexican settlers in 1850 and planted the sweet green Muscat
grapes in this part of Southern California. In 1873 a group from
Indiana arrived in California with the intention of founding an
agricultural community. They planted citrus trees and named the
land "Pasadena," a rough translation of a Chippewa Indian word
for "crown of the valley." When Pasadena was incorporated in 1886,
the city elders passed restrictions on the sale of alcohol and closed
the one saloon.[1] To this town came Upton and Mary Sinclair.

Mary Craig describes Pasadena then as a "small city, occupied
mostly by retired millionaires and those who served them. It had
a good library, a theater, a reasonably liberal newspaper—all those
things which Upton had missed on the Mississippi Coast."[2] The
town was home to one of America's earliest theater groups, the

Pasadena Community Playhouse, founded in 1917 (two years after Sinclair's arrival). Pasadena historian Cedar Phillips describes the twenties as the city's golden age, when its architectural masterpieces, including City Hall, were designed and built.[3] Pasadena residents rode the Pacific Electric Red Cars to travel into downtown Los Angeles and everywhere else.[4]

The Sinclair house stood on the edge of a slope, with the valley of the Arroyo Seco to the west. Craig described their garden: "A rosebush aflame with crimson blooms covered half the lot. ... On the other side of the cottage, a jacaranda tree waved fernlike branches laden with violet blossoms."[5] That first year, Craig wrote a sonnet to her new home.[6] It begins:

> Like honey pouring from a golden jar
> The days of autumn pour upon the hills
> Whose peaks are purple while the sunlight fills
> The vistas where the valley winds afar

The house was unfurnished, so Craig would walk several blocks to the streetcar, ride a couple of miles downtown, and shop at secondhand furniture stores. Novelist Irving Stone remembered that their home was "a little mad, but it worked for them."[7] Eventually they connected the original bungalow to four small wood framed houses that Craig bought and relocated to their property. Sinclair wrote that the house looked like a camouflaged battleship until a few years later, when Craig had it painted pink.[8]

In 1916 about forty thousand people lived in Pasadena. Every Sunday morning Sinclair played doubles tennis at the Valley Hunt Club with local businessmen: "one of my opponents here in Pasadena called me 'the human rabbit.'" He added, "I played tennis with the utmost delight."[9] His victories in tournaments were reported in the *Pasadena Star-News*, which characterized him as "mild-mannered and living a simple life."[10] Sinclair joined the local chapter of the Socialist Party and became its chair. Along with a group of new friends, he helped found the Workers Cooperative

So. Cal. Tennis Championship
Tournament
Long Beach, Cal.
1917

7. Sinclair playing tennis. In Pasadena he played doubles tennis every Sunday morning with prominent businessmen. By 1926 he was rated the eighth top tennis player in town. Courtesy of the Lilly Library, Indiana University, Bloomington.

Association of Pasadena. The members traded magazines, books, clothing, shoes, coal, coke, wood, fuel oil, and food.[11]

Once settled in Southern California, Sinclair rarely left. In an interview, he remarked that since moving, he had never wanted to be anywhere else. When friends asked how he could stand the reactionary politics, and the antiunion atmosphere, Sinclair responded, practically, that "people are much the same the world over, but here the climate makes it possible to be so much more active."[12]

Early visitors to Pasadena included King Gillette, founder of the razor fortune, a man with "an almost hypnotic cloak of easy-going, clubbable charm."[13] King Gillette, whose face was on every package of Gillette razor blades, was a Utopian Socialist who had published a book titled *The Human Drift* in 1894, advocating that all industry should be taken over by a single corporation owned by the public. *World Corporation* (1910) was a prospectus for a company set up to create this vision. Gillette offered Theodore Roosevelt the presidency of the company for a salary of a million dollars—but Roosevelt declined the offer. Gillette's final book, *The People's Corporation* (1924), was written with Upton Sinclair. Gillette paid Sinclair five hundred dollars a month for twice-weekly editing sessions.

Another resident of Pasadena, whom Sinclair befriended, was Henry Ford, wintering there with his wife and son, Edsel. Henry Ford had introduced the Model T in 1908. The car was simple to drive, and easy and cheap to repair.[14] Ford wanted to improve the lives of his workers. Efficiency, he argued, meant hiring and keeping the best workers, so in 1914 he offered a wage of five dollars per day, which more than doubled the rate of most of his workers. The best mechanics in Detroit flocked to Ford, bringing their human capital and expertise, raising productivity, and lowering training costs. Ford also experimented with reduced workweeks.[15] His competitors were forced to raise wages or lose their best workers. By 1918 half of all cars in America were Model Ts.[16]

Sinclair took Ford hiking in the San Gabriel Mountains. While lunching within the shady groves of sycamore and oak, Sinclair suggested a meeting between Ford and King Gillette. Mary Craig commented: "Mr. Gillette was as ardent in behalf of his remedy for the world's ills as Henry Ford was in behalf of more and better gadgets."[17] After a two-hour meeting, no one changed their minds. King Gillette thought it a waste of time, Henry Ford was sure he had won the debate, while Upton Sinclair was confident that eventually Ford would see the wisdom of socialism.[18]

The Sinclairs' closest friend in Pasadena was Kate Crane Gartz, the daughter of the millionaire Chicago plumbing magnate Charles Crane. Their friendship trio was unusual; Mary and Upton each had their own warm relationship with Gartz. Mary Craig wrote a sonnet in Gartz's honor.[19] It concludes:

Oh, hear the mothers of the sheltered say:
"What can we do?" But you! Maternal ease
Has not sufficed for you! Oh, wide and free
Your pity flows, a world-maternity!

Like many of the characters in Sinclair's novels, Gartz used her inherited fortune to promote and defend activists in causes ranging from workers rights to civil liberties. In his 1920 novel *100%: The Story of a Patriot*, he modeled the character of Mrs. Godd on Kate Crane Gartz, described by Paul Jordan Smith as "a massively handsome woman, almost regal in appearance, with wide-open great liquid eyes for those who earned her disapproval."[20] Upton Sinclair was always interested in the role of "parlor reds" (wealthy liberal sympathizers) in social change.[21]

Mary Craig described the Sinclairs' first dinner for Mrs. Gartz: "I had no china and no silver, no tablecloth, no cloth napkins."[22] She sent Upton to buy a beef roast, potatoes, and celery. He had always cooked their steaks in a frying pan, and she had never roasted meat. He had brought yellow yams instead of sweet potatoes. The meat burnt and the potatoes were dry: "No one could cut even a potato without a struggle and soon no one tried to keep from laughing."[23]

Sinclair's first published work from California was *The Cry for Justice*, a collection of five thousand works of poetry, philosophy, and fiction. Published in 1915, it was a pioneering anthology of proletarian literature. He dedicated the book to "those unknown ones, who by their dimes and quarters keep the socialist movement going."[24] The book begins with poems by John Masefield, Edwin Markham, and Thomas Carlyle and concludes with work by Walt Whitman, Charlotte Perkins Gilman, and Olive Schreiner. Jack London wrote the introduction, and Sinclair published the book himself.

Sinclair quickly began fencing with the *Los Angeles Times*, which he later described as "the most reactionary paper in America, a bitter-hate paper that never by any possibility wished any favor to

8. Kate Crane Gartz. She was one of the Sinclairs' closest friends in Pasadena. Sinclair's monogamous marriage allowed him to have authentic and supportive friendships with many women. Courtesy of the Lilly Library, Indiana University, Bloomington.

any kind of radical. Of course, I was a special target for its impoliteness."[25] Sinclair rebutted the *Times* through articles that he published in various small presses. Harrison Gray Otis was the publisher of the *Los Angeles Times*; "no man in all the United States hated organized labor more, and it is certain that few did more to obstruct its advance."[26]

Otis detested Sinclair for everything from his labor advocacy to his interest in healthy diets. He used to his advantage the discourse about what constituted acceptable masculinity initiated by Theodore Roosevelt a decade earlier. Amid attacks from the *Times*, Sinclair continued to support women's rights. On October 16, 1916, Margaret Sanger opened the first birth control clinic in the United States in Brooklyn. Nine days later, police closed down the clinic and confiscated its literature and devices. Sanger and her staff were arrested and charged with maintaining a public nuisance. Sanger wrote to Sinclair: "It is the trick of the authorities to try and kill the great interest upon the subject of BIRTH CONTROL as well as to exhaust me physically, spiritually, and financially."[27] She asked him to write to Judge Dayton at the Federal Court in New York demanding her speedy trial or release from persecution. He wrote the letter.

By 1917 Sinclair had finished *King Coal*, the first half of his planned two-volume novel based on the Colorado coal strike, which he had begun immediately after the searing events at Ludlow. In the novel, a college student turned organizer named Hal Warner visits the mining camps, trying to help the workers organize against the theft of their wages. Andrew Lee writes: "*King Coal* was part of Sinclair's massive attempt to do what Zola in France had done: create a national myth and consciousness through fiction."[28] His Macmillan editor, George Brett, admonished him: "Bear in mind that it is a novel you are writing and not a work of history or controversy."[29] Mary Craig had written Brett that she fully agreed, but that part of her husband's stubbornness was simple fatigue. She added that Sinclair respected her literary judgment and would listen to her.[30]

Peggy Prenshaw notes that Craig's contribution to the literary partnership with Sinclair was "her ability to add vivifying detail to the fiction, what she and he came to call 'putting the clothes on Mary Burke' [the heroine of *King Coal*]."[31] When Floyd Dell, who read *King Coal* in manuscript, suggested that the characterization of a labor leader as a self-seeking scoundrel would add dramatic impact, Sinclair rejected the idea because he believed that such an addition would distort history.[32] Instead, he added a factual appendix to authenticate his story. Macmillan ultimately published *King Coal*, but by that time, Americans had turned their attention to World War I.

A War to Save Democracy?

Ironically, just like Otis's cherished "red-blooded men," Sinclair supported America's entry into World War I. He had always believed that all war was motivated by a search for profit. Though he was not a complete pacifist, he had argued that socialists should work to prevent war because it was workers who did the fighting and the dying. His friend Henry Ford opposed the war and supported the decision of the Woman's Peace Party to organize a peace conference in Holland. After that conference, Ford was contacted by Jane Addams. She suggested that he sponsor a further conference in Stockholm to discuss ways to avoid war. Ford sent a delegation of pacifists to Europe; he chartered the ship *Oskar II*, which left New Jersey at the end of 1915 and reached Stockholm in January 1916. But the Europeans attending were unable to bring in Britain, France, or Germany—and were thus unable to negotiate an armistice. When the United States entered the war, the American Socialist Party split; while the majority opposed war, a minority supported U.S. intervention.

Upton Sinclair began receiving letters from friends in Europe and America, who forcefully argued that German workers needed help in overthrowing the autocracy. Peter Kropotkin implored, "Does not the thunder of the war reach you in America? I am writing all the time letters in all directions asking everyone to support France and Belgium in their great struggle against the barbarian invasion."[33] George Herron, who had moved to Italy and become a confidential agent of President Wilson, wrote hopefully that "the outcome will be social revolution in every country and the sweeping away of all the old institutions of government."[34]

In 1916 Sinclair began to circulate a letter that endorsed the war from a socialist perspective. The group who signed it believed that President Wilson was correct when he argued that the war was necessary to save liberal democracy. Wilson, originally from Virginia, had taught at Princeton, where Sinclair had happily researched *Manassas*. He was, Sinclair believed, an enlightened Southerner. Yet there was continued disagreement among his progressive community. George Bernard Shaw had urged his friends to "rally the world's intellectuals to prevent the world war."[35] Yet philosopher John Dewey argued that the war highlighted "the supremacy of public need over private possessions," thus expanding the social contract.[36] Sinclair was drawn to Dewey's way of thinking, based on his respect for Dewey as an authority on the political issues of his day, including women's rights, race relations, and international peace.[37] Significantly, Dewey had been an occasional guest at Helicon Hall and a member of its board of directors.

Woodrow Wilson had already signed legislation regulating child labor and providing an eight-hour day for railroad workers—a protection few workers enjoyed. To ensure that the needs of the military were met, the government involved itself in business operations to a degree previously unknown. The National War Labor Board guaranteed collective bargaining and mediated labor disputes. The government nationalized telephone, telegraph, sleeping-car, and express companies, as well as warehouses and terminals. Late in 1916, Sinclair decided to join the Social Democratic League, a group that had split from the Socialist Party and was both socialist and prowar. Yet he found himself in an uncomfortable situation: "I don't like the company I am in while I am supporting the government," he explained in a speech he gave in early 1918.[38] He decided to create a magazine, primarily in order to explain his position. He called it *Upton Sinclair's*, and it was funded solely by income from sales and subscriptions. Sinclair produced his magazine from home, doing much of the work himself.

Sinclair was fully aware of the risks of losing civil liberties during wartime, since he had described those events in *Manassas*. He voiced concern that the espionage laws were being used to silence war critics.[39] Since it would be his friends who would be prosecuted, he decided that in supporting the war, he would also have to criticize the way it was prosecuted, seeing himself, Mattson says, as "an in-house critic of Wilson's policies."[40] As is often the case with people trying to compromise, his position antagonized antiwar and prowar friends alike. Sir Arthur Conan Doyle wrote that as much as he admired Sinclair's books, his ideas on the war demonstrated a "half-and-half limited ability" that would guarantee the triumph of the German Kaiser.[41]

Meanwhile, war critics in America were imprisoned, most notably Eugene Debs, a hero to Sinclair and millions of other Americans.[42] Eugene Debs had begun his working life as a locomotive paint-scraper. He became a leader in organizing railroad workers. After leading the American Railway Union in a confrontation with federal troops sent to break up the 1894 Pullman Strike, Debs was jailed for six months for contempt of court. Upon release he became a featured speaker for the Socialist Party and their nominee for president in 1900. Debs's greatest success was in 1912, when he campaigned against Democratic nominee Woodrow Wilson, incumbent President Taft, and former president Theodore Roosevelt. He received almost a million votes. Six years later, Debs was arrested under the terms of the Sedition and Espionage Acts.

Sinclair condemned the jailing of political dissenters and implored President Wilson to release Debs.[43] At Sinclair's alma mater, Columbia University, psychologist Jay McKeen Cattell was fired for criticizing the war. A week later, historian Charles Beard resigned from the Columbia faculty in protest. Beyond the attacks on socialists and intellectuals, local vigilantes used the war as an excuse to attack immigrants and labor organizers, lynching German Americans and breaking up Socialist Party meetings. In Bisbee, Arizona, vigilantes in league with state officials rounded up 1,200 copper miners belonging to the Industrial Workers of the World (IWW), threw them into railroad cars, and left them in the New Mexico desert.

The IWW had been founded by Bill Haywood, Eugene Debs, and Mother Jones in 1905 with the vision of wage earners around the world joining into "one big union." Historian Patrick Renshaw notes that while the Progressive movement was "the response of those who were displaced or dispossessed by the march of American capitalism," the IWW represented "immigrant and migratory workers, the unskilled, unorganized and unwanted, the poorest and weakest sections of labor."[44] IWW membership rarely exceeded one hundred thousand at any one time, but at least a million workers held IWW cards at some time between 1905 and 1923, and referred to themselves as "Wobblies." Workers joined the IWW in Canada, Great Britain, Scandinavia, Australia, New Zealand, South Africa, Mexico, South America, Norway, and Sweden.

Among the IWW activists arrested was Ralph Chaplin, who wrote the labor anthem "Solidarity Forever" in the winter of 1915. By 1918 Chaplin was incarcerated in Leavenworth, Kansas. He remembered, "It was letters from the outside world that helped me most to keep courage. . . . Scott and Nelly Nearing kept in touch with me all the time. So did Upton Sinclair."[45] While Chaplin was incarcerated in Kansas, a group of Wobblies were jailed in California. Close to fifty rank-and-file men were locked up for months in a disease-ridden jail in Sacramento where five of them died. Twenty-four were sentenced to ten years in prison. The men proudly walked out of the courtroom singing "Solidarity Forever."

By Armistice Day, November 11, 1918, 48,000 American soldiers had died in combat, and 56,000 more had died of disease. But

European losses were even more staggering: Germany lost 1,800,000 men, France lost 1,385,000, and Britain not quite one million.[46] Initially, Sinclair did not regret his support of the war. "I am, so far as I know," he wrote in 1918, "unique among American Socialists who supported the war, in that I did not lose, for a moment, my vision of the evils, both of our own country and our allies."[47] Sinclair strongly believed that the Allies should never have humiliated the people of Germany, especially when it came time to draw up the terms of peace.[48] However, President Wilson agreed to sign on to Article 231 of the Versailles Treaty, later termed the "war guilt clause," which forced Germany to take sole responsibility for the war and to pay billions of dollars in reparations to the Allies. Sinclair cabled Wilson's advisers: "All Liberals aghast at President Wilson's surrender. Urgently implore less drastic terms."[49] Such pleas had no effect.

Sinclair sent a second telegram to Wilson. He asked that "all territory taken from central powers in this war shall be neutralized and made forever independent under international guarantee."[50] Yet almost immediately, European powers claimed land throughout Africa, and colonies liberated from Germany were turned over to France and Britain. An outraged Sinclair accused Wilson of befriending the "reactionary forces of France and Italy and the entrenched power of triumphant British commercialism."[51] Sinclair's last hope was that the League of Nations would succeed. He embraced its goals, and Wilson returned from Europe in order to convince Americans that their country had a moral obligation to enter this international compact. President Wilson asked Henry Ford to run for the Senate as a Democrat from Michigan in 1918. Ford ran as a peace candidate and a strong supporter of the proposed League of Nations. He almost won. But the United States Senate rejected the League of Nations on November 19, 1919.

Sinclair believed that the terms of the peace treaty and the rejection of the League of Nations would determine the future of the twentieth century. He commented grimly that "I think I have supported my last capitalist war."[52] Wilson allowed industry to immediately attack labor unions following the armistice and, notes Kevin Mattson, "like the influenza epidemic a year earlier, which prevented Sinclair from going to the public library for a spell, the red scare of 1919 worked its way into the Los Angeles area like a virus."[53] Upton Sinclair wrote angrily in the *Appeal to Reason* that the government was now "seizing radicals and throwing them into jail, deporting them if they are foreigners, holding them at prohibitive bail if they are American citizens."[54] He wrote also of what he heard about treatment of prisoners that seemed to verge on torture.

As Upton Sinclair usually did when he felt strongly about an injustice, he wrote a book. In 1919 he published *Jimmy Higgins*, about a worker in the socialist movement who decides to enlist, overcoming his pacifist politics. When he is asked to fight the Bolsheviks, he faces a crisis of conscience. German critic Utz Riese notes that Jimmy Higgins was an imagined Socialist Everyman, a loyal worker in his movement.[55] This kind of foot soldier was rarely chronicled, even by radical historians, and Riese argues that Sinclair legitimized this kind of activist through his novel. Novelist Gertrude Atherton wrote Sinclair, "I have been intensely interested in *Jimmy Higgins*, as it gives me a progressive point of view that I could not get else-where."[56] Within the novel, one of the characters states what Sinclair himself felt: "If at the beginning of 1917 I had known what I know today, I would have opposed the war and gone to jail with the pacifist radicals. I cannot forgive him [Wilson]; it is not merely that he made a fool of himself, but he made a fool of me!"[57]

In *Jimmy Higgins* Sinclair took on more than participation in World War I. Sinclair biographer Leon Harris noted that "half a century before industrial pollution would arrest the attention of most Americans, except for a few cranks," Sinclair lamented in *Jimmy Higgins* "how factories were pouring chemicals into every stream."[58] Japanese critic Sachiko Nakada points out that "the restoring forces of Mother Nature" had already been introduced in *The Jungle*: "how the sounds and sites of the field, meadows, woods, and rivers made the poor man restore himself as a proper man."[59] Since 1906 Sinclair's novels had been translated into Japanese. He enjoyed a fervent following in Japan.

Defending Liberty

Upton Sinclair's folded in February 1919. Sinclair recalled, "I got letters of praise and letters of fury, and published them side by side. The more bad names I was called, the more amusing I found it; and my readers let me know that they too enjoyed it."[60] But he was losing money, and his health was suffering. When in early 1919 editor Emanuelle Haldeman-Julius took over the *Appeal to Reason*, Sinclair proposed that they merge the two magazines. Haldeman agreed, changed its name to *Haldeman-Julius Weekly*, and gave Sinclair one full page called *Upton Sinclair's* in which to express his ideas. Now he had an audience of nearly half a million. Sinclair possessed a mailing list and a means of distribution that enabled him to self-publish his books for the next twenty years. Utz Riese argues that Sinclair practiced "self-authorization," a prescient invention of self-publishing.[61] Any profits were used to underwrite the cost of printing the next book.

The first of his series of social critiques, which Sinclair titled the Dead Hand series, was *Profits of Religion*. The book's message was that the profit motive of organized religion was in contradiction with true Christianity. Sir Arthur Conan Doyle wrote that he found the book "brave and strong, and good . . . but don't run down Spiritualism . . . the one solid patch in the whole quagmire of religion."[62] He added that he ran a psychic book store in London and "if ever I can send you any books let me know."[63] Anthony Arthur comments that *Profits of Religion* was "deliberately incendiary and intensely autobiographical."[64]

Sinclair followed *Profits* with a religiously themed novel. *They Call Me Carpenter* was set amidst the Armistice Day parades of 1921

9. Pasadena house where the Sinclairs moved in 1916. Craig had her room at the south end and Upton practiced violin at the north end. Courtesy of Dana Downie, 1971.

when uniformed veterans protested showings of the German film *The Cabinet of Dr. Caligari* in Los Angeles. In Sinclair's novel, the figure of Christ steps down from a church window to become part of the crowd in the street and quotes the Bible—and the crowd responds by accusing him of being a Red. John Ahouse suggests that one of Jesus's sermons in the book echoes Sinclair's own socialist and Christian beliefs.[65]

Sinclair did admire many qualities in the historical Jesus (and eventually wrote a book on the topic). He was drawn to those characteristics in friends like naturalist Luther Burbank, whom he described as a "kind and gentle man."[66] Burbank invited the Sinclairs and David to visit him in Santa Rosa. He wrote that one of Mary Craig's sonnets was the "finest thing of the sort ever born of the human mind."[67] He added, "Your son seems to be a genius too. . . . I am like him, *I like figs*, and think them about the best fruit that ever grew."[68] David Sinclair was living with his father and stepmother from the summer of 1917 till January 1919, when he returned to Mississippi to finish high school.

That eighteen months was the longest period David had ever spent with his father since his parents' divorce. The distance in space and time that characterized their relationship from 1915 to 1945 may have been based on Craig's seeming need, and perhaps his own, to create distance from this son of his first marriage. Mary Craig and Upton Sinclair had no child of their own; contact with David generated memories of Meta and would bring a constant reminder of that perhaps more passionate if less successful marriage.

Meta Sinclair had meanwhile married Lester Keene in New York City in 1916, a marriage that would last until Keene's death in 1947. By the time David joined the Sinclairs, the Workers Cooperative Association from their early years in Pasadena had disbanded, but Sinclair and Craig were still buying in bulk: Leon Harris wrote that David remembered eating oatmeal on a daily basis. David also told Harris how his father would pace up and down through the jasmine and rose hedges in the backyard, thinking out his books, his concentration so intense that he would wear a rut several inches deep. Every so often he would stop to shovel dirt into the ruts and then resume his pacing.[69]

After David returned to Mississippi, Upton Sinclair privately published *The Brass Check*, the manuscript he had been working on during David's stay. About the book he wrote: "I had made notes and had envelopes full of clippings, and a head full of memories and a heart full of rage."[70] He chose for his title the cost of a prostitute, a brass check purchased at the entrance. One source of inspiration for the book were the reports that American suffragist Alice Stone Blackwell sent him.[71] She described how "the news carried by the great press agencies on the subject of women's suffrage was habitually twisted and the twist was almost always unfavorable to suffrage."[72] She detailed how defeats of woman suffrage were publicized while its success was ignored: "A good many women, I think, learned a wholesome distrust of press reports during the suffrage struggle."[73] It was examples like these that impelled Sinclair to write the first exposé of bias among newspaper publishers, editors, and reporters.

Anthony Arthur comments, "Because he subordinated everything to what he saw as the need to work for social justice, the institution that should have been Sinclair's natural ally, the press, became his deadliest enemy, bent on destroying him."[74] The first half of *The Brass Check* is personal memoir, detailing the newspapers' attacks after *The Jungle* and their refusal to print his rebuttal: "I have been persecuted for twenty years by prostitute Journalism"—"an animal in a cage" whose "bars were newspapers."[75] The second half of the book documented how American newspapers represented private rather than public interests. When Sinclair had shown the manuscript to an attorney, he was warned that it contained fifty criminal libel cases. Although both the Associated Press and the *New York Times* considered lawsuits, Sinclair correctly believed that any litigation would give his claims publicity. Max Eastman wrote a preface for the book. He argued that bias in American journalism was a "monstrous and malignant growth.... Upton Sinclair proves this statement for the first time."[76]

When Sinclair received the initial printing of *The Brass Check*, he showed it to Gaylord Wilshire, by then also living in Pasadena. Wilshire phoned him to say it was "inconceivable that the publication of this book would be permitted in America."[77] He urged Sinclair to distribute his copies to socialist and labor groups and bookstores, and to tell them to hide the books. Although the book was ignored by the newspapers he profiled, for media scholars, it became a permanent classic.

Later that year, Sinclair wrote *The Book of Life* to continue the exploration he had begun in *Good Health and How We Won It*.

Remembering a childhood diet of "fried chicken and hot biscuits and chocolate cake," Sinclair aimed to offer a fuller guide to his working-class readers seeking healthy a diet and life-extending habits.[78] This information, he wrote, was known only to "a little group of adventurous persons known as 'health cranks' and it has been my pleasure to watch the leading ideas of these 'cranks' being rediscovered one by one by medical authority."[79] Sinclair dedicated the book to Kate Crane Gartz, for her "unceasing efforts for a better world, and her fidelity to those who struggle to achieve it."[80]

Ever since that fateful visit to John Harvey Kellogg's clinic in 1909, Sinclair had been an enthusiastic supporter of preventive healthcare. He saw the achievement of physical wellness as integral to a life of intellectual work and political activism. The 1924 issue of *Physical Culture* magazine featured a cover story by Upton Sinclair on "My Life and Diet." Sinclair was unlike the caricatures of humorless health-food reformers: he enjoyed poking fun at himself and joked about the "picketing diet" he developed at Ludlow. He told his readers to find themselves a simple diet of natural foods, "then learn as quickly as possible to forget your diet and all the rest of your physical problems and interest yourself in something worthwhile in life—somebody or some cause outside of yourself."[81]

Upton Sinclair briefly turned his attention to Hollywood in these years. Filmmaking had become the biggest industry in California. Southern California's climate was ideal for filming, and the studios open shop practices provided cheap labor. Sinclair's melodramatic screenplay *The Adventurer* had been produced in 1917 as a silent film by the U.S. Amusement Corporation, and he continued to be fascinated by the potential of film as a political and educational tool.[82] During the conservative Republican climate of the 1920s, Hollywood was emerging as a corporate entity; studios tried to expand their audience base and increase profits by creating an experience of fantasy for a cross-class audience. They built exotic "picture palaces" and produced lavish films designed to turn movie going into an experience that encouraged individualism rather than collective action.[83]

10. Upton Sinclair in Hollywood in 1923, standing in the garden. The twenties were rich and productive years for Sinclair. Courtesy of the Lilly Library, Indiana University, Bloomington.

In 1922 Sinclair wrote a biting essay for *Screenland*, in which he contrasted the laudatory response of the press to *Birth of a Nation* with the removal of *The Jungle* from theaters. Sinclair described a conversation with *Birth of a Nation* filmmaker D. W. Griffith. He had expressed his "abhorrence of the incitement to race hatred which makes the essence of his picture." Griffith's answer was that "he had merely been concerned to tell an effective story."[84] Sinclair's essay "Big Business and Its Movies" was published not in an obscure radical newspaper, but in a Hollywood screen magazine, next to ads for "The Book of Fate: What Is Going to Happen to You?" or "Have You an Idea for a Movie Star?" That same year, industry representatives created a new position of "movie czar," whose job was to issue a code of ethics for the movies. Most film historians cite the censorship of sexual and feminist imagery as first occurring in this period.[85] Meanwhile, Sinclair's article points to a much earlier purging of films like *The Jungle* in favor of Griffith's white supremacist memoir of the South.

Sinclair's third book in the Dead Hand series targeted higher education. He traveled from California by train to universities in Montana, Oregon, Wisconsin, Illinois, Pennsylvania, and New York. At the University of Wisconsin he visited David, who was wavering between a major in music or physics (he chose physics). At each institution, Sinclair met with professors and documented the way that administrators, like those he had observed at Columbia, were subservient to conservative boards and often fired professors for espousing their beliefs in the classroom. Novelist Irving Stone remembers walking through Sather Gate at the University of California, Berkeley: "right across the narrow street, was Upton Sinclair with a box and on top of it about a dozen copies of *The Brass Check*." Stone asked him why he was selling the book on the street corner "instead of where he belonged, on campus, with a dignified table loaned to him by the university."[86] Sinclair replied that he had applied and been refused permission.

In *The Goosestep*, published in 1922, Sinclair documented how groups ranging from the National Association of Manufacturers to the Chamber of Commerce pushed for colleges to create obedient workers who would not question the system. Upton Sinclair delighted in including an exposé of President Nicholas Butler of Columbia University: "President Butler's career at Columbia has been like that of a drunken motorist in a crowded street; he has left behind him a trail of corpses."[87]

Describing what he observed of campus politics, Sinclair noted dryly that the average professor will watch a college president abuse a colleague with the same indifference that a rabbit observes a ferret chase down another rabbit and drink its blood.[88] Social critic John Jay Chapman wrote Sinclair that his reporting "will remain as a valuable deposit, a sort of lurid mass of hot smoldering coals, at which historians may warm their hands."[89] In 1923 this book stood alone as a rare and prophetic critique of higher education in America.

During this period Sinclair hired Delia Spencer Williams as a secretary. One of his unique qualities was that in writing for "everyman," he often reached "everywoman" as well, that is, the mass public. Delia Williams, who had earlier enjoyed reading *King Coal*, would work for Sinclair for the next twenty years, undoubtedly making possible much of his most productive period.[90] In his next book, *The Goslings*, Sinclair eviscerated the grade school system. The book begins in Southern California, documenting the control of the *Los Angeles Times* over the school board and the selection of superintendents. It also investigates education in towns ranging from Spokane, Butte, Denver, Kansas City, St. Louis, and Chicago, to Minneapolis, Boston, New York, Philadelphia and Washington DC. Educational reformer Jack Nelson celebrated the book as a valuable contribution on the political economy of education, "which foreshadowed the current applications of critical theory to schooling."[91] Sinclair addresses corruption, nationalistic impositions on texts and teachers, censorship, teacher unions, and the role of foundations like the Rockefeller and Carnegie Funds.

Sinclair's critique of education pointed out the history that was *not* taught in the classroom. The strike of militant longshoremen, sailors, and oil workers in the Los Angeles harbor at San Pedro is part of the forgotten history of California.[92] In "Pedro," as in Ludlow, Sinclair would place himself directly into a labor struggle. Many writers were sympathetic to the struggles of organized labor in California, but few put themselves in harm's way, as Sinclair did at Liberty Hill. The IWW had met in San Pedro only four months after its founding in 1905, and Wobbly composer Joe Hill's IWW card was issued by the San Pedro local 167.[93] In the spring of 1923, the Wobblies in San Pedro called a general strike to pressure for the release of state political prisoners, to protest "Fink Halls" (anti-union employment offices) and the criminal-syndicalism law, and to agitate for higher wages for dockworkers. At San Pedro, some three thousand longshoremen tied up the port. The local police began mass arrests of strikers, raiding IWW halls.

Sinclair had continued to lodge public protests from Pasadena on behalf of jailed radicals and to keep them supplied with books. In her memoir, Craig described a visit from a longshoreman's wife who "vividly described atrocities when a hired mob raided a meeting, beating workers, throwing a little girl into a receptacle of boiling coffee, scalding her almost to death."[94] Longshoreman Art Shields, who knew Sinclair from the picketing of Rockefeller headquarters after the Ludlow massacre, phoned him and asked for help. Although Sinclair was not the major figure in either Ludlow or San Pedro, his participation was crucial in developing sympathy for the strikers. Inspired by groups like the Women's Trade Union League and the suffrage movement, Sinclair initiated some of the first efforts by intellectuals to gain widespread support for striking workers. By involving himself on behalf of these workers, Sinclair became, notes Dieter Herms, not only a chronicler of history but also a participant.[95]

When San Pedro strike sympathizer Minnie Davis heard that the striking dockworkers needed somewhere to meet, she offered the use of her rented land behind Third and Fourth Streets, on a hill overlooking the harbor.[96] The workers promptly dubbed it Liberty Hill. Art Shields remembers: "There was more singing than speaking on Liberty Hill. . . . I've heard 'Solidarity' on many picket lines in the last sixty-two years, but I've never enjoyed it as much as I did on Liberty Hill."[97] Eighty or so men, armed with clubs and guns, began climbing the hill. The two thousand strikers continued to sing as each was arrested. The strikers decided to carry their message from door to door. Thousands of men, women, and children wound through the streets singing, with the jailed workers singing back from inside the San Pedro jail. Although a housewives' committee was feeding many dockworkers, others were going hungry. Art Shields telephoned Upton Sinclair again.

Police Captain Plummer announced a ban on street meetings. Sinclair notified the strikers that the next move of the police would be to take over Liberty Hill. He would bring friends to challenge the police order. Sinclair's group huddled into a nearby café to strategize; it included his brother-in-law Hunter Kimbrough, along with Kate Crane Gartz (who had come with her overnight bag all packed, prepared for jail). Sinclair told reporters, "We're testing the right of police to suppress free speech and assemblage. You'll hear what I say if you climb Liberty Hill."[98] When Sinclair and his friends reached the summit, he stepped on a speaker's box. Captain Plummer shouted, "I'm taking you in if you utter a word." "My right to speak is protected by the U.S. Constitution," Sinclair replied, and recited the First Amendment. As Art Shields remembered, Police Captain Plummer "grabbed the people's novelist by the collar" and arrested him.[99]

Hunter Kimbrough began to read the Declaration of Independence and was arrested, along with Prince Hopkins and Hugh Handyman. The officers, under orders not to arrest women, ignored Mrs. Gartz. Hunter Kimbrough wrote his own account of the arrest, describing how he rode on the running board of the overloaded police car, and how Sinclair lay on the floor in his cell rather than risk the lice-ridden cots. Kimbrough called the policemen's attention to the patriotism of the ancestors of those arrested.[100]

The men were not allowed to consult an attorney and were held incommunicado. Mary Craig believed that the police planned to harm Sinclair and to make it appear that either the iww or the Ku Klux Klan was responsible.[101] The Los Angeles papers carried an unconfirmed report that the Klan planned to capture the four men. Mary Craig was visited by a Klansman during the time she was frantically trying to find her husband, who assured her that there was no plot on the part of his organization.[102] Art Shields issued a press statement saying Sinclair might be a victim of foul play. Two days later Upton Sinclair was released from jail.

Sinclair's valiant efforts did not save the San Pedro walkout. Sailors left for distant ports, and the iww's isolation from the rest of organized labor meant that the San Pedro strike was one of the final actions of the Wobblies before the split in the organization in 1924 and its subsequent decline.[103] A week later, Upton Sinclair, out on bail, reappeared on Liberty Hill. Yugoslav-American writer Louis Adamic recounted: "Sinclair, a triumphant note in his intense voice, conducted doubtless the biggest meeting of his strike-following career, while over the bay of San Pedro hung a very full and very serene moon."[104] Adamic concluded that the night that Upton Sinclair spent in jail for trying to read the Constitution was "among the pleasantest incidents of his career."[105]

Police Chief Oaks stated to the press, "I hope Sinclair goes to jail if convicted. . . . I would rather deal with four thousand iww than one man like Sinclair, who is what I consider one of the worst types of radicals."[106] After he was released, Sinclair wrote an open letter to Chief Oaks, which was printed as a leaflet and widely circulated in Los Angeles. It began, "I thank you for this compliment, for to be dangerous to lawbreakers in office such as yourself is the highest duty that a citizen of this community can perform."[107] Eventually Oaks was fired as one of the conditions of Sinclair's dropping his civil suit for false arrest. Martin Zanger suggests that Sinclair's

11. *Singing Jailbirds* cast and stage set. After his 1923 arrest for reading the Bill of Rights to striking longshoremen, Sinclair publicized the episode as a means of launching the Southern California branch of the American Civil Liberties Union. He dramatized the plight of political prisoners in the play *Singing Jailbirds*, 1924. Courtesy of the Lilly Library, Indiana University, Bloomington.

experience at Liberty Hill may have stimulated his willingness to run a campaign for governor, noting that "subsequent California history might well have evolved differently had Mary Craig Sinclair held her husband to his promise to stay out of the Wobbly strike."[108] Sinclair's own version of the events and their aftermath can be found in the introductory chapter of *The Goslings* and in the postscript to *Singing Jailbirds*.[109]

Upton Sinclair went on to launch the Southern California branch of the American Civil Liberties Union, raising funds from wealthy sympathizers such as Charlie Chaplin, Congressman William Kent, and King Gillette. Sinclair hoped the ACLU would work for prison reform and release of political prisoners. Ella Reeve Bloor was still a good friend twenty-five years after she had helped him research

The Jungle. She wrote after a visit to iww members at Walla Walla Prison in Centralia, thanking him for his "prompt reply to my sos." About the prisoners, she wrote, "It's a wonder that they keep up their spirits as they do, after being away from Life itself for ten years."[110] Sinclair wrote the play *Singing Jailbirds* to draw attention to the injustices that Bloor described.

Singing Jailbirds was set in the jail in San Pedro where the striking dockworkers were imprisoned. German critic Dieter Herms writes: "The generalization of the tragedy is achieved by means of the iww chorus whose songs of proletarian solidarity punctuate the play in leitmotif fashion."[111] In his postscript to the play, Sinclair noted that similar conditions could be found in prisons throughout the country and that if anyone doubted this, "he is advised to read 'In Prison,' by Kate Richards O'Hare."[112] After World War I, Socialist Party organizer O'Hare had condemned the way mothers in America were encouraged to raise children for the military. She was sent to jail for five years, where she organized fellow prisoners.

Journalist Miriam Allen deFord wrote Sinclair that she found *Singing Jailbirds* to be "a remarkable contribution to expressionistic drama. I should like immensely to see it adequately performed."[113] But Sinclair needed funding for such a performance. He appealed to the readers of the *New Republic*—"We who care about free speech confront a difficult situation out here on the Coast. . . . I undertook to raise the money to finance a production of *Singing Jailbirds*"—explaining that he would take no royalties.[114] Following successful performances in Berlin in 1927, the play ran for two months at the New Playwrights Theater in New York. Later the play toured in both France and India.

Upton Sinclair continued to correspond with other women like Edith Summers Kelly, who had been a resident at Helicon Hall. She wrote him to announce the publication of her feminist novel, *Weeds*, and to ask that he and Mary Craig publish positive reviews: "Congratulations on the measure of success that you have attained in your Los Angeles fight. It takes much courage and strength of

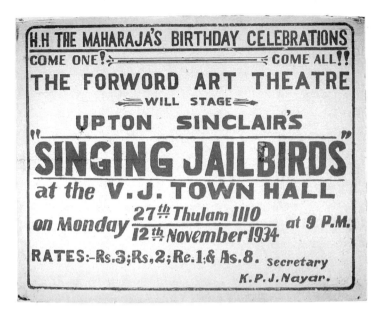

12. Poster from India for *Singing Jailbirds*. Sinclair's play ran for two months in New York and was also produced in Germany and France. Courtesy of the Lilly Library, Indiana University, Bloomington.

purpose to think anything worth fighting for in these dark days."[115] A month later Kelly wrote again that she was "very much pleased to have you devote so much space to *Weeds* and to praise it so highly. . . . I got a lot of satisfaction out of writing the book even though I had to do it under most unfavorable conditions."[116]

In 1982 the Feminist Press republished *Weeds* as a forgotten proletarian classic. In her afterword, Charlotte Margolis describes Kelly's memories of Helicon Hall: "Kelly celebrated the fact that because of these kitchens and nurseries, mothers were able to eat their meals in peace and converse freely with other adults."[117] Kelly herself wrote that "Helicon Hall is one of the beauty spots of the past."[118] Her subsequent letters to Sinclair reveal how the demands of housework and childcare on her California ranch devoured her writing time; she was never able to write another book. An examination of the Kelly-Sinclair correspondence reveals that Sinclair devoted his funds and energy to ensuring that *Weeds* would be published in German, Russian, and French.

Kelly's novel may have reminded Sinclair of the struggles in his first marriage, particularly with its eloquent evocation of a mother's frustrations. In 1924 David Sinclair graduated from the University of Wisconsin with a degree in physics. (David's half-brother, Meta's second son, Lester, would also study physics.) Sinclair did not attend his son's graduation, but his grandmother, Priscilla Sinclair, did. A reporter described her as "a very dignified and aristocratic old lady, with such a fashionable Parisian hat."[119] The article noted that Mrs. Sinclair enjoyed playing bridge and talking about her famous son. It must have been disappointing to David that his father did not cross the country for his graduation.

Instead Sinclair was absorbed in the discovery of oil in Long Beach near Signal Hill where Craig had bought several lots. She describes the meetings held among property owners like herself, who were "awakened to the fact that they must organize and stand together . . . otherwise the oil companies could buy a few scattered lots and from there proceed to drain all the oil from under the adjoining lots."[120] After a half-dozen trips from Pasadena, Upton Sinclair was also carrying a notebook, but not for recording legal opinions. He was instead taking notes for a new novel. Sinclair told his wife, "Don't you see what we've got here? Human nature laid bare! Competition in excelsis! The whole oil industry—free, gratis, and for nothing! How could I pass it up?"[121]

After the first oil strike, the Hill was transformed into a forest of wooden derricks by the mid 1920s, replacing every last one of the homes on the ocean side. Roberta Nichols, former curator at Rancho Los Cerritos museum and historic site, describes the pumping rigs, which had first displaced commercial flower growing and truck gardens. These rigs "swept aside the rows of vegetables, the rabbit hutches and the modest cottages" on what came to be called Signal Hill.[122]

In 1926, as Sinclair completed his novel about the oil industry, the Sinclairs moved closer to their Signal Hill properties in Long Beach, right across the harbor from San Pedro. From there he wrote to his readers: "Too many visitors got my Pasadena street address. I wish I were double, one to see visitors and be human, and the other to study and write books. As it is, MCS and I have eloped and are hiding in a post office box."[123] "Station B" was the name of the post office at Redondo Avenue. With the two houses they purchased on Fifty-seventh and Fifty-eighth Streets, he and Craig found the space for the home and office that they both craved.

Sinclair hired a local printer, George Moyle, to produce his mass mailings. Moyle's son, William, often delivered the twenty-five thousand letters printed in his father's shop. They were folded, stitched, and trimmed, but Sinclair had to stuff the envelopes. Roberta Nichols interviewed Moyle. She writes: "On warm days, Sinclair might be in swim trunks, propped against the railing, with the typewriter in front of him.... With no regular staff in evidence to stuff and seal them, Bill Moyle assumes the Sinclairs did most of it themselves."[124] Sinclair treasured the freedom to print whatever he chose, but self-publishing brought a heavy burden of assembly and distribution. He hoped that with the new novel, the one he thought of as *Flowing Gold*, he would earn enough to pay for a secretary to assist him.

Sinclair's novel was published in 1927 by Albert and Charles Boni and titled *Oil!* The entire book is based on actual events, though names were fictionalized. Sinclair writes in the preface: "The picture is the truth, and the great mass of detail actually exists. But the cards have been shuffled: names, places, dates—everything has been dealt over again."[125] According to critic R. N. Mookerjee, it was the investigative reports about the leasing out of the Elk Hills oil reserves in California that were the actual source of Sinclair's materials.[126]

The novel tells the story of an oil developer and his son and contrasts the father's practicality and conservatism with the son's idealism and sensitivity. Their story begins around 1910, roughly coinciding with the discovery of the Union Oil gusher in Kern County. "I read it with interest, and consider it a splendid novel of fact," wrote D. H. Lawrence. The novel's thirty-one chapters are arranged to balance the lives and viewpoints of the two worlds being contrasted, those of wealth and of deprivation. In J. Arnold Ross, the oil magnate, Upton Sinclair created of the most sympathetic portrayals of a businessman in American literature.

Oil! is set in California's rolling hills and valleys, and in the tiny beach towns that were transformed by the oil boom. In *Oil!*, "Beach City" is really Long Beach and "Prospect Hill" is Signal Hill. In the first chapter of the book, the reader gains a vivid sense of the California that once was, as the oil tycoon and his son drive up the Central Valley, passing miles of wheat fields, green in the sun: "'Are you looking for a Home?' inquired a friendly sign. 'Santa Ynez is a place for folks. Good water, cheap land, seven churches.'"[127]

The Literary Guild chose *Oil!* as one of its major selections. Two months after its publication, the Los Angeles–based Julian Petroleum Corporation collapsed after an over-issue of five million shares of stock. Tens of thousands lost money, while a handful of stockbrokers made large profits. This collapse illustrated Sinclair's narrative and the book became a bestseller. Initially, *Oil!* was banned in Boston, for its discussion of abortion and birth control. A bookstore clerk who had sold a copy of *Oil!* had been arrested and was scheduled to go on trial.

Sinclair spoke to a Long Beach reporter about Boston, where "a group of self-appointed critics tried to say what is and what is not a true reflection of life in a state 2,500 miles away.... If necessary, I'll go to Boston and fight it out with them."[128] Sinclair asked his printer to prepare 150 copies of the paperback edition and to replace the nine offending pages with "cancel" leaves printed with a page-size fig leaf in silhouette."[129] He took these to Boston in summer 1927, pausing en route in New York to visit with David, who was attending Columbia and was engaged to be married. Sinclair sold the "fig leaf" copies of *Oil!* on the Boston Common to passersby, and was briefly arrested, drawing publicity and further sales to the novel.

As *Oil!* was selling thousands of copies, the first biography of Upton Sinclair was published. Sinclair had suggested to Floyd Dell that he write it. Born into a poor family, Dell became a factory worker and then a reporter. In 1914 he moved to Greenwich Village, where he became assistant editor of *The Masses*, working with Max Eastman. After that paper was indicted under the Espionage Act, Dell and Eastman then founded *The Liberator*, and although they tried to self-censor, they were put on trial. The jury deadlocked, and Dell continued editing *The Masses* until 1921.

Floyd Dell wrote to Sinclair, describing his visit to Priscilla Sinclair. He had liked her very much: "a nice, hard-headed, conventional old reactionary—don't you tell her I said that! . . . If the world were made up exclusively of people like her, there would be no progress; if it were made up exclusively of people like you, it would prematurely explode!"[130] He concluded that he liked both kinds of people and found it "very amusing that you should be her son."[131] Dell began his biography by noting that citizens of the world, looking to America for an explanation of world events, often found help by reading Upton Sinclair. Dell described Sinclair at forty-nine as "a slight, wiry, graying figure, an excellent tennis player, an eager talker . . . wearing the cast-off clothes of a rich young friend, very boyish, impulsive, trustful, stubborn, fondly regarded as impractical by those who love him."[132]

The *Rocky Mountain News*' review of Dell's biography was illustrated by a caricature of Sinclair holding a spotlight on himself. Sinclair sued the paper for libel because the review made him appear "a snob and a publicity-seeker."[133] In his account of his legal defeat, Sinclair describes the trial, during which the defense attorneys turned him into the offender, grilling him for three days straight, for a total of eighteen hours. Sometimes the questions involved strategic omissions: "Did Dell state that Upton Sinclair is a guide conspicuously lacking in tolerance?" Sinclair could only answer yes—not able to add the rest of Dell's line: "for drunkenness or debauchery."[134] It must have been embittering, even to such an optimist as Sinclair, to have his biography and character attacked just as the novel *Oil!* was being celebrated.

Sinclair adapted the novel into a play in 1929. In Japan, the *Bungei Sensen* carried two hundred pages of Maedako's translation of *Oil! A Play*. Japanese critic Kinzo Satomura wrote that Sinclair's work reminded him of the disillusionment that occurred in his own childhood "in the darkness of some temple. Just in such shock and wonder, Sinclair unfolds the whole mechanism of the United States, capitalist kingdom, for us. He is a great writer who writes society itself."[135] However, the screenplay itself was rejected by Hollywood; as he later wrote: "*Oil!* has been read by every concern in the business, and never have they reported but one thing: 'magnificent, but dangerous.'"[136]

CHAPTER FIVE

How I Ran for Governor
[1928–1939]

Who scrapes from grimy pots and pans a certain kind of truth?
Who tells the world to "Open Wide" and spots a hollow tooth?
Who disavows the Here and Now and swears by what's ahead?
Who thinks the word "undignified" is better left unsaid?
Sinclair is that most valiant man—
If anyone's to vouch for it, then I'm the one who can.
ALBERT EINSTEIN, translated by John Ahouse, 1933

In August 1927 Upton Sinclair wrote to Kate Crane Gartz that he was no longer interested in fighting over the publication and distribution of *Oil!* in Boston: "The situation there is too tense and serious for that kind of joking. What I want to do is to go very quietly and gather the material for a big novel, and take a couple of years to write it."[1] Seven years earlier, Italian immigrants Nicola Sacco and Bartolomeo Vanzetti had been arrested in Brockton, Massachusetts, charged with the robbery and murder of a shoe-factory paymaster and his guard. Their supporters insisted that the two men were targeted only because of their political identity as anarchists and that the attack on these immigrants was part of the nationwide backlash against radicals following World War I.

After a trial that attracted little publicity, the men were sentenced to death. Sinclair had visited Vanzetti in Charlestown Prison immediately after the trial. Vanzetti, like Sinclair, was a vegetarian and a Prohibitionist. He wrote in his limited English to Sinclair:

"I will never forget your visit nor what your golden pen—that so many good battles valiantly fought in behalf of the truth and of the freedom—had wrote in my defense."[2] The case began to draw national—indeed, international—attention, but the campaign to overturn the death sentences failed to sway Massachusetts authorities, and the two were executed on August 23, 1927. Howard Zinn explains that Sinclair wrote *Boston* in nine months, "in what seems like a barely controlled anger, right after the execution."[3]

Sinclair chose to tell the story through the voice of a sixty-year-old woman. His protagonist, Cornelia, deserts her aristocratic family to live with poor Italians, work in a factory, and walk a picket line. German critic Ingrid Kerkhoff suggests that "Sinclair might have been inspired by the women who worked in the Sacco and Vanzetti defense committees."[4] Cornelia is the quintessential Sinclair hero: a wealthy and cultured American who identifies with the struggles of the oppressed. Like Kate Crane Gartz, Cornelia resists the life of privilege she has inherited in favor of social action. British scholar Dennis Welland points out that through knowing Cornelia, "Vanzetti came to understand that goodness is not a matter of class."[5] Historians Lewis Joughin and Edmund Morgan wrote that the book's "combination of completeness, accuracy, and penetration places *Boston* in the front rank of historical novels."[6]

But Thornton Wilder, not Upton Sinclair, won the 1928 Pulitzer Prize for the novel *The Bridge of San Luis Rey*. The chairman of the Pulitzer Selection Committee wrote to Sinclair that *Boston* "only missed winning because of its socialist tone."[7] That year Sinclair turned fifty. Two years later, when Sinclair Lewis won the Nobel Prize in Literature, he scolded the judges for not having honored his mentor Upton Sinclair, "of whom you must say, whether you admire or detest his aggressive socialism, that he is internationally better known than any other American artist whosoever, be he novelist, poet, painter, sculptor, musician, architect."[8] Lewis's *Elmer Gantry* was inspired by *The Profits of Religion*. Later, Albert Einstein, Bertrand Russell, and George Bernard Shaw would also sign unsuccessful petitions advancing the candidacy of Upton Sinclair to the Nobel committees.

The Wet Parade and Women's Culture

While the male companions of his youth—George Sterling, Jack London, and Eugene O'Neill—had perished, many from alcoholism, Sinclair was full of vigor and imagination. His friendships with women, already flourishing, deepened during the thirties, offering badly needed camaraderie and validation for these activists and writers. Such friendships were possible because they neither threatened his marriage nor impinged on the women's independence.

An impressive record of Sinclair's rapport with women writers can be found in his unpublished correspondence, which offers evidence that Upton Sinclair read books *with* his wife, read and applauded books *by* women, and then shared the books with friends. He wrote to Kate Crane Gartz that he and Craig had just read Agnes Smedley's autobiographical novel *Daughter of Earth*: "We found it extremely interesting, and we thought of it as a book you would like on account of her interest in the freedom for India movement. I am sending you the book."[9] After finishing her novel, Smedley left India and moved to Shanghai. She spent the rest of her life reporting on the independence struggle in China. Helen Keller, another of Sinclair's correspondents, contacted him on behalf of the Chinese blind, whose school had been destroyed in 1938. He wrote her back immediately, noting that her signature "gave me quite a start, because when I was a boy, I had an autograph collection and that signature of yours was one of its most prized features."[10]

While Sinclair corresponded with Smedley and Keller about India and China, he was mindful that there was much in America that still needed to be recorded. His old friend Ella Reeve Bloor wrote him: "I still feel that you should write the saga of the South."[11] She pointed out that while the press was heralding the South's industrial progress, "thousands of women and little white American children work there in the textile mills twelve hours per days and 65 percent

of the white adult workers can't read or write."[12] The book he did
write about the South, *The Wet Parade*, would instead document
the alcoholism that destroyed families like his own.

Sinclair's commitment to fidelity has been a source of derision
among many biographers and critics who have mistaken monogamy for unmanliness. Sinclair chose to celebrate his marriage to
Mary Craig in a 1937 article called "My Lifelong Love Affair," published, interestingly, in *Personal Romances Magazine*, and primarily
directed to a female audience. There between a recipe for "Ambrosia
Supreme" and a joke called "Gentlemen First," Sinclair's article
stood in the heart of women's culture. What are the implications
of a man who was also a public figure writing a testimonial to
monogamy, arguing that "the long love affairs are the most useful
and worthwhile ones?"[13] In the article, Sinclair sought to connect
with ordinary Americans, while still retaining his identity as a
radical man. Unafraid of ridicule, he argued that monogamous
marriage worked best for families and individuals.

Sinclair therefore encouraged his wife's interests in psycho-
logical exploration, which were shared by others in their circle.
Friends would come to Pasadena for evening discussions; Mary
Craig describes an evening when Mary Wilshire arrived, "lovely
and very striking in her cream satin dress, heavily embroidered in
red and gold."[14] That night, Wilshire explained to her friends how
Carl Jung's theories differed from those of Freud. Freud's deeply
conservative views about women and about human nature would
have been antithetical to this group; Jung's more holistic world
view and his ideas about archetypes would be a welcome alternative.

In America investigations of psychic phenomena were inter-
twined with the development of psychology and psychiatry, topics
of particular interest to the wives of Gaylord Wilshire and Upton
Sinclair. While Mary Wilshire studied psychoanalysis, Mary Craig
developed an interest in dreams and extrasensory perception.
Roberta Nichols notes, "Dolly [Craig's sister] and her husband
Bob lived in the Sinclairs' Pasadena home off and on during these

years and frequently joined Mary Craig and Upton to participate in their mental experiments."[15] Kevin Mattson suggests that Sinclair's openness to telepathy was part of his worldview "that related back to his socialism. His spiritualism helped him look beyond present day social arrangements to a world where all souls were equal."[16]

Sinclair's *Mental Radio* is an enthusiastic account of the Sinclairs' experiments with telepathy. One story in the book recounts how Sinclair had received a periodical published by Sacco and Vanzetti supporters. As he was reading an article attacking Charles Lindberg for his pro-fascist sympathies, Craig came downstairs to tell him about her dream of Lindberg flying across the ocean.[17] Upton Sinclair began corresponding with Mahatma Gandhi, a man whose personal and political choices echoed many of his own. Sinclair wrote to Gandhi in Yerwada Jail in Bombay: "Ask for anything that you find in the enclosed list ... and that applies also to any of your friends who might be interested to have them."[18] He sent Gandhi *The Book of Life*, *The Cry for Justice*, *The Brass Check*, *The Goosestep*, *King Coal* and *Oil!*[19] He also sent *Mental Radio*. Receiving it, Gandhi wrote dryly to Sinclair: "Nobody in India would, I think, doubt the possibility of telepathy but most would doubt the wisdom of its material use."[20]

Like Gandhi, Albert Einstein's public presence as a moral authority was equal to his scientific stardom.[21] Einstein admired *Mental Radio* and he and Sinclair began a correspondence. Sinclair began it: "I just read in last Sunday's New York Times an account of your experiments with telepathy and clairvoyance."[22] He offered to send Einstein a copy of *Mental Radio* in German translation, and later wrote that he had received correspondence from people around the world about the book, but there were no reviews in America. Publishers in Germany were not interested.

Sinclair thanked Einstein for his offer to write an introduction to the book, "as I am sure that will make it easier to find publisher and audience."[23] Almost alone among his books (except for *The Jungle*), *Mental Radio* has been continuously in print.[24] Sinclair

13. Photograph of Sinclair playing the violin out of doors. Courtesy of the Lilly Library, Indiana University, Bloomington.

then sent Einstein an anthology of antiwar poetry that included five of Mary Craig's sonnets, "not so bad for a Socialist writer."[25] When he heard Einstein was going to be working at Cal Tech, near Pasadena, he wrote, "I am considered a very dangerous person down at Cal Tech, so do not mention to anybody there that you have ever heard of me! If you want a quiet garden to come to and be let alone in, we will provide it."[26]

Albert Einstein did visit, and the two played duets on their violins. As Sinclair promised, he saved the last figs on their trees for Einstein and his wife. Other visitors to Pasadena included Bobby Scripps from the publishing family, oil heiress Aline Barnsdall, Eugene Debs, and Clarence Darrow. When H. L. Menken visited, Lionel Rolfe writes, "They argued about booze and Jack London. Mencken was, of course, firmly committed to booze."[27]

In 1930 Sinclair saw a poll by *Literary Digest* suggesting that sentiment in the country might lead to repeal of Prohibition.[28] One poll showed about 30 percent of the population still supported it, 30 percent wanted modification, and 40 percent supported repeal.[29] He wrote to Gandhi congratulating him on his endorsement of Prohibition, and added, "I have completed work upon a long novel called *The Wet Parade* . . . and would like very much to send it to you."[30] Alcoholism was the one social problem Sinclair had not yet exposed. He wrote *The Wet Parade* to remind the country why Prohibition had been passed in the first place.

When the Eighteenth Amendment was ratified in 1919, Congress had given the Prohibition Bureau only three thousand employees and less than $7 million for nationwide enforcement. Yet Prohibition was effective in regions where temperance movements had historically been successful, many of which were already "dry." However, large urban centers were strongholds of bootlegging. By 1930 the country was deeply divided about Prohibition.

While magazine stories of the era were evenly balanced between "dry" and "wet" perspectives, ridiculing Prohibitionists was considered sophisticated by Hollywood, and movies reflected this bias.[31] Addiction researcher Robin Room investigated the films released between 1929 and 1931; almost half showed intoxication, and over 90 percent had some reference to liquor.[32] As *Variety* noted, "Mention of repeal naturally met with applause from the Broadway audience. Hisses greeted expressions of dry sentiment."[33] Despite the misery and destruction it produced, intoxication was treated humorously, and heroes in film were three times more likely to be shown drinking than were the villains.

As the feminist son of an alcoholic, Sinclair continued to try to focus national attention on the reasons for the Eighteenth Amendment even as sentiment increased for its repeal. Sinclair commented that his liberal friends who read *The Wet Parade* "found it sentimental and out of the spirit of the time. To them I made answer that the experiences of my childhood were 'reality,' quite as much so as the blood and guts of the Chicago stockyards."[34] Those who grew up despising liquor and the destruction it created rarely are featured as the protagonist in films; more often, they are simply the victims of the main character—the fascinating and self-destructive alcoholic. Sinclair chose to construct a different narrative; he wanted to remind the country of the origins of the Prohibition movement in the tragedies of alcoholic families. The protagonists of the novel—and the later film—are a young couple who have both been victimized by alcoholism in their families. What is striking about *The Wet Parade* is that the narrative is framed quite overtly against alcohol and for temperance. The struggle of the enforcers is portrayed as a noble and courageous battle.

Although H. L. Mencken relished Sinclair's critiques of the press and education, he mocked his friend's temperance views.[35] In his review of *The Wet Parade*, Mencken wrote, "Mr. Sinclair undertakes a feat unprecedented in swell letters: he makes a Prohibition agent his hero."[36] Edith Kelley wrote to Sinclair: "I read Mencken's review of *Wet Parade* in [the] *Nation* and was disgusted at this abuse of the reviewer's privilege. Everybody will agree that it was most malicious and unfair."[37] But the novel sold well, and Irving Thalberg bought the film rights in 1931 for twenty thousand dollars—even though he didn't like Sinclair's politics and barred him from the MGM lot during shooting.[38] When the film premiered at Grauman's Chinese Theater in March 1932, the audience called for Sinclair to speak, but owner Sid Grauman, who also disliked socialists, refused, with the excuse that Sinclair was not wearing a tuxedo.[39] Unfazed, Sinclair arranged to set up a table in the lobby to sell the book, inviting all the various temperance groups to join him.

Sinclair organized a debate on Prohibition between Aimee Semple McPherson (who argued for Prohibition) and *Wet Parade* star Walter Huston (who argued against it). *Wet Parade* suggests that the major cause of Prohibition's failure was the lack of enforcement and the corruption created by the demand for illegal liquor. However, most reviewers echoed Mencken's response to the novel. The *New York World-Telegram* critic wrote that he could find nothing to recommend in *The Wet Parade*: "What started out to be an

14. Program for premiere of *The Wet Parade*. Upton Sinclair's choice of temperance as a political issue is one of the many aspects by which contemporary historians might reevaluate him. Courtesy of the Lilly Library, Indiana University, Bloomington.

authentic reflection of the typical American scene in the first twenty years turns into an incoherent diatribe. . . . *The Wet Parade* is not a credible nor entertaining piece of work. Indeed, it is excessively tedious."[40] Many reviewers were determined to demonstrate their acceptance of alcohol as a normative part of life.

Robin Room explains: "Drinking and heavy drinking became entrenched among middle-class people after the mid-1920s, in much the way that tobacco or coffee spread in Europe."[41] Richard Watts of the *New York Herald-Tribune* commented snidely that Prohibition agents are normally not the sympathetic hero and heroine and that the film was absurd "in the efforts to make a dry snooper sympathetic by casting Jimmy Durante as a noble dry agent. . . . Now let's all go around the corner and lift one."[42] *The Wet Parade* was disconcerting to viewers, clearly illustrating how economic and political interests were served by the distribution of liquor during Prohibition.

In stark contrast to other critics, Regina Crewe wrote that the film was "a grim indictment of our times, sprayed with bitter laughter. It may make people think."[43] During that period, the largest single category of major writers with a reputation for heavy drinking or alcoholism were part of a particular cohort that came of age in 1909–21.[44] When Alcoholics Anonymous was founded in 1935, the face of alcoholism was transformed into the private stories of individual alcoholics. A poll about Prohibition in 1937 shows a striking gender gap: 15 percent of men, yet 30 percent of women, wanted complete prohibition reinstated.[45]

In 1932 Mina Maxfield and Lena Eggleston of the Board of Temperance, Prohibition, and Public Morals converted *The Wet Parade* into a play.[46] That year, with the twenty thousand dollars from the film, the Sinclairs decided to relocate. Sinclair's studio work meant driving to Culver City daily, through traffic that was worsening. They moved to 614 North Arden Drive, in Beverly Hills, that fall, "just a bit at a time and mostly in our own car," as he wrote to his daughter-in-law Betty (whom David had married in 1928.) He added that he was still planning to use part of the profits from *The Wet Parade* to support the Socialist Party and hoped that she and his son would "not think he had 'gone Hollywood.'"[47]

In 1932 Sinclair's autobiography, *American Outpost*, was released. Although he had finished the work in 1929, he waited until after Priscilla Sinclair's death to publish it. His mother had objected to some parts that Sinclair had shown her, and he delayed publication for three years rather than alter what he had written. Over the years, Sinclair had written his mother rarely, and she never visited him in California. In August 1931 she wrote that she would like very much to read *The Wet Parade*, but was too sick to do so. She died of heart disease two months later. Sinclair wrote to his son that he "grew beyond her, and she wouldn't follow or couldn't. If she'd let me alone, it would have been alright; but she still thought I was a child and still stubbornly sought to direct my life and *mind*."[48] In his review of *American Outpost*, Edmund Wilson commented that "practically alone among the writers of his generation, he [Sinclair] put to the American public the fundamental questions raised by capitalism in such a way that they could not escape them."[49]

Producers and Scenarios

After the success of *The Wet Parade*, Irving Thalberg invited Sinclair to write another screenplay about the contrasting lives of the rich and the poor. Sinclair received ten thousand dollars for a first draft of what he called "The Gold Spangled Banner." He never heard back from Thalberg. His unpublished novella *The Golden Scenario*, written sometime during the Depression, reflects his bitterness about his treatment by the movie industry: the novella exposed script mills and studio manipulation of story ideas, abuses which he himself had experienced.[50]

Upton Sinclair continued to have a contentious relationship with the movie-industry moguls (he even wrote a preface to a pamphlet called *Sodom and Gomorrah: The Story of Hollywood*), but developed close friendships with actors Charlie Chaplin and Douglas

Fairbanks.[51] Chaplin considered Sinclair one of his two mentors in Hollywood; the other was Rob Wagner, editor of *Script*, the Hollywood trade magazine. Sinclair and Chaplin were frequent dinner guests at Wagner's home in Beverly Hills, and Sinclair often visited the sets of Chaplin's films. Journalist Greg Mitchell describes how the friendship began en route to Sinclair's home in Pasadena when Sinclair asked Chaplin "in his soft-spoken way, whether he believed in the 'profit system.'... Sinclair had exposed a true paradox—want in the midst of plenty—and from that moment on Chaplin looked at politics through the prism of economics, not history."[52]

It was Charlie Chaplin who persuaded Sinclair to finance a project by Russian filmmaker Sergei Eisenstein that was to be a short feature film shot in Mexico. Anthony Arthur comments that Chaplin's refusal to provide funding himself for Eisenstein laid the groundwork for "the series of events that Sinclair would come to regret for the rest of his long life."[53] Charlie Chaplin was a wealthy man who spent his money cautiously, and so he chose not to invest in the film. In 1930 Paramount Studios had brought Eisenstein to Hollywood to study the new techniques of sound motion pictures. Four months after his arrival, his contract was terminated because the studio did not want the negative publicity of being associated with a known communist. Sinclair, who had been fascinated by Eisenstein's famous 1925 film *The Battleship Potemkin*, wrote to the filmmaker that "a great artist was to be permitted to make one picture the way he wanted it."[54]

The Sinclairs took out loans on several of the properties that Craig had bought, so the contract was in her name. She was required to provide twenty-five thousand dollars—a huge sum at the time—to Eisenstein. Sinclair sent his brother-in-law, Hunter Kimbrough, to Mexico, supposedly as the Sinclairs' business manager, but really to chaperone Eisenstein. As Kevin Mattson wryly describes it, "A Southern man nursing a drinking problem would go to Mexico to keep a Russian Jew and avant-garde director on schedule."[55]

By the summer of 1931, Sinclair was trying to raise seventy

15. Charlie Chaplin. Chaplin, along with Douglas Fairbanks, was one of Sinclair's closest friends in Hollywood. Courtesy of the Lilly Library, Indiana University, Bloomington.

16. Eisenstein at a film shoot in Mexico. *Left to right*: Sergei Eisenstein, Hunter Kimbrough, and cinematographer Eduard Tisse, 1933. Courtesy of David Lesser.

thousand dollars more for the project but questioned Hunter about why he hadn't seen any actual footage. Eisenstein sent back some film; Sinclair was not impressed—although his friend Mary Beard (a pioneer in American women's history) wrote, "The Eisenstein pictures are so wonderful that Charles and I believe they will make one of the world's greatest films."[56] She hoped that the Sinclairs would come for dinner "when the Mexico party is safely at home and headaches are a thing of the past."[57]

Sinclair did send more funds, but as banks collapsed across the country, he became anxious. The financial stress brought on health problems serious enough to hospitalize him in 1931. He wrote to Albert Einstein: "The Eisenstein party is still working in Mexico.

17. Eisenstein's crew filming *¡Qué viva México! Left to right*: Castro Padilla, composer; A. A. Leiva, critic; Dr. Adolpho Best-Maugard, artist; unidentified journalist; Hunter Kimbrough; Sergei Eisenstein; Julio Saldivar, composer; Sr. Garibay, interpreter. Hacienda Tetlapayac, 1933. Courtesy of David Lesser.

They are sending home a lot of wonderful stuff, but it has been a hard strain on me, because it has taken three times as much time and money as we expected."[58] When he got out of the hospital, he returned to a frightening letter from Hunter Kimborough: "Eisenstein has not the slightest regard for the interest of the investors or for you and Sister.... He is thinking only of his artistic triumph."[59] The Eisenstein project was wreaking havoc on the Sinclair marriage.

Sinclair turned to the Soviet government for assistance. The Soviet response was to order Eisenstein home immediately.[60] Eisenstein returned to the USSR without his footage, which Sinclair gave to a friend, film editor Sol Lesser. Lesser edited the film, *¡Qué viva México!*, into a much shorter picture, and then renamed it *Thunder Over Mexico*. When the film opened in Los Angeles in 1933, members of the Communist Party picketed the theater. They believed Lesser's editing was illegitimate, though actually no radical scenes had been cut. In the end, Sol Lesser was unable to distribute the film.

That year, Sinclair himself published *Upton Sinclair Presents William Fox*, about which he wrote, "No melodrama that I have been able to invent had been more packed with crimes and betrayals, perils and escapes, than the story of William Fox."[61] The book documents the war between Fox, an independent producer, and the corporate financers of motion pictures. Fox Studios forbid its employees to read the book. Sinclair's exposé of Fox and the Sergei Eisenstein fiasco would contribute to the film industry's adversarial response when Sinclair began his campaign for governor of California later in 1933.

The EPIC Campaign

Early in September 1933, Upton Sinclair changed his party registration from Socialist to Democrat. A group of Santa Monica Democrats had persuaded him that he might be able to win the gubernatorial primary in a weakened Democratic Party.[62] If he did win the primary, he would have the advantage of facing the Republican, Frank Merriam, an unpopular governor. Later that month, the Sinclairs traveled to New York for the premiere of *Thunder Over Mexico*. While there, they planned to see David and Betty. Sinclair packed his just completed copy of *I, Governor of California and How I Ended Poverty*, intending to give it to his son.

David was still working on his doctorate in physics at Columbia and had not seen his father since 1927. The couple brought their infant daughter, Diana, with them to the train platform. The meeting was difficult. David and Betty, who considered themselves socialists, immediately began to express their disapproval over several issues. They condemned Sinclair's purported insult to Eisenstein by the release of Sol Lesser's Hollywood movie. They also disagreed with Sinclair leaving the Socialist Party to run for governor, and they blamed Craig for encouraging what they saw as Sinclair's defections from socialism.[63] The argument continued at the Algonquin Hotel in front of a reporter from the *Herald Tribune*. According

I, GOVERNOR OF CALIFORNIA

And How I Ended Poverty

A True Story of the Future

BY

UPTON SINCLAIR

This is not just a pamphlet.

This is the beginning of a Crusade.

A Two-Year Plan to make over a State.

To capture the Democratic primaries and use an old party for a new job.

The EPIC plan:

(E)nd (P)overty (I)n (C)alifornia!

The Best Selling Book in the History of California
150,000 in Four Months

PRICE 20 CENTS

END POVERTY LEAGUE 1501 SOUTH GRAND AVE. LOS ANGELES, CALIFORNIA
INCORPORATED
(ADDRESS ALL LETTERS AS ABOVE)

18. *I, Governor of California*. Sinclair presented his vision in this pamphlet that became the principal organizing tool of the campaign. He narrated the story backward from the fictional future of 1938, in the style of Edward Bellamy's utopian novel *Looking Backward*, 1888. Courtesy of the Lilly Library, Indiana University, Bloomington.

to the reporter, David told his father, "I wish you'd go back and read all your books again and become converted by them!"[64] The reporter added that Sinclair "frowned, then smiled tolerantly" and reminded everyone present that he had written about these conflicts as early as 1907.[65]

After returning from New York, Sinclair wrote to his son attempting to explain his decision: "So long as I was a Socialist, I was just one more crank; but when I call myself a Democrat, I become a man worth listening to."[66] *I, Governor of California* imagines Sinclair implementing reforms in Depression-era, ravaged California with innovations such as scrip, co-ops, and what he called "production for use" rather than "production for profit." Sinclair centered his campaign on groups of citizens who had been disenfranchised: small property owners, the unemployed, the poor, seniors, widows, and the disabled. Historian James Gregory comments about how effective Upton Sinclair was "with these hundreds of thousands of modestly educated Californians, his self-presentation as teacher-with-all-the-answers was powerful and self-affirming. He was the teacher, but he taught that they were experts."[67]

In June 1934, Will Rogers told his readers that the famous author Upton Sinclair was running for governor—"a darn nice fellow, and just plum smart, and if he could deliver even some of the things he promises should not only be governor of one state, but president of all of 'em."[68] Sinclair's campaign, which was titled EPIC (End Poverty in California), touched people's intimate lives: when an unemployed Los Angeles couple became parents of a baby boy on primary day, they named him Upton Sinclair Marshaw.[69] The depth of support for Sinclair was so strong that he received more votes in the August 1934 Democratic primary than his six opponents put together.

Like much of the Progressive population, Sinclair had a deep respect for President Roosevelt. When Sinclair visited Hyde Park in 1934, FDR talked while Sinclair listened, telling stories "with gusto" about overcoming opponents who were trying to frustrate his New

Deal programs; he recalled that his mother had read *The Jungle* to him at the breakfast table when he was a boy.[70] Sinclair referred to Roosevelt as "open-minded and loveable," "a very cheerful-hearted man," and a tonic for the country.[71] Later Sinclair said the meeting constituted some of the most fascinating hours of his life. He had hoped for an endorsement, but never received it.

After the primary, Webb Waldron, correspondent for *Today* magazine, drove across the curving Arroyo Seco Bridge into Pasadena to interview the candidate. He described Sinclair's house as a shabby structure in a working-class neighborhood. When he knocked, Sinclair opened the door in his bathrobe: "His face showed only faint lines of fatigue, and he answered one question after another, sharply, concisely, and soothingly. His words rang with urgency but his voice was soft, his manner boyish, charming, bemused."[72]

William Randolph Hearst was in Germany visiting with Mussolini and Hitler when he learned of the victory. Journalist Greg Mitchell describes the reaction to Sinclair's winning the nomination: "Up and down the state, terrified Republicans and outraged Democrats faced a nightmare of their own making."[73] These men included Earl Warren in Oakland, A. P. Giannini in San Francisco, Herbert Hoover in Palo Alto, Harry Chandler in Los Angeles, and Irving Thalberg in Hollywood, all of whom were determined that California not be won by the "scourge of the ruling class, and now Democratic nominee for governor, Upton Sinclair."[74] As soon as Sinclair won, *I, Governor* became the best-selling publication in the history of California.

Sinclair followed it with EPIC *Answers*, based on questions gathered from his audiences during his speaking tour. Los Angeles County was the center of the movement; over eight hundred EPIC clubs were formed, most of them in or around Los Angeles. Carey McWilliams describes the campaign as one of the most successful experiments in mass education ever performed, with Sinclair's pamphlets exhibiting "matchless skill, lucidity and brilliance."[75]

With scrap paper obtained free from a paper mill and printed on a mimeograph machine, featuring material contributed by writers and artists, one co-op turned out leaflets in support of EPIC.

Decades later, Faye Blake and Morton Newman gathered a group of former campaigners to discuss their memories of EPIC and the cooperative movement. LaRue McCormick was a community activist and organizer in Los Angeles who attributed her enthusiastic entry into the local consumers' cooperative in part to her youthful readings of Sinclair's works. The Unemployed Exchange Association began with a small group of women operating a handloom in Berkeley, and eventually included thousands of unemployed workers who hauled crops, wood, and fruit from farmers unable to sell their produce, in exchange for all kinds of services. McCormick told Blake and Newman about the informal co-op organized in her own home. Its participants bought "milk at a quarter a gallon, day-old bread at five cents a loaf, macaroni ends at two cents a pound, and vegetables from a truck gardener at a penny a bunch."[76]

Sinclair supporters began publishing the EPIC News, which was sold for a nickel a copy and achieved a weekly distribution of over one million copies. Lorna Smith established an EPIC club in her Glendale home and worked for Sinclair's election with her husband. When the time came for Sinclair to speak in the Glendale Auditorium, she "went to the churches and asked for notices in their Sunday bulletins, explaining to the ministers, 'I am sure all churches would like to end poverty in California.'"[77] In the crowded auditorium, she sat along with the other officers on Sinclair's platform. Smith's account gives a vivid sense of the empowerment that citizens received from their work with EPIC. Smith left her church, where she had played the piano for the children, in protest of the church's silence in the face of the distorted campaign against Sinclair.

What was unique about the EPIC Campaign was its use of popular culture to reach the public in an electoral contest, with events like a grand rodeo complete with "rough riders," foot races, "aeroplanes"

19. EPIC Campaign song. Everywhere that EPIC clubs met, people sang this and other songs to strengthen their commitment to the campaign. Courtesy of the Lilly Library, Indiana University, Bloomington.

releasing parachutes, and cowboy bands. When a group of unemployed actors formed an EPIC troupe, Upton Sinclair found the time to write a one-act satire for them entitled *Depression Island*, which was performed in June at the Shrine Auditorium in Los Angeles.[78]

Charlie Chaplin spoke at the rally, the first time (as far as Sinclair knew) that Chaplin had ever made a political speech.[79] EPIC clubs in every community in California sponsored barbeques, picnics, sewing bees, dances, and athletic competitions. Woulden Howell staged an EPIC pageant created by his art students in the Pasadena schools.[80] Lorna Smith recalls that during the EPIC Campaign, she took her son to an open-air meeting and asked Sinclair to autograph his copy of *The Wet Parade*, "though my son was too young to read it. Thoughtfully, Sinclair said he would find *King Coal* more interesting."[81]

In response to Sinclair's growing success, the *Los Angeles Times'* owner, Harry Chandler, called a war council with members of the Chamber of Commerce, who hired the advertising firm of Lord and Thomas to create "a media blitz to discredit EPIC in every way possible."[82] Ed Ainsworth had the job at the *Times* of selecting out-of-context quotes from Sinclair's novels to be printed in large black boxes on the front page to confuse the voting public. Ainsworth recalls: "In my role, I became, in the terse lexicon of Sinclairese, one of the 'hired liars' trying to defeat him. In our lexicon, Sinclair became a hodgepodge of menace."[83] Numerous front groups were organized to circulate six million pamphlets using partial quotes from a number of Sinclair's books in order to "prove" that the candidate was an atheist who "advocated revolution, Communism, free love, and the scientific care of children."[84] Sinclair commented: "When you have twenty or thirty such garbled extracts made into a pamphlet, the results are terrifying."[85] Two hundred thousand billboards smearing him were erected throughout the state.

The *Los Angeles Times* sent its political writer Kyle Palmer to work with Will Hays, president of the Motion Picture Producers and Distributors of America, to organize the movie industry's

20. "Sincliar" dollar. Hundreds of thousands of these "dollars" printed in red ink were circulated throughout the state to discredit his campaign. Courtesy of the Lilly Library, Indiana University, Bloomington.

participation in the anti-Sinclair campaign.[86] MGM Studios, run by fiercely Republican Louie B. Mayer, created and disseminated fake newsreels. The *Hollywood Reporter* bragged, "This campaign against Sinclair has been and is DYNAMITE. It is the most effective piece of political humdingery that has ever been effected."[87] Studio workers were docked one day's wages to pay for the production of the newsreels. Jean Harlow and James Cagney led an actors' revolt against this loss of pay. The studios forced theater owners to show the newsreels if they wanted their feature films. Sinclair supporters reacted by shouting their objections when the "newsreels" came up on the screen.

Actors Melvyn Douglas and Frederick March plunged into the campaign, bitterly condemning MGM's smear tactics.[88] Just before the election, the Allied Churchmen invited evangelical Aimee Semple McPherson to participate at an anti-Sinclair rally at Shrine Auditorium. When the campaign began, a Sinclair supporter had invited McPherson to hold a public debate on the EPIC plan. Greg Mitchell writes, "Surprisingly Aimee commented that she favored EPIC and suggested that they hold the debate at the Angeles Temple."[89] It was rumored that bankers had threatened to foreclose the mortgage on her temple if she endorsed the EPIC plan. Instead she accepted money to stage the anti-Sinclair rally just before Election Day.

At the event, titled "America! Awake! The Enemy Is at Your Gates!" Aimee McPherson lowered the American flag and raised the Russian flag.[90] Accusing Sinclair of being a communist was a favorite tactic of Republicans during the campaign, ironic considering that the American Communist Party was condemning Sinclair both for his betrayal of Eisenstein and for joining the Democratic Party. Earl Behrens, the *Chronicle*'s political editor, began every story with the words, "Upton Sinclair, erstwhile Socialist."[91]

The only three newspapers that were at all favorable to Sinclair were the *San Francisco News*, the *Illustrated Daily News* of Los Angeles, and the *Turlock Tribune*. The *Los Angeles Times* headline of October 15 was "Sinclair Candidacy Is Opposed by Ninety-eight Per Cent of State Newspapers Taking Stands."[92] It offered quotes from papers ranging from Sonoma to Monrovia, from Pasadena to Oxnard, to Red Bluff. Since all the major newspapers ignored the campaign, supporter Aileen Barnsdall paid for radio time over national hookups and used billboards on Olive Hill to educate the public with the information that the local papers would not publish.[93]

Sinclair supporters began to fear for his personal safety. The candidate even wrote a pamphlet titled *Last Will and Testament*, noting that members of the campaign had been begging him to accept a bodyguard. He resisted their pleas because he liked to sit in the sunshine and take walks: "I think my best security lies in making plain to the opposition that my death would not accomplish what they desire, but on the contrary would intensify our movement."[94] Sinclair did finally agree to accept a German shepherd as a guard dog, whom he named Duchess.

Just before the election Upton Sinclair was on the covers of *Time*, *Literary Digest*, and *Your Astrology Magazine*. With a week remaining in the race, supporter Frank Hoyt circulated a pamphlet with

IMMEDIATE EPIC

The Final Statement of The Plan

BY

UPTON SINCLAIR

The book, "I, Governor of California, And How I Ended Poverty," was written in August, 1933, and has been for a year the best selling book in the history of the State.

But meantime the crisis has deepened, and California draws every day nearer to bankruptcy.

Plans for bond issues, which seemed practicable a year ago, are seen in September of 1934 to involve too great delay.

The EPIC Plan has been revised in the light of a full year's criticism. We have learned from our friends how to improve the Plan, and from our enemies how to present it more effectively.

This is the final statement of the Plan, and supersedes all other statements.

PRICE 15 CENTS

END POVERTY LEAGUE

1501 SOUTH GRAND AVE.
LOS ANGELES, CALIFORNIA

21. Immediate EPIC brochure. Courtesy of the author.

22. Sinclair with his beloved dog, Duchess, during or after the EPIC Campaign. Courtesy of the Lilly Library, Indiana University, Bloomington.

his own "Open Letter to the Voters." Decades later, he described his blue-and-white "magic Sinclair button" and remembered the responses it drew. In Los Angeles, a department store clerk told him, "All the clerks here are for Sinclair but the boss doesn't know it." A young man in Long Beach said he'd been told by his manager that "to keep our jobs we must vote for Merriam and carry his stickers on our automobiles. There are sixty of us in the department who are using the stickers, but we are all voting for Sinclair." When Hoyt boarded a streetcar, the conductor told him, "If he isn't elected, we're sunk."[95] In Japan a reporter commented that although the odds were against him, Sinclair was "now having advantages in the campaign, because of his popularity as a writer, of his Puritan way of life as well as his outlook, of his sympathy with the proletariat."[96]

In the days before the election, nine thousand people jammed the Civic Auditorium in Pasadena to hear Upton Sinclair speak. Organizers turned away six thousand more, so Sinclair came out to the front steps to address them. He explained that he had argued for twenty-five years with H. L. Mencken "about the wisdom and the true nature of 'the people': I have been Mencken's prize boob because I believed in you. Now, we shall find out which of us is right."[97] When all the ballots were counted, incumbent Merriam received one million votes to Sinclair's nine hundred thousand, but Sinclair had received twice the number of votes of any previous Democratic candidate in California.[98] Mary Craig wept in relief at the news of her husband's defeat.[99]

Sinclair was both massively relieved and very disappointed. Being governor of California would have changed the rest of his life and he might well have never written again. But the opportunity to try social reform on a grand scale would have been worth the sacrifice, for him. Sinclair also believed that he had literally dodged a bullet. According to son David, he had barely avoided being murdered. On election night, a businessman had written out his will, stuck a pistol in his pocket and set out for a radio station where Sinclair was scheduled to speak. If Sinclair had won, the businessman would have shot him dead on the spot.[100] But Sinclair's followers were inconsolable; Lola Dominguez, a twenty-eight-year-old woman from East Los Angeles, drank poison when she heard the election returns on the radio.[101]

Several days after the election, Will Rogers observed that if Sinclair had had only a few more dollars, he would have won.[102] In evaluating the cause of his defeat, Sinclair later said he regarded *Profits of Religion*, which he had written some sixteen years before, as the most important single factor.[103] Yet Sinclair's campaign was, Theodore Dreiser concluded, "the most impressive political phenomenon that America has yet produced."[104] Although Sinclair was defeated, fifty other EPIC-backed candidates won races for the state legislature. His EPIC Campaign had established the Democratic Party as a progressive force in California.[105] State party chair Culbert Olsen wrote, "Upton Sinclair has re-founded the Democrats in this state, and we take up where he left off."[106] In 1936 Olson beat Merriam for governor by over two hundred thousand votes, and Sheridan Downey, Sinclair's former running mate, was elected senator.

Three days after the election, Upton Sinclair started dictating his campaign memoir, *How I Ran for Governor and Got Licked*. Dozens of newspapers purchased the serial rights; by November 19, the *San Francisco Chronicle* was publishing chapters daily. Shortly after the election, at a party in Beverly Hills at the home of Fredric March and Florence Eldridge, "Irving Thalberg quietly announced, 'I made those shorts.' 'But it was a dirty trick!' Frederic March protested. 'It was the damnedest unfair thing I've ever heard of.' 'Nothing is unfair in politics,' Thalberg replied."[107] "After 1934," screenwriter Philip Dunne later told Greg Mitchell, "we said, 'Never Again.' EPIC created a liberal climate in Hollywood for the first time."[108]

Years later Carey McWilliams would find the slogans of the EPIC Campaign "painted on rocks in the desert, carved in trees in the forest, and scrawled on the walls of labor camps in the San Joaquin Valley."[109] Toward the end of his life Sinclair remembered: "When I talked to Franklin Roosevelt I told him my immediate demands in the EPIC movement. Sinclair reports of FDR that "he checked them off his fingers and said 'Right, right, right,' and so on. He brought about a great many of those changes."[110] Sinclair's biographer, Floyd Dell, was among those who found a job with the Works Progress Administration in 1935. Sinclair believed in the New Deal, and his view was that pushing from the left would embolden the national leadership to try the social experiments being advocated by former social workers like Frances Perkins.

The EPIC movement itself collapsed after Sinclair's defeat, and he had to go on the road to raise funds to pay off his campaign debts. Mary Craig received a warning letter from her brother Orman, who admitted that although Craig had worried about threats to Sinclair, "I've never thought so until now. Last night I heard a broadcast by Goebbels from Germany in which he warned Upton Sinclair of the fate he was earning for himself by his public attacks on the Nazis."[111] Craig reacted: "Now Upton proposed to set off alone on a tour of the whole country in our Ford! I informed him that if he went, I would go along."[112] In July 1935, with Duchess, they headed north in the new car, purchased for $774.

They traveled first on the newly built Highway 101 through the redwoods, which Sinclair had never seen before.[113] He marveled at the giant trees and the masses of ferns: "And I imagined little gnomes living in those ferns. Because I always think of stories, you see, I had the idea of a little girl wandering among those ferns."[114] What he produced was his only book for children. In the thirties, children's literature was just emerging from the moralistic fables of the nineteenth and early twentieth centuries; British socialist E. Nesbit was inventing the children's adventure story.[115] Nesbit was a founding member of the Fabian Society in Britain, along with George Bernard Shaw; Sinclair would have likely known her work. Considering that Sinclair had begun his writing career as a teenager, penning dime novels for boys, it is significant that his protagonist was a girl.[116] He dedicated *The Gnomobile* to his granddaughter, Diana.

The book uses the familiar Sinclair convention of an innocent being educated, and its setting in the redwoods allows the author to lyrically describe their beauty. The first chapter of the book ends, appropriately enough, with the sound of a car; nine years after *Oil!*, the California landscape was being transformed. *The Gnomobile* may well have been the first children's adventure story with an ecological message—in this case, saving the redwoods.[117] When the book was published, Rob Wagner thought it would make a good movie, so he took Sinclair to see Walt Disney. Disney responded that the story wasn't right for cartoon characters, but promised he would consider making a film of it if the studio ever switched to live actors.

The Sinclairs set off on a second lecture tour in order to continue paying off campaign debts. As they traveled from Washington State toward the Midwest, they chose to travel on unpaved roads, passing through small town after small town. On a country road at the end of a humid summer's day, they pulled the car over to let their dog explore. Duchess spotted a rabbit and disappeared into a field of high weeds. They set off into the alfalfa fields following her. Their high-spirited dog had fallen into an open cement hole, a deep, round basin swirling with underground irrigation water. Sinclair dropped to the ground next to the basin and Mary Craig braced him so he wouldn't fall. For months they had been surrounded by swarms of people—campaign workers, reporters, advisers, even a bodyguard—but now in the stillness of this late afternoon, the sun dropping onto a flat horizon, nothing but alfalfa encircling them for miles, they were utterly alone. Sinclair leaned in farther, grabbed Duchess's front paws, and managed to lift her fifty pounds out of the drainage basin and onto the ground beside them.

Despite all the traveling, Sinclair published a second book in 1936. *Co-op* was a novel about the cooperative movement in California.[118] He based the novel partially on his interviews with the residents at Pipe City, in Oakland, a settlement from the winter of 1932–33, when about two hundred people moved into the large concrete pipes in the storage yard of the American Concrete and Steel Pipe Company. They elected their own mayor, and a volunteer police force kept the peace. They shared cash from odd jobs, food, and clothing, and came up with the idea of the cooperatives.[119] Mary Craig noted wryly that "Upton's kind of people loved it and the rest of the world cared for it not at all or only mildly."[120] Sinclair himself wrote to Eleanor Roosevelt, asking if she had the copy that he sent: "I think it is a book which will especially appeal to you."[121] Alice Stone Blackwell wrote to Sinclair, asking that copies of *Co-op*, *Oil!*, and *The Gnomobile* be sent to four other women friends. Weeks later she wrote again that she had a friend working in the book section of a large department store. Blackwell had sent her friend *The Gnomobile* and "she liked it very much, and has sold about a dozen copies.... Your friend (and admirer in her eightieth year) Alice Stone Blackwell."[122] In 1990 Ingrid Kerkhoff, speaking of *Co-op*, noted that "no critic, so far, has praised it for its feminist content. *Co-Op* is a pleasure to read for every gender-conscious reader." With its "matter-of-fact women who know what they talk about, politics and economics not excluded," where "the new life within the co-operative has restored their dignity."[123] As Kerkhoff points out, his identification with women and feminist issues "lends considerable poignancy to his writing."[124]

CHAPTER SIX

World's End
[1940–1949]

I wish I were terribly rich, I wish I had an inexhaustible quantity of paper: for I would supply a whole set of the Lanny Budd novels to every boy and girl graduating from high school. I think they would then have a better chance of entering the adult world with an understanding grasp of what life holds for them.

IRVING STONE, 1947

In 1937 Sinclair published *No Pasaran!* Intellectuals in America and around the world were aware that the first war against fascism was being fought in Spain, and if the Spanish Republic was defeated, fascism could succeed in neighboring countries. Sinclair wrote to Alice Stone Blackwell: "I am trying to make my contribution to the Spanish cause in a novel. I have worked out a plan to get it printed in cheap edition for mass circulation."[1] Blackwell responded that she would send five dollars in support, "though I fear the die is cast, and all that can be done is to expose the iniquity."[2]

A month later, Seattle educator and journalist Anna Louise Strong wrote him. She'd been at the Spanish battle front and had recently reported her observations to Eleanor Roosevelt. Strong proposed to Sinclair that they "exchange some of my knowledge of Spain for yours of California," explaining that she was planning to "get to Los Angeles to see Mrs. Barnsdall and Mrs. Gartz."[3] These letters reveal Sinclair's inclusion in the powerful alliances of Depression-era women activists like Roosevelt, Strong, Gartz, and Aline Barnsdall.

Elizabeth Gurley Flynn was a socialist and feminist labor organizer who by the thirties was a member of the Communist Party. In a 1939 letter, Flynn wrote to Sinclair. She disparaged the "New York radicals who seem to think it's all there is of America," and who spent their time in "endless debate and personal affairs. Especially amorous ones." She wrote that he had been wise to leave the East for the solitude of California: "I admire your industry and your devotion to the cause during the last twenty years when so many of the promising radical writers of yesterday have fallen by the wayside."[4] Despite the dispute between the socialist and communist parties, which had grown ever more bitter, the Gurley-Sinclair friendship continued even after the Eisenstein debacle.

George Bernard Shaw and his wife, Charlotte, came to visit in 1936. The Sinclairs were sad to find Shaw much aged at eighty. Mary Craig wrote, "Mrs. Shaw, stout and blonde, looked as if she would live longer than her husband. But Shaw's smile was as sweet as ever."[5] In 1937 Sinclair wrote to Albert Einstein, by then one of his closest friends, requesting assistance for David, who was having a difficult time as the son of the infamous Upton Sinclair. Although David and his wife were members of the Norman Thomas Socialist Group, Upton wrote, "they have never carried their political convictions into their work, and they have never taken part in any activities which conventional people would consider objectionable."[6] He asked Einstein to find a physics department "which will judge a man on his merits and not on his father's politics."[7] Einstein replied within a week to say he would help, and Sinclair thanked him: "Just a line to express my gratitude at your great kindness to David. I hope to have a new story to send you in a couple of weeks. It deals with Henry Ford and his struggle with the labor unions."[8]

The project was called *The Flivver King*. Mary Craig believed this book was the way for Upton to succeed, as he had described before their marriage, upon "the path he would follow in future, if it lay

23. The arrival of two hundred thousand copies of *The Flivver King: The Story of Henry Ford* at the office of the Ford Organizing Committee in Detroit. Sinclair is shown standing with auto workers next to a van advertising the book, in 1937. Courtesy of the Lilly Library, Indiana University, Bloomington.

in my power to keep him on it. No matter how attractive he was as a platform speaker, he reached more people with the printed page."[9] Victor Reuther, vice president of the United Auto Workers, printed two hundred thousand copies of *The Flivver King* in order to educate autoworkers. "This excellent book," Reuther declared in a German documentary made in 1978, "was a very useful weapon; the workers passed it secretly to organize; it publicized conditions of the Ford workers."[10] Feminist novelist Vera Brittain wrote to Sinclair how much she looked forward to reading the book: "I was driven over the Ford Works when I lectured in Detroit in 1934, so your story will mean more to me than to most English readers."[11]

Brittain, who had written the acclaimed antiwar novel *Testament of Youth*, must have been delighted to see the inclusion of Henry Ford's peace mission to Europe. Ingrid Kerkhoff notes that "the fact that he lends 'visibility' to the Woman's Peace Party shows his sense of historical truth."[12] Walter Reuther told Sinclair that all over the world Ford workers slipped the pamphlet of *The Flivver King* into their pockets: "If you didn't have a coat on, it stuck up about four or five inches, a green signal of defiance."[13] Sinclair suggested to the United Auto Workers that he could produce *Flivver King* as a movie, with workers buying advanced tickets to fund the filming.[14] Although this plan never materialized, Ford workers unionized four years after his book was published.

Later Sinclair recalled that when Ford workers struck, Ford threatened to close his plants rather than recognize the union: "Then without any explanation Ford reversed his position and he went the whole hog. He recognized the union, he met with them, he made decent terms with them."[15] Sinclair began to correspond with a close associate of Henry Ford and discovered that Mrs. Ford had threatened to leave her husband if he closed his plants. Sinclair remembered "that quiet little woman sitting over there against the wall in that rented home, listening to me outline the idea of social democracy to her husband, and I just say to myself, 'I had something to do with that.'"[16]

After the publication of *The Flivver King*, Upton Sinclair produced another one of his experiments in genre. *Our Lady* is a time-travel fantasy, about which Sinclair later wrote, "I think I love that best of all my books."[17] In this book, the biblical Maria appears at the annual Notre Dame football game in the Los Angeles Coliseum. She meets two Catholic clergy and an Aramaic scholar to whom she describes the world of the Bible. John Ahouse notes, "Sinclair must have thoroughly enjoyed describing the contradictions of modern life seen through the eyes of a visitor from another time."[18] Sinclair's promotional leaflet for *Our Lady* offers a summary of the story as a play with act and scene divisions. When he sent a copy to Helen Keller, she responded, "I am glad of the irony with which you brush aside the ceremonies and church paraphernalia that tend to blot out the sweet human story. But I can hardly imagine Mary wanting to look into Jesus's future on earth. To my way of thinking, she was too happy in the spiritual atmosphere He created for her. Perhaps some of your delicate suggestions have escaped me. Such a book calls for many auditions."[19]

Lanny Budd and the Popular Front against Fascism

One of Upton's Sinclair's most significant accomplishments, in his own view as well as that of his readers, was the eleven-volume World's End series (1940–49).[20] Critic Sally Parry called it "The Allies' Secret Weapon against the Third Reich."[21] Sinclair continued the series throughout the forties, making it the most widely read narrative of the war. World's End gave the reading public popular history written so nimbly that one could expect to find the latest book for sale in every train station across the country.

Michael Riherd has investigated Sinclair's creation of the first volume of the series in October 1938, "a time when Sinclair was becoming convinced that democratic society was doomed."[22] After they heard a radio broadcast describing Hitler's invasion of Czechoslovakia, Mary Craig turned to him and said. "Well, our world is at an end; I don't see how anyone can fail to realize that."[23] Yet the near unanimous mood in the country was that the United States should avoid involvement in another war.[24]

Public opinion was in fact "perhaps more isolationist than at any time since before the World War."[25] As many as 70 percent of Americans thought that World War I had been a mistake, and, as Frederick Allen notes, "When people spoke of the 'fascist menace,' most of them meant the menace of an American fascist movement."[26] Although Roosevelt harbored deep concerns about Hitler, "the President would not tell the country about the gravity of the situation. When Secretary of the Interior Harold Ickes urged him to do so, he said the people simply would not believe him."[27] In October 1937 FDR gave the "Quarantine Speech" in which he proposed that warmongering states be treated as a public health menace. Yet he secretly stepped up a program to build long-range submarines that could blockade Japan.[28] At the time of the Munich Agreement in 1938, Roosevelt promised that the United States would not join a "stop-Hitler bloc" under any circumstances, and in the event of German aggression against Czechoslovakia, the United States would remain neutral.[29] In late September of 1940, the Republican candidate, Wendell Willkie, began to tighten the race by charging that if FDR won a third term, "you may expect that we will be at war." Roosevelt countered that he would not send Americans to fight in "any foreign war."[30]

Critic Sally Parry reports that an examination of Sinclair's letters at the Lilly Library shows his intent in the late thirties to write a "long novel on the rise of fascism."[31] She contends that his hope was that "the hero would learn, just as he hoped his readers would, that fascism was a menace to world peace and could not be ignored but must be destroyed."[32] Those Americans who had gone to Spain in 1937 to defend the Spanish Republic had also seen the necessity of early resistance to fascism. John Ahouse notes that "*No Pasaran!* points the way to the later books of the World's End series with their novelistic treatment of contemporary world events."[33] Sinclair set out to create what may be one of the first antifascist spy novels written. German critic Dieter Herms maintains that Sinclair wrote the World's End series as "propaganda entertainingly packaged in the wrappers of popular literature."[34]

Six weeks after the invasion of Czechoslovakia, while walking in his garden one night, Sinclair experienced a vision of the entire series: "a novel came rolling into the field of my mental vision." It had happened before, "but never with such force, such mass and persistence. There was no resisting it, and I didn't try."[35] Within several days of the vision, Sinclair had written the first draft of the novel, based on ninety-two pages of notes, which included characters, events, and information about life in Europe before the war and about the peace conference. He wrote to a friend, writer

Fulton Oursler, that his idea "kept me busy all day and most of the night—the biggest story I have ever written. . . . It was perfectly marvelous the way the thing just unfolded itself."[36]

As soon as he completed the first few chapters of *World's End*, the first novel in the series, Sinclair sent them out to experts for critique. He had visited Germany with Mary Craig prior to World War I, but not during the Weimar or Hitler eras. Michael Riherd's research documents that Sinclair received seventy critical suggestions from about eighteen people, including Ray Stannard Baker (biographer of Woodrow Wilson); Adolf Berle (delegate to the Paris Peace Conference of 1919 and later assistant secretary of state to FDR); Isaiah Bowman (director of the American Geographical Society and territorial specialist to the Paris Peace Conference); and William Bullitt (ambassador to the USSR from 1933 to 1936, and then to France from 1936 to 1940).

Riherd writes, "Emerging from Sinclair's creative imagination and his intellect was a newly constructed whole that did not so exist in history: a tragic vision of European society."[37] He compares Sinclair's use of historical sources to that of Shakespeare, using the raw material of history to construct his dramas, and suggests, "Maybe you could call it 'story history.' I really got the Versailles meetings from the book in a way I never could have from any other source."[38] But the novel was rejected by four publishers. Mary Craig recalls: "Then by happy chance Upton thought of an old friend, B. W. Huebsch of Viking Press. Ben had been a Civil Liberties Union man from early days and would understand what Upton was driving at."[39]

Huebsch took it on one day in 1940—and was ready to publish by the next. Thus Sinclair's course was set for the next dozen years. When Elizabeth Gurley Flynn wrote in August 1941 asking Sinclair to join a citizens committee to free Communist Party General Secretary Earl Browder, he regretfully declined: "I have had to make a resolve to drop all committee work. . . . I am giving all my time and energy to a series of novels about Europe, which I believe represents my proper job."[40] Sinclair wrote the early novels in the Pasadena garden, surrounded by rose bushes. Duchess would lie still beside him as he typed. Mary Craig remembers how he would occasionally rise and so would Duchess: "He would pat her head, then walk up and down on the garden path, while she raced around joyously and barked at birds in the fig trees."[41] When he sat down again, so did she.

The first book in the series, *World's End*, describes events in Europe from 1911 to 1919. The last novel, *O Shepherd, Speak!*, is set in the closing days of World War II; John Ahouse notes that "the author saw fit at the end of the tenth volume to provide an index—surely unique in a work of fiction—in which real and imaginary figures are mixed without differentiation."[42] Each title in the series carries its own significance; for instance, *Between Two Worlds* refers simultaneously to the world between the wars, the contrasts between poverty and luxury, and the conflicting viewpoints about fascism in Europe and America. *Dragon's Teeth* and *Dragon Harvest* refer to the Versailles Treaty as sowing dragon's teeth in the ground of Europe—the inevitable source of future bloodshed.

In 1940 novelist Thomas Mann, who had left Germany when Hitler rose to power, visited the Sinclairs. Mary Craig thought that he lacked humanity, but noted that "Upton, whose outflowing of interest in his fellow man was his chief characteristic, did not seem to miss this quality in Thomas Mann."[43] To Sinclair, Mann was a fascinating source of information about Europe. Sinclair set the first chapter of the World's End series at a dance recital attended by George Bernard Shaw, who later wrote that he regarded Sinclair "not as a novelist, but as a historian; for it is my considered opinion that records of fact are not history."[44]

Vera Brittain also came to Pasadena that year, later writing, "It was a joy to meet your wife and to have that delightful conversation. . . . It was a most important experience to me to be able to identify the name with a real person at last."[45] Sinclair responded by urging her not to return to England: "Why don't you arrange to stay in this country until the bombing is over? . . . You can render much greater service to your country on this side and your country will have fewer mouths to feed."[46] The Sinclairs' friendship with Brittain was deepening since her initial correspondence with Sinclair about *The Flivver King*. As with many of their female friends, the Sinclairs' companionate and companionable marriage provided a space to welcome many female—and male—friends without fear of infidelity or flirtation.

Almost two years later, America itself was bombed at Pearl Harbor. As President Roosevelt intoned, "December 7, 1941: a date which will live in infamy—the United States of America was suddenly and deliberately attacked by naval and air forces of the Empire of Japan."[47] Sinclair must have heard those words from the Bendix radio, which stood tall in the Sinclair living room in Pasadena. He had probably just finished his breakfast of rice and fruit, and Mary Craig was perhaps not yet up.

He may have left the house quietly, heading for the bench in his garden, next to the fig tree. He might have sat there in the cold thinking of his father and grandfather, who had hoped he would become a military man. He may have thought of Albert Einstein, who would no doubt be enlisted to help develop cruel weapons against the Germans and Japanese. He might have thought about his women friends, so passionately involved in the antifascist effort of the Spanish Civil War. He may have been overwhelmed by having lived long enough to watch this next war unroll, for the chance to be its chronicler and even its propagandist. He might have opened his garden gate and walked silently through the streets, where people sat on porches, talking of nothing but Pearl Harbor and Mr. Roosevelt.

That year, Upton Sinclair was sixty-three years old; he would spend the rest of the war writing book after book featuring Lanny Budd, an American expatriate turned presidential agent. The series used everything he knew about American business from his Baltimore childhood and his investigative reporting; everything he had learned about European history from Thomas Mann and George Bernard Shaw; and the craftsmanship he developed back in 1903 as he wrote *Manassas*.

Many of Sinclair's heroes, like Lanny Budd, had been privileged Americans. Critic Arun Pant has noted the role of such characters in *Oil!* and *Boston*, reflecting "the beginning of a certain introspective trait among the rich over their own role in the making of social order when confronted with inequality and human misery."[48] Lanny Budd feels a growing sense of responsibility for his friends in Europe. Family connections and his expertise in fine art enable Lanny to move freely behind Axis lines once war is declared, making him valuable to the Allied powers and to Franklin Roosevelt in particular. Lanny straddles two political worlds, but his patriotism and devotion to the Allied cause are never in doubt. When *World's End* was published later in 1940, Theodore Dreiser wrote, "I am reading your novel. Talk about novelized history, economics, sociology, greed, and what not! Here they strut the stage as characters."[49]

Each of the World's End novels was a bestseller, translated into twenty languages. The first eight found over one million buyers in the United States alone.[50] With these novels, "Sinclair regained his 'lost' audience. The novels introduced Sinclair to the grandchildren of the immigrants who had lauded him in the early years of the century."[51] Historian Perry Miller wrote of the series, "It is a version of modern history, and it is more coherent than most.... I am struck with admiration for the monumental simplicity of the conception, and sighing like Lanny over the muddle of the world, I eagerly await my next installment."[52] This turned out to be a common experience; Germaine Warkentin remembers reading, along with her mother, the Lanny Budd books from the public library, which became her introduction to modern history: "I simply devoured them, over the summers of 1947 and 1948.... The vision of history the books communicated has, I am sure, powerfully influenced my present social democrat views."[53]

Sinclair cared most about the effect his books had on individual readers. Edward Allatt, an English soldier, was profoundly affected by the books. In 1947 Allatt was stationed with the British Occupation Forces in the Hartz Mountains of Germany. By his own account, as an average reader who grew up on "penny dreadfuls," Allatt made frequent use of the Civilian Service Library, where he chanced on the novel *Dragon's Teeth*. When interviewed many years after the war by Robert Hahn, he explained that he felt the novel "mystically to say, 'read me more, read me more.'"[54] John Ahouse adds, "On returning to London, he began to visit the American Embassy Library and British Museum . . . in hope of finding additional titles by this American author, whose notion of social justice held a deep appeal for him."[55]

Jeffrey Youdelman inherited a set of the series from his father (who had read them a dozen times) at age fifteen, and writes, "Through Lanny, I first saw many of the 'events' in history I would learn more about later. . . . I liked learning the poetry along with the stories and history."[56] Youdelman also notes, "Here in the boundaries of a novel were, to cite a few, Edward Bellamy, Hilaire Belloc, Bergh of Bismarck, Leon Blum, Eva Braun, British Intelligence, William Blake, Neville Chamberlain, Himmler, Eugene Debs, Hearst, Tom Mooney, Tom Paine, and Wordsworth."[57]

Lady Bird Johnson was another reader who "gained a more vivid recollection of foreign affairs through the adventures of Lanny Budd, than through reading the newspapers at that time!"[58] Hugh Sidney, Time-Life journalist, similarly wrote, "The Lanny Budd series were the first serious books I read discussing the political-social problems of this age."[59] Sinclair also drew praise from Mari Sandoz, the foremost interpreter of the Nebraska historical experience. She wrote to a friend: "One book that surprised me was *World's End*, the new Upton Sinclair book . . . not a line that read like a tract, and an interesting, to me at least, portrayal of the pre-war, war, and post-war European scene."[60]

Dragon's Teeth, the third book in the series, was the last to be written in Pasadena. Gertrude Atherton wrote that *Dragon's Teeth* was "enthralling and bloodthirsty. . . . I would revel in seeing with my own eyes Hitler *et al* boiled in oil."[61] She incorrectly assumed that Sinclair must have spent long periods in Europe in order to

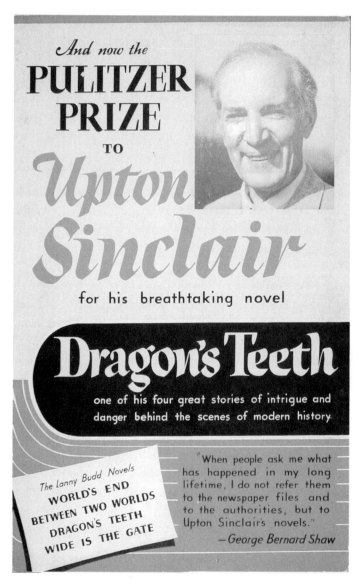

And now the
PULITZER PRIZE
TO
Upton Sinclair
for his breathtaking novel

Dragon's Teeth
one of his four great stories of intrigue and
danger behind the scenes of modern history

The Lanny Budd Novels
WORLD'S END
BETWEEN TWO WORLDS
DRAGON'S TEETH
WIDE IS THE GATE

"When people ask me what
has happened in my long
lifetime, I do not refer them
to the newspaper files and
to the authorities, but to
Upton Sinclair's novels."
—*George Bernard Shaw*

24. *Dragon's Teeth* book cover. In a letter to Sinclair, dated 1942, Margaret Sanger wrote that she had been living with "your Lanny ... again and again I wondered how you could know these people so well unless you had lived each life yourself." Courtesy of the Lilly Library, Indiana University, Bloomington.

"learn so much, not only about the psychology of peoples, but of art, music, literature—no man ever lived a busier life."[62] Thomas Mann wrote that it was painful reading matter, particularly for a German, "but the pain is turned into pleasure by the art of the presentation—a pleasure, of course, constantly mingled with rage and shame. Whoever knows Nazi Germany will admit that not a word in your book is exaggerated."[63]

The Sinclairs experienced the war at home in Southern California. On February 1942 the *Los Angeles Times* mistakenly reported that Japanese planes had bombed the city.[64] Emergency regulations mandated that in case of bombing, every household needed a pail of sand and a shovel, with a nearby ladder in order to climb up the roof to shovel sand over the fire. Mary Craig remembers, "Our house was over ninety feet long, and we could not have even carried a tall-enough ladder from one corner to the other, to say nothing of climbing up with shovel and sand and putting out a fire."[65] But they managed to get the ladder, the sand, and the shovel, which could not have been easy since gasoline was rationed.

In October 1942 the Sinclairs began to look for a new house—for their papers, their books, and themselves, somewhere, as Craig remembers, "farther from the center of industry, traffic and smoke."[66] Upton Sinclair wrote to David that the move was Craig's idea.[67] They could no longer manage the upkeep of the house in Pasadena: black widow spiders, silverfish, termites, and rats were running through the stacks of papers and books. Mesquite and creosote bushes overgrew the gully next to the house, a real fire hazard in the dry summer months of Southern California. They found a two-story concrete residence for sale on the edge of the town of Monrovia where, Craig wrote, they "later counted twenty-two varieties of fruit trees; we would have something to eat, free of charge, every week of the year."[68]

The new house on North Myrtle Drive was importantly within walking distance of both the post office and library. Craig insisted that her husband give their address to no one and receive mail at the post office. On May 3, 1943, the phone rang and the editor of the Monrovia paper told Upton Sinclair that *Dragon's Teeth* had been awarded the Pulitzer Prize. Craig remembers that her husband "was as happy as if he had inherited enough money to buy the world and make it over according to his life-long dream."[69]

One of the Pulitzer jury members wrote that Sinclair was almost unique among novelists because "contemporary history, as it comes through to us every day in the headlines, has become so overpowering that many individuals can have no significant emotional life apart from it."[70] George Bernard Shaw agreed; he wrote to his friend expressing his admiration for the way he "rescues facts from the unintelligible chaos of their actual occurrence and arranges them in works of art."[71] Sinclair continued to write at least a thousand words a day on the World's End series, hammering "on my little typewriter for three hours every morning . . . revising every afternoon, and walking in the garden every evening, composing the next day's work."[72]

Sinclair's own personal narrative had altered with the move to Monrovia. Don Wolfe, who visited them there, described driving "up a long street to an abrupt end, where the barren canyon slopes loomed on the horizon, brown and sun-burned by day, purple and cool in the evening light."[73] Craig's niece, Liz Clements, remembered the home as surrounded by a forest, dark inside, with windows covered by large thick drapes. The house was full of bookcases and second-hand furniture. "Material things did not mean anything to them," Clements later told an interviewer.[74] Few people were invited to visit; and David was not one of them. Father and son continued to have political disagreements.

David's mother married a third time, in the late 1940s, this time to John Stone, who was thirteen years younger than Meta. John Stone remembered Meta's complaints about Sinclair, which she believed led David to three years of daily psychoanalysis. Stone wrote, "I've met David several times and he seems to be okay now and he eats the same as most people. He even drinks, quite regularly, and likes a pre-dinner cocktail."[75] During the war, David Sinclair was part of a group of scientists doing research for the government at Columbia University. They invented an aerosol generator used to create protective smokescreens for Allied troops during the invasion of Normandy.

David and Betty Sinclair had divorced in 1939. David, like his father, would have one child with his first wife followed by a successful second marriage. David married Jean Weidman in 1944, and Jean would soon smooth the path to reconciliation between her husband and his father. David sent his father a card after his wedding, explaining that he had been hired by the Johns Manville Company. He thought that his research project at Manville on the cause and cure of automobile brake squeal "might be of interest because it was caused by the same physical process as the tones of the violin."[76] He may have been reaching out to his father through their mutual love of music.

John Ahouse comments, "I like to think of Lanny Budd as Upton's fantasy version of David. They were born at the same time (to start the new century), and the opening book, *World's End*, begins with the eurhythmics at the private school episode, which corresponds to David's experience."[77] Sally Parry believes Lanny was modeled on Ernst "Putzi" Hanfstaengl, a Harvard graduate who was kept in Hitler's entourage to entertain but was secretly advising the United States.[78] She speculates that since one of his parents was American and one German, Sinclair may have taken the parentage from him as well as the occupation of being an art connoisseur. They would have been in New York at the same time, prior to World War II, and Hanfstaengl does show up as a character in the Lanny Budd series. Parry writes that "after he fell from favor with Hitler, Hanfstaengl provided much information on Hitler to the oss, including details of Hitler's personal life. Since Lanny works as a secret agent for FDR in a number of the books in the second half of the series, this was probably inspired by Hanfstaengl."[79]

Andrew Lee compares the World's End series to the series

Episodos Nacionales, by Benito Pérez Galdós: "Supposedly, the model for Lanny Budd was one of the founders of the Rand School of Social Science, George Herron. The Rand School library is the basis for the Tamiment Library."[80] George Herron had been a close friend since he introduced Sinclair to socialism in 1902. Perry Miller declared that "the character of Lanny Budd is surely one of the more fabulous creations of our time ... possessing the insouciance of D'Artagnan, the penetration of Sherlock Holmes, the elegance of Beau Brummel ... [and] the sociological profundity of Herbert Spencer."[81]

Another possible real-life inspiration for Lanny Budd was Cornelius Vanderbilt Jr., scion of America's plutocratic ruling family, and one of a small number of friends invited to Monrovia. The Sinclairs met Cornelius, known as Neil, early in their California life. "I liked him, and what was more important, Craig liked him; we saw a great deal of him, and watched his gallant fight to finance a liberal newspaper in a reactionary community."[82] When Sinclair was working on the fifth volume in the series, Vanderbilt dropped by, one of the few visitors welcomed by Mary Craig. Sinclair recalls that while his wife played matchmaker for her visiting nieces, he sat out by their little homemade swimming pool and listened to Neil's stories about his work with Franklin Roosevelt. "I said with some excitement and hesitancy, 'That would make a wonderful story for Lanny Budd.' Neil said, 'That's why I'm telling it to you.' It was a magnificent gift."[83]

Lanny Budd, open-minded, morally passionate, absorbed in ideas, yet able to meet and influence most of the leading figures in Europe, lived a life that seems the opposite of that of Upton Sinclair, but Delia Spencer Williams, who worked over several decades as a secretary to Sinclair, recalls a parallel. She was "summoned one night in 1940 or 1941 to type an urgent letter on the growing threat of war."[84] She believes that this letter was indeed sent to FDR. Although Sinclair did not visit with Roosevelt after 1934, he did write to him, and to Eleanor.

In 1944 Upton Sinclair wrote to Eleanor Roosevelt that his wife had "commissioned me to send to you this message. 'May you live long to prosper him.'"[85] He told Roosevelt that they had debated if that was a feminist statement since it implied that the president was more important than his wife. For a couple to debate in the mid-1940s as to whether something was feminist or not was highly unusual, more characteristic of either the 1920s or the 1970s. But the Sinclairs suspected—and Mrs. Roosevelt knew— that FDR had very little time left: he was exhausted and very ill by the end of the war.

Sinclair chose to end his only collection of published letters with Cornelius Vanderbilt's description of his last visits with Franklin Roosevelt. Vanderbilt remembered sitting with FDR in the presidential yacht when Roosevelt commented that the Bay cities, the Peninsula, and the area as far north as Petaluma were more "in fitting with the world labor movement than any other part of America. He was especially impressed by how black, yellow, and white men *and WOMEN* work hand in hand without trouble doing a supreme war job."[86] During their last visit, Vanderbilt reported that Roosevelt "talked almost entirely on the need of STOPPING WAR FOREVER. . . . [T]he international bankers must not only have their wings shorn, but must have nothing left to fly with save the stump."[87]

Franklin D. Roosevelt died in Warm Springs, Georgia, on April 12, 1945. Mary Craig recalls, "I watched Upton's distress as he paced the room, trying to think what the effect of the loss would be. This first shock must have engraved itself upon his mind, for later he wrote it into the novel *O Shepherd, Speak!*"[88] Sinclair sent a telegram to Eleanor: "We have lost the greatest statesmen of our time and it is a personal loss to every man and woman in this country whether they know it or not."[89] That year, as the country moved from World War II into the Cold War, Sinclair chose to end the World's End series with a focus on FDR. In *One Clear Call*, Lanny explains that he "considered Franklin Roosevelt the greatest man in the world."[90] In the last book of the series, Roosevelt dies, and Lanny Budd founds a newspaper to advocate for world government. He also participates in séances, in which the ghost of FDR speaks.

Many readers saw the World's End series as a natural for cinematic treatment, but it would have a tangled history as a film or television project. Helen Taubkin writes, "I read and enjoyed the entire Lanny Budd series. I even tried to persuade Tyrone Power, whose secretary I was when he was under contract at 20th Century Fox in the 1940s, to have the studio buy the series as a starring vehicle for him."[91] Screenwriter Malvin Wald believes that due to Sinclair's condemnation of Henry Ford's business relationship with the Nazis during World War II, the project lost sponsorship by the Ford Motor Company.[92] CBS, and producer Abby Mann, optioned the World's End series, but year after year something intervened to prevent production. This long process is documented in Jean Sinclair's correspondence.

Sinclair wrote again to Eleanor Roosevelt in 1946. She was in London with the United Nations Organizing Delegation. He enclosed a New Year's message written by Mary Craig: "It deals with the subject of the atomic bomb, and it seems to me unusually eloquent."[93] In 1948 Sinclair published *A Giant's Strength*, a play about the threat of atomic weapons. Sinclair's third publication that year was titled *Limbo on the Loose*. It was a reissue of *The Way Out: What Lies Ahead for America* (originally published in 1933). Sinclair added an introductory sketch, "Limbo on the Loose," a melancholy and somber meditation about the waning of his own life, and possibly, that of the world. Sinclair subtitled the story "A Midsummer Night's Dream"; the setting is lyrically Southern California, brown hills full of large rocks, lit by a waning moon. Sinclair titles himself "Hopeful," a person who "sees that now a time limit has been set; there are no more half-centuries; there may not be even half decades."[94] "Hopeful" meets real friends from his past (Lincoln Steffens, Henry Ford, King Gillette) and characters from previous books.

25. Monrovia house. The Sinclairs moved to Monrovia in 1942, from where they could see the Pacific Ocean some twenty or thirty miles away when the air was clear. Courtesy of Dana Downie, 1971.

Although he would write another eight books, and update his *Autobiography* in 1962, this sketch stands as Sinclair's own elegy for his life and work and leaves him in the reader's mind where he most loved to be—alone in nature, conversing with his friends "in that place called limbo, where, according to the ancients, the dead await the living."[95] In 1943 George Bernard Shaw had written Sinclair: "My wife died on the 12th of this month. During her long illness, she read the Lanny Budd saga over and over and over again."[96]

In 1949 David wrote that he was experiencing a difficult period with his sixteen-year-old daughter, Diana, so that he understood better now what his father had experienced with his own adolescence. Sinclair began to write more often to his son; he told David, for example, how thrilled he was that his work was being published by the Atomic Energy Commission.[97]

Mary Craig describes their life as they entered the new decade: "It was a balmy summer evening. Standing at the window, we listened to an owl hooting in the trees and a coyote barking in the hills. In the morning when Upton went out, there was a deer under one of the orange trees."[98]

CHAPTER SEVEN

A Lifetime in Letters
[1950–1968]

My dear Upton:
So you, like me, "are there." We are tough ones, you and I. Certainly
I am pleased if you have found any of my letters interesting enough
to publish. Go ahead! Yes, Upton, the "world do move," if we care to
push hard enough and care to have it move.

MARGARET SANGER, 1957

In early 1950 the Sinclairs rented out the house in Monrovia and
moved to the desert town of Corona, hungry for cleaner air and
needing family support. Craig's brother Hunter Kimbrough had
moved to nearby Riverside in 1948 with his family to open an automobile insurance business. He knew that his sister and Sinclair were
growing too old to look after themselves without some assistance,
so he checked regularly to see that bills were paid and the house
maintained. When Hunter relocated to Phoenix, Arizona, Craig
and Sinclair followed and bought a tiny house in a nearby suburb,
where they lived until 1952.

The Impact of the Cold War

They returned to California only after Craig's heart attack in 1954,
in order to be closer to her doctors. Once back in Monrovia, they
kept the curtains drawn, and Upton installed an escalator seat to
carry his wife up and down the stairs. The shut-in life fostered their

isolation and their exposure to the mainstream Cold War narrative.[1] In 1951 the editors at the *New Leader*, a bastion of Cold War liberalism, told Sinclair that the Lanny Budd books were too soft on Communism.[2] By 1952, during the Korean War, Sinclair endorsed U.S. containment policy toward the USSR. "I do not think that we are under any obligation to unify Korea," he explained, once U.S. troops had pushed North Korea and its Chinese allies back to the Thirty-Eighth Parallel, "and I think we have done what we set out to do, which was to teach the Reds that they cannot go on seizing territory and enslaving new peoples."[3] Thus he wrote *The Return of Lanny Budd* and published it in 1953 as a Cold War spy story.

In 1951 Sinclair had attempted to release the full footage of *Thunder Over Mexico*, but ironically—given his growing anticommunism—the politics of the McCarthy era made the release impossible. The film was stored in a vault from 1951 to 1954 and was finally donated to the Museum of Modern Art by Bud Lesser in 1954. Sinclair would never vote for a Socialist Party candidate for president again; he even declined to support Henry Wallace in 1948 because, as he wrote to Clinton Taft, he considered Wallace's Progressive Party a cover for the communists.[4] Instead he supported the two Democratic candidates of 1956 and 1960, Adlai Stevenson and John F. Kennedy. Sinclair embraced Americans for Democratic Action (ADA), the leading anticommunist liberal organization of the postwar years.[5] Like Sinclair, the ADA advocated for labor unions, the welfare state, civil rights for African Americans, and civil liberties for all.

But he never became as conservative as his old friend Max Eastman, who had renounced his radical past and by the 1950s was writing for the *Reader's Digest*. In the *New Leader*, Sinclair argued that Eastman was "for resistance to Soviet dictatorship, and I am with him completely, but I am not willing to shut my eyes to the defects of the economic system we have at home."[6] Elaine Tyler May's point that "Cold-war ideology wove together several strands of American political culture [which] included a belief in individual freedom, unfettered capitalism, the sanctity of the home, and a suspicion of outsiders," helps contextualize Sinclair's life in the fifties.[7]

For the Sinclairs, the Cold War turned personal quickly with the loss of their friendship with Kate Crane Gartz. As Sinclair notes in *Mental Radio*, the two were so close that Craig had been able to intuit when Kate Gartz would phone, and often Gartz and Craig dreamt the same dream. In 1946, at Craig's request, the Sinclairs began to avoid Kate Crane Gartz, as she tried to include them in her embrace of the Communist Party. She came to Monrovia and pressed them with invitations to her home. They ignored her.

Sinclair wrote to a friend that Crane Gartz "asked us [to] come [to] her home and answer the Communists," but "Mary Craig had made up her mind to do no more." She had "seen enough of their trickery," and marked out all names of communists from their address book.[8] Elaine Tyler May explains that "at the dawn of the atomic age, protection against external dangers took the form of a nuclear arsenal; protection against internal enemies took the form of a nuclear family. The two were profoundly connected."[9] The end of their friendship with Gartz would have been very painful.

Perhaps Sinclair's way of writing Kate Gartz out of their lives was to cast her in his first book of the fifties. Gartz was the model for the employer in *Another Pamela: or, Virtue Still Rewarded*, a variation on Richardson's classic epistolary novel, set in the Southern California of the 1920s, an era to which Sinclair may have looked backward with some nostalgia. In the novel, a young working girl takes a job as a servant to a wealthy radical woman and is courted by her employer's son. Ingrid Kerkhoff notes that the heroine is ready to marry her suitor, but "she will only accept him at *her* terms, which stipulate that she will continue to work," and that Charles, her suitor, will step out of his class and work for a living.[10]

Mary Craig's paranoia and desire for isolation was exacerbated by her failing health. She had an enlarged heart and found breathing the ever-growing smog increasingly difficult. The Sinclairs bought a trailer and began traveling in the mountains outside of Monrovia.

There they encountered numerous fundamentalist churches holding revival meetings, and Sinclair—ever curious—went in to listen. In response he wrote *A Personal Jesus*, which focused on the historical Jesus.[11] It took him two long years to find a publisher for the book, and he was finally forced to advertise in a magazine. Albert Einstein wrote indignantly that "the attitude of the publishing world towards your beautiful work corresponds somewhat with the attitude of the official world toward the memory of the hero of your book whom you have so lovingly depicted."[12] *A Personal Jesus* was finally published in 1952.

The Congress for Cultural Freedom and the State Department were promoting Ezra Pound, William Faulkner, and the paintings of abstract expressionists as part of the erasure of politically radical voices in the arts that characterized the McCarthy Era.[13] Kevin Mattson notes that "Sinclair's middlebrow literary and artistic tastes, even if they were to the liking of Harry Truman (who claimed to have read the Lanny Budd series), didn't seem to project the necessary complexity and sophistication America's foreign policy elite wanted to show off around the world."[14] Despite his endorsement of the dominant Cold War ideology, Sinclair was treated as irrelevant.[15] Granville Hicks wrote that Sinclair had been "either dismissed or patronized by the majority of critics and literary historians."[16] Sinclair wrote to Carl Jung, who had reviewed *A Personal Jesus*: "In the past four years or so I have written six books, large or small, and found a publisher for only one."[17]

In 1955 Jean and David traveled west to visit the elder Sinclairs in Monrovia. David had not seen his father or stepmother for more than twenty years. By this period in the early fifties, Upton Sinclair was a staunch supporter of the Democratic Party and of the Cold War, while David considered himself a liberal socialist. Jean's compassion, David's loyalty to his father, and the changing needs of the elder Sinclairs as they aged were all factors in the reconciliation.

Don Wolfe describes his visit to Upton Sinclair that year in Monrovia: he saw "a short slender man with a great oval head of sparse gray hair, bright blue eyes, and an almost luminous fair skin." Mary Craig came downstairs on an escalator; Wolfe saw "a pale, thin woman with bright brown eyes and a warm Southern accent." When he asked Sinclair which of his books had the most profound social impact, Sinclair told him, "It's either *The Jungle* or *The Brass Check*." And which book in his judgment had the best claim to literary quality? "His answer surprised us: *Oil!* or *World's End*."[18] This comment by Upton Sinclair demonstrates an astute understanding of the stylistic and aesthetic value of these two novels, both almost forgotten (although the 2007 Paul Thomas Anderson film adaptation *There Will be Blood* was loosely based on *Oil!*), one written when he was forty-five and the other twelve years later.

In 1956 the *Los Angeles Times'* reporter Graham Berry visited Monrovia. In the coy parlance of the era, Berry titled his article "A Prolific Puritan of the Pen," describing Sinclair as "lean and fit in his short-sleeved sport shirt, white duck trousers and the inevitable tennis shoes . . . working on one of his most successful crusades, bringing back the health of his wife. . . . [T]hat crusade has included cooking 3,000 pots of rice."[19] Sinclair told Berry that he had tried unsuccessfully for a year to find a publisher for *The Cup of Fury*, his book about alcoholism. When it was published in 1956 by the obscure Channel Press, Sinclair was horrified to learn that its editor went door to door to try to sell his book.

The Cup of Fury grimly examines the effects of alcohol on his friends, including Eugene Debs, "one of the noblest and kindest men," among his list of alcoholics.[20] By the 1950s the cultural narrative in books and films of alcohol as a disease separated the debate from the realm of political and social analysis.[21] Sinclair wrote that "most of them [his friends] started with vision and courage, but in the end the example they give us is of sickness of mind and soul. They have helped bring about an America in which people feel they 'must' drink. And America is drinking, more than ever before."[22] Male writers—Ernest Hemingway is a famous example—were still expected to be reckless in their lifestyles as a badge of masculinity— drinking heavily and with impunity, unkind or indifferent to the women in their lives.

In 1957 Upton Sinclair's papers were sold to Indiana University for fifty thousand dollars. The Huntington Library in Southern California had turned them down. Mary Craig had guarded the collection since 1915, eventually building four storerooms to protect it from fire. There were some 250 cardboard cartons of files, original manuscripts of one hundred books and pamphlets; and eight hundred volumes of foreign translations, from fifty-five countries in sixty languages. The vast collection of papers and books was transferred to the Lilly Library. Cecil Byrd, associate director of the Indiana University Libraries, recalls how Sinclair, then nearly eighty years old, sat with him as he sorted the papers, "maintaining a continuous and enthusiastic commentary about the background of each of the items, as Mary Craig came in occasionally to remind Sinclair not to bother the man from Indiana while he was trying to work."[23]

"What More Can a Man Do with His Life?"

In 1957 Mary Craig's memoir *Southern Belle* was published. Much of the manuscript was in Upton's handwriting; she wrote David Randall at the Lilly Library to explain that she had been too ill to write herself, so had dictated the book, but "none of it was written by Upton."[24] The Honnold Library at Claremont College holds the original diary from which *Southern Belle* was composed.[25] As John Ahouse notes, "That should give the lie to suggestions that Upton 'ghosted' her work."[26] Anthony Arthur argues that had Sinclair been the true author, he wouldn't have written it in the same way. In addition to confusing the location of Helicon Hall, he did not alter Craig's critical description of Thomas Mann: "In the first instance Sinclair, now nearly eighty years old, let slip an error he could not have made. In the second, he may have been resisting the chance to censor his wife's opinion when it varied from his own, in keeping with his long-avowed feminism."[27]

Only recently have women's memoirs been given credit for the insight they offer.[28] When *Southern Belle* was published, *Time* magazine's reviewer called it a "truly romantic as well as a wonderfully goofy story . . . irresistible to students of U.S. life and manners," referring to Sinclair as "that strange, admirable, preposterous figure of a vanished America—a man with every gift except humor and silence."[29] It is a mark of how far Sinclair had fallen since the heady days of the Lanny Budd series just ten years earlier, and a hint of the condescension with which subsequent biographers would regard him. A reviewer for the *New Republic* commented that Sinclair's world of utopian socialism "seems as dead as the carrier pigeon." He does note that the book is more of a biography of Sinclair than an autobiography by Craig, featuring "a parade of half-forgotten figures."[30]

Craig's original intent was to write a biography of Upton Sinclair. She wrote Hunter, "Upton always said he wanted me to write his biography—and of course I'm the only person who really can."[31] When the book was ready she asked Hunter to read it for errors, having considered and rejected Floyd Dell because Dell "knows nothing about the South and will probably be bored to death (even angry) with the Southern stuff and therefore unable to judge it reasonably."[32] Craig was offered only a thousand-dollar advance for her book. She decided it was more important to get published while she was still alive. Peggy Prenshaw comments on "the depth of desire—and the lifelong conflicting impulses for self-sacrifice and self-achievement—that prompted the last line of the ten-page letter to her brother: 'I want something before I leave this earth—so I'm happy about the contract.'"[33]

In 1960 Ron Gottesman began to catalogue the collection at the Lilly, and he tried to meet Sinclair in person that year. The author had sent Gottesman his telephone number, with the warning not to release it because Craig was still afraid that he was marked for assassination. When Gottesman called from the airport, Craig asked him what he wanted, and then hung up on him. He rented a car and drove to Monrovia where he stood outside the locked gate of the house on Myrtle Avenue. He called out, but there was no response. A neighbor suggested that he might wait around and catch Sinclair on one of his walks to the post office. The local Western Union clerk laughed when Gottesman tried to send a telegram, telling him to save his money and do what they did: tie his message around a rock and throw it over the fence.[34] He was unsuccessful: Sinclair remained secluded inside the house, caring for an increasingly fragile and ill wife.

One evening, Sinclair saw a notice in TV *Guide*, announcing a "new adventure series, Lanny Budd, Presidential Agent, based on the Upton Sinclair novels" that went into "production here in October for ABC syndication."[35] The Lanny Budd series was indeed optioned for television, but it was never produced. Upton Sinclair also received a letter from Walt Disney announcing that he would now keep his promise, producing *The Gnomobile* as a live action film. Sinclair was so elated—a film starring Walter Brennan and the child actors from Mary Poppins!—that he ignored his agent. He asked almost nothing for the rights to his book; this was going to be the first film adaptation of his work since *The Wet Parade* thirty years earlier.

In 1960 Sinclair published *My Lifetime in Letters*. Mary Craig had set aside seven thousand letters and the book could only contain three hundred, so "you can imagine the arguments we had—I putting in and she taking out, or vice versa."[36] The decision to limit the book to the two early decades of his career meant that the important and fascinating correspondence of the thirties and forties was largely omitted. What previous biographers have not discussed is the remarkable democracy and equity of Upton Sinclair's friendships. That he chose to publish these letters is a testament to the centrality of friendship in his life, but *My Lifetime in Letters* was not received with enthusiasm. A sarcastic review in the *New Republic* prompted Sinclair to write a letter to the editor—Ronald Sanders had criticized the book for a lack of consistent theme. Sinclair wrote, "But how can one 'organize' Bernard Shaw and Ezra Pound, Julia Ward Howe and Thomas Mann, Edith Wharton and Gandhi, Einstein and Vanzetti? I couldn't."[37]

On April 26, 1961, five days after their forty-eighth wedding anniversary, Mary Craig died. He had cared for her at home until her death, a task that had become increasingly frightening and difficult. When she died, Sinclair felt "a sense of desolation beyond my powers to describe."[38] Miriam Allen deFord wrote: "Craig was a lovely person and you made her very happy. You had a long beautiful time together and I envy you the many years you had, but if you couldn't go together, than it is better that she went first."[39] Craig left instructions for her return to her native state: "I want again to be a part of the soil of Mississippi. I want to be buried there."[40] From his now empty house Sinclair wrote to a friend: "I literally do not know one human being in the town where I live."[41] Sinclair had been a married man since he was twenty years old and wanted a companion for his old age.

Richard Armour, a friend who taught English at Scripps College, recalled that Sinclair asked him: "Get me someone who's literate, and get me a Democrat."[42] The Armours invited him to meet Mary "May" Elizabeth Willis, the recently widowed sister of Frederick Hard, the president of Scripps College. Before the two were formally introduced, Armour recalled that May "sat down on a sofa that was covered with a treacherously smooth fabric and slid to the floor, holding her whiskey and soda aloft like the Statue of Liberty. Unembarrassed, she burst into laughter." Mrs. Armour nudged Upton Sinclair's shoulder and instructed him, "That's the woman for you."[43]

Sinclair was eighty-three and May was seventy-nine when they married on October 16, 1961. Sinclair did not expect romantic love with this final marriage, but Anthony Arthur notes that "he found something even more valuable, almost a literal rejuvenation. Sinclair had said that he knew not a soul in Monrovia after living there for twenty years, but May was as gregarious as Craig had been solitary."[44] Former EPIC supporter Lorna Smith describes how May vowed repeatedly to "put the 'social' in 'socialism,' the 'sin' in 'sinclair,' and the 'rove' in 'Monrovia.'"[45] She insisted that her new husband buy a new suit, arguing that he could consider the cost a donation to the garment workers' union.

When he was interviewed for *Personal Close-Up* in 1963, Mike Wallace asked him about his sex life. Sinclair laughed and suggested that he and May were having a good time.[46] Part of that "good time" consisted of making new friends, one of the most surprising of whom was Ed Ainsworth, who had once used selective quotes from Sinclair's novels against him during the EPIC Campaign. Sinclair spent many happy hours at the Monrovia Public Library where Ainsworth's wife, Katherine, was chief librarian, and they became friendly. Ed Ainsworth recalls that "finally my wife said to me: 'Why can't you quit harboring grudges and go meet him and learn to like him? I've gotten to know him and he's a sweet, kind, courtly old gentleman.'"[47]

That year the Ainsworths ran into Upton Sinclair at a Hollywood television studio where the two men were speaking about their new books. Ed recalls that Sinclair only knew him as the librarian's husband who worked for the *Los Angeles Times*. After the event, the Sinclairs needed a ride to Monrovia. "My wife offered, and they accepted, a ride in our car which was one of a fleet belonging to the *Times*."[48] When interviewed about the friendship, Katherine Ainsworth remembered that although everyone else considered Sinclair "a rabble rouser . . . my husband was dissolved by his personality and little jokes."[49] Sinclair forgave Ainsworth for what he had done during the EPIC Campaign. Ed Ainsworth remembers how Upton Sinclair introduced Richard Armour at a meeting: "After the introduction, Uppie disdained the stairs and—at eighty-five—vaulted from the stage to sit beside his bride."[50]

Sinclair and May went East in 1962 where he received a Page One Award from the New York Newspaper Guild and a Social Justice Award from the United Auto Workers. That year, Ron Gottesman finally was able to interview Sinclair for the Columbia Oral History

Project and Upton Sinclair updated his original 1930 autobiography, *American Outpost*. In reviewing the revised book for the *Saturday Review*, novelist Howard Fast describes reading Sinclair in the thirties: "I learned what no schools taught—a philosophy of social justice. You read a book by Upton Sinclair then, and you were never quite the same as before."[51] German critic Renate von Bardeleben notes that Sinclair, "though a traditional storyteller, does not build his account around a single change, since they are too numerous in his long life." The events that apparently cut much deeper, she believes, were the divorce from Meta Fuller, his marriage to Mary Craig, her death, and his final marriage to May Hard.[52]

Edward Allatt, who had first read the Lanny Budd series as a soldier in Europe, wrote to Sinclair in 1958 and the two began corresponding. John Ahouse writes, "If Sinclair had made Allatt a reader, a collector, then a writer, he ultimately made him a bibliographer."[53] Allatt's collection moved from the living room to a bedroom to a library room in a new house. Until Gottesman's catalogue was published, Ahouse adds, "aside from short lists inserted in the dust jackets of some of Sinclair's works and personal additions from the author himself, researcher Edward Allatt was on his own."[54] Allatt worked a day job as a film editor in order to finance his work, traveling to bookstores on lunch hours and after work.

Both Edward Allatt and Ron Gottesman were able to visit with the Sinclairs in 1963. Allatt filmed Sinclair driving confidently along the freeways in his pink Nash Rambler. Allatt meticulously recorded every scene with his camera: the exterior of the Monrovia home; Sinclair and May at the front door; Main Street in Monrovia; Sinclair driving Allatt to Disneyland; Sinclair at the Honnold Library, Claremont College; the garden in Monrovia; Edward Allatt talking with Sinclair (this part filmed by May Sinclair). In the film, the mountains still gleam against the sky of 1963.[55]

When Ron Gottesman finally visited, he found that "Craig's camellias were long gone, as were the heavy velvet curtains. . . . The room was flooded with sunlight" as he sat down with them.[56]

May asked him what he would like to drink. Thinking of Sinclair's temperance beliefs, Gottesman answered that "whatever she was having would be fine with him. 'None of that, young man,' May admonished him. 'What are you going to drink?' Then she took pity on him, and said, 'I'm having a margarita!'"[57]

Sinclair and May enjoyed long games of Scrabble; he noted by early 1963 that they had played 890 games. Of the 100,000 points accumulated so far, May was ahead by 300, but he had just made his "highest score ever, 410!"[58] He wrote to David and Jean, his "blessed children," to describe a "wondrous" Christmas party he had attended with May.[59] Sinclair also kept up his efforts to understand his son's scientific work, of which he was very proud, especially David's patented device for making air-pollution particles visible, called the Sinclair Phoenix Smoke Photometer. "Say all the loving things that are in your heart," May advised him, and his letters to David after 1955 reflect that advice.[60]

In 1963 Ron Gottesman published *A Catalogue of Books, Manuscripts, and Other Materials from the Upton Sinclair Archives*. In October of that year, Sinclair traveled to Bloomington for the dedication of his collection at the Lilly Library. The event was arranged by library director David Randall and Ron Gottesman. The chairman of the Lilly Foundation had written an anxious letter—worried about Sinclair's radical past—to David Randall, but the librarian disregarded the complaint. He had the support of Indiana University's powerful president, Herman Wells.

Local newspapers reported that Sinclair shook his head in amazement as he viewed the display of books, letters, and posters filling some forty cases in the library, mildly protesting that "it seems very egotistical to be looking at them." Sinclair shared his political opinions that President Kennedy was doing a fine job, the Martin Luther King speech on the mall in Washington was "the most wonderful thing I've seen in years," and Barry Goldwater was alternately horrifying and comic, a racist but an amiable man, and "one of the most amusing spectacles" on the current scene.[61]

26. Ronald Gottesman and Upton Sinclair, on the occasion of Sinclair's visit to Indiana University, 1962. Courtesy of the Lilly Library, Indiana University, Bloomington.

In Bloomington, Sinclair gave interviews to librarians and archivists in attendance, charmed Gottesman's English class by reading a humorous love poem that he had written as a boy, and spoke to over four thousand guests at the banquet in his honor. When dinner was served, Sinclair "politely refused the roast beef that was placed before him, dining instead on cold rice in a silver bowl that he always carried with him."[62] Sinclair left Bloomington to travel to Milwaukee, Chicago, and New York City. He was especially pleased at being invited to speak at his alma maters: City College of New York and Columbia University. Edgar Johnson, the Dickens biographer who taught in the English Department at ccny, invited him, recalling his early appreciation of Sinclair's attacks on President "Nicholas Miraculous" at Columbia. Johnson told Sinclair that he remained a "devout follower" of Lanny Budd.

In 1964 the *Washington Post* published Arthur and Lila Weinberg's account of their visit to Monrovia. When he introduced them to his third wife, May told them, "I've never known anybody more saintly. He is the most placid, serene person I've ever met in my life. An unhappy thought never crosses his mind."[63] Sinclair explained to his visitors that he had restricted his diet to brown rice and fresh fruits three times a day, seven days a week. He added that although friends expressed interest, "not one has been moved to try it—not even my wife."[64] Visitors to Monrovia always reported on Sinclair's eating habits, although in his *Lifetime in Letters* he had explained that "most of my life I was looking for a diet that would permit me to overwork with impunity. In my old age I found it, and am a vegetarian again."[65]

Rather than his diet, Sinclair wanted to talk about civil rights: "I am in sympathy with it. It is the crucial issue of our time and I think it's winning."[66] After his friend Lorna Smith marched for civil rights with Stokeley Carmichael, she remembered that "Sinclair wrote to me, saying he had not known I was down in Mississippi, and he honored me for it."[67] That year, forty years after the events at Liberty Hill, civil rights and free speech warrior Mario Savio urged, "You've got to put your bodies upon the wheels, upon the levers."[68] Upton Sinclair was one of the very few writers who had dared to do exactly that.

Recalling his labor activism, he told the Weinbergs he had given the Auto Workers Union the house after he and his wife died. He was hoping that they would "put up a fund and award a prize for the best literary work in the cause of labor and social justice. The author could use the upstairs to live—two bedrooms, a study and a bath."[69] Curiously, the gift of the house was never realized. Before the Weinbergs left, Sinclair spoke to them about the threat of nuclear weapons: "If they are used, it's the end of our civilization. We better sit up and end social injustice and mass starvation before some poor people get hold of the bomb and drop it on New York. It's a prime target."[70]

One of Sinclair's plays, *The Enemy Had It Too*, describes a family who moved from New York City after a nuclear attack, only to be rescued by Martians. "We created a terrible means of destruction," one character explains, "but we did not have the moral force to control ourselves, and we were not fit to be trusted with such weapons."[71] The election of 1964 centered on the public's fear of nuclear weapons, a fear reflected in the famous—and infamous—"daisy" television ad against Barry Goldwater.[72] Sinclair spoke to the Weinbergs about the upcoming election: "I think the Democratic Party will win. I can't imagine a greater horror than seeing Senator Barry Goldwater win the election."[73]

After Johnson's election, Upton Sinclair was heartened by newspaper reports of his accomplishments: civil rights legislation that demolished segregation and disenfranchisement in the South; Head Start, providing preschools for impoverished kids; Medicaid, offering assistance with medical costs for poor people, and Medicare for the elderly. As Bill Moyers, who worked for LBJ, writes, "They laid down the now-endangered markers of a civilized society: legally ordained minimum wages, child labor laws, workers' safety and compensation laws, pure foods and safe drugs, Social Security, Medicare."[74] Kevin Mattson comments that for Sinclair in 1965, many of his visions had been realized: "the glacier of socialism moved ahead in the guise of American liberalism."[75]

Sinclair was eighty-seven years old when filming finally began on his book *The Gnomobile* (the film's title became *The Gnome-Mobile*). At Disney's invitation, he visited the set in 1965. He wrote to David that he was impressed by how the furniture was created to make adults look small. Sinclair hoped that the film's message of ecological awareness would reach a new generation. When the book was reprinted accompanying the release of the film, he dedicated it "to all who love and protect our forests." His ecological concerns, which sprang from his love of the nature poets, and of the land itself as he camped along the river with Meta in 1901, had never diminished.

By the time the film was released in 1967, Sinclair's legs were not strong enough for him to walk into the theater, and he had to be carried into the screening. He left no record of what his thoughts

27. Walt Disney (*right*) and Upton Sinclair. When Sinclair finished writing *The Gnomobile* in 1936, a mutual friend brought him to meet Walt Disney to discuss adapting it as a children's film. Disney promised to do so when he switched from animation to live characters; the film was released in 1967 (as *The Gnome-Mobile*), a year before Sinclair's death. Courtesy of the Lilly Library, Indiana University, Bloomington.

were as he watched the film. The year of the film's release, he and May accepted their family's invitation to move to Washington DC, although they never really moved out of the Monrovia house.

President Johnson invited Sinclair to the White House twice, once for lunch, and again to celebrate the passage of the Wholesome Meat Act. Sinclair arrived in a wheelchair—and shook the president's hand. Along with the Democratic Party leadership, Sinclair still supported the war in Vietnam, but he wasn't asked his opinion about it when he delivered his last public speech at the University of Buffalo in 1967. Students in "tight-fitting blue denim pants and long hair" filed into the auditorium, according to the local papers, who reported that Sinclair was taken aback at receiving a standing ovation.[76]

May Sinclair died on December 18, 1967. Upton Sinclair had now outlived all three of his wives. We have no letters to describe the desolation he must have felt over losing her. Following May's death, David took over his father's care. Sinclair endured multiple medical problems in 1968 and was moved to a small nursing home a mile away from Jean and David's home in Martinsville, New Jersey. In October of that year David wrote to the curator of the Lilly that his father was doing "amazingly well," still dictating responses to letters and enjoying drives with them to see the autumn foliage.[77] On November 26, 1968, just three weeks after Richard Nixon's election as president, Upton Sinclair died.

The *Baltimore Sun* described Sinclair's final visit to the city of his birth three years earlier. He seemed to know, wrote the reporter, that he was seeing it for the last time: "At 87, he walks slowly, but with a firm step. A few days earlier he had climbed the 228 steps of Baltimore's Washington Monument. 'If I was not always right, I was always looking for the right. What more can a man do with his life?'"[78] He had begun his life at the end of the nineteenth century; it ended in the pivotal year of 1968, when political and cultural reform movements of all kinds were once again flourishing, often reflecting—even without knowing it—the ideas of Upton Sinclair.

A World to Win

[1969–2011]

The past that has not been tamed with words is not memory, only
a sort of spying.

LAURA RESTREPO, 2010

After Sinclair's death, Ryo Namikawa wrote an obituary for Japanese
readers, lamenting that "the merry days of America have passed away
with him."[1] There is no longer any published journal about Sinclair,
no scholarly society, no home or museum in which to teach new
generations about his role and significance in American life.[2] Yet
despite this neglect, Sinclair and his legacy remain vitally relevant.

In 1969 Lorna Smith and Edward Allatt, readers whose lives were
transformed by Upton Sinclair, published the first reminiscences
of the writer. In the early seventies, several dissertations and Ron
Gottesman's compilation of Sinclair's literary manuscripts were
published. The stage was set for a full biography, and when Leon
Harris wrote *Upton Sinclair: American Rebel*, he framed the discussion of Sinclair for the next thirty-five years. John Ahouse writes,
"Someone put forward Leon Harris, a sort of journeyman writer
whose background (moneyed Texans) hardly permitted him a
very sympathetic view of Sinclair's activities."[3] Harris's biography

is noteworthy for its dismissive tone.[4] Leon Harris was not the biographer to appreciate the Sinclairs' companionate marriage. He enshrined the idea that Sinclair was a "bluenose," defined by the dictionary that year as "a person with strongly puritanical moral convictions; one who believes that having a good time is immoral; an ultraconservative."[5] Hardly accurate!

After Harris's work was published, David Sinclair wrote Irving Stone that he was sorry that Stone hadn't written the biography: "Your description of how father's mind worked agrees with my own estimate."[6] In the 1940s Upton Sinclair had told Irving Stone he was looking for a biographer, and asked if Stone would write it. Mary Craig overheard and objected. Stone believes that it was her fault that the project was abandoned.[7] Irving Stone would certainly have been a more sympathetic historian of Sinclair's life; rather than ridiculing the Sinclairs' experiments with telepathy, David Sinclair believed that Stone understood that the mysticism wasn't his father's "own inclination, but Craig's. But of course, he was not averse to exploring and remaining open-minded, as he was about most things. Except liquor!"[8]

Literary scholar Jon Yoder also published a book about Upton Sinclair in 1975 that focused on his disappearance from academic writing. Yoder noted that both Sinclair's socialist politics and his interdisciplinary oeuvre have left him without an academic home, since "truth, in American universities, is usually dispensed by departments."[9] Yoder argued that Sinclair did not fit neatly into any academic discipline, and this, he suggested, was one reason for his absence from scholarly consideration.

In 1976 historian John Graham published the balance of Sinclair's reporting on the Ludlow Massacre under the title *The Coal War*. In his introduction, Graham notes, "Sinclair set an opposing truth before readers besieged daily with misinformation and outright lies. . . . He is one of the very few American novelists who had not only an impact on the ideas of his time, but on the social and economic conditions as well."[10] Graham's work represented part of the new interest in class struggle and labor history that engaged historians in the post-Vietnam era. In that context, Graham called for a renewed recognition of Sinclair's relevance.

Nine years after Sinclair's death, Robert Hahn, of California State University–Los Angeles, initiated an extraordinarily fertile period of Sinclair scholarship. Hahn offered a course through American Studies on Upton Sinclair, one of the first (and last) ever offered. He and his students decided to publish a journal to promote "Sinclairiana," as Hahn affectionately termed it, and in 1977 the first issue of *Uppie Speaks* emerged.[11] The cohort of women and men most affected by Sinclair were coming to the end of their lives, and the journal sought to record their memories and ideas while there was still time.

In 1978 Hahn organized an Upton Sinclair centenary event at the university. Speaking at the centenary commemoration, David Sinclair told a reporter that his father was "as much a Democratic Socialist when he was old as when he was young, but the world finally caught up with father. He helped to clean and protect the meat on your table."[12] David Sinclair also credited his father with encouraging reporters to form unions, publicizing conditions in mining, founding the California chapter of the American Civil Liberties Union, and helping organize the United Auto Workers.[13] David Sinclair wrote to Robert Hahn that he and Jean were thrilled to see that Hahn had "imbued so many young people with excitement over a man whom they have only read or read about."[14] David and Jean Sinclair would be financial supporters of Sinclair studies for the rest of their lives.

California State University–Los Angeles published the *Upton Sinclair Centenary Journal* later that year. The journal includes an essay by Lorna Smith—"My Life Was Changed by Upton Sinclair." Smith grew up in Centralia, Washington, and retained a vivid memory of the Armistice Day clash between Legionnaires and IWW members there in 1919. She recalls her father telling her, "When you go into a meat market and see the government seal on a quarter of beef, you will know it is there because of Upton Sinclair."[15] She went to the library, got *The Jungle*, and read it. "My entire life was changed and I owe it all to Upton Sinclair. His quotation, 'I aimed at their hearts and I hit their stomachs,' did not apply to me. He hit my heart."[16]

In the late seventies, German filmmakers visited Los Angeles to film a documentary for German television. In an early issue of the *Upton Sinclair Quarterly*, Robert Hahn wrote a brief account of the adventures of the visiting German film team, who were part of this exciting albeit brief era in Sinclair research. Hahn reports that the Germans worked "with the kind of zeal and intense association which Sinclair's career stimulated. . . . We were saddened by the realization that on this 100th anniversary, only the West Germans were interested in preserving the last of the Sinclair scene for posterity."[17] The history of Upton Sinclair's German readership still largely remains unknown, as Marion Schulz has noted, and would be an important addition to the scholarship.[18]

At the request of this author, Ilka Hartman translated the documentary, which remains the only film biography of Sinclair ever made.[19] At the end of the film, poet Erich Fried notes that Sinclair was the most-read American writer of the twentieth century in thirty other countries: "He had the genius to describe societal connections simply. Literary critics may wrinkle their noses but his books are in all libraries of workers in Germany and Austria."[20] In 1989, Dieter Herms's biography *Upton Sinclair: Amerikanischer Radikaler* was published in German. It is still untranslated.[21]

As the seventies ended, Michael Riherd wrote his doctoral dissertation on the creation of the World's End series, and the John Rylands Library at the University of Manchester acquired Edward Allatt's collection of Sinclair materials.[22] Edward Allatt epitomizes what Virginia Woolf called the "common reader," a man without formal education whose life was transformed by his reading, collecting, and eventual friendship with Upton Sinclair.[23] In 1980 *Uppie Speaks* was retitled the *Upton Sinclair Quarterly* and was edited by John Ahouse until spring 1986.[24] In one issue French critic Andre

Muraire discusses Sinclair's short novel *Zillions of Dollars: A Truth Story*, arguing that Sinclair's last novels exhibit "a growing use of positive female characters to contrast with the coarseness, violence, and eventual failure of their male counterparts."[25]

Robert Hahn was interviewed for another issue about his and wife Genevieve's production of *Oil!* in Altadena. David and Jean Sinclair attended and photographed the performance. Robert Hahn recalls, "People jumped on ladders and started yelling, warning everybody in the audience, it really got them excited and involved."[26] The Hahns showed slides of old Los Angeles and passed out hard hats to help the audience imagine the scenes in the oil fields.

Robin Room and Denise Herd assembled a four-night series "Alcohol: Images in American Film" at the Pacific Film Archive in 1982. Room comments, "I found *The Wet Parade* really fascinating. . . . What is most striking about *The Wet Parade* to the modern viewer is the degree to which alcohol is a political matter."[27] Room notes that since Prohibition's repeal, there has been a renewed privatization of alcoholism: "What had been a matter of public discourse and action has become again a matter of private anguish."[28] The work of feminist scholars has been instrumental in interrogating the caricature of temperance advocates that has been common in histories of the period.

In the recent documentary on Prohibition by Ken Burns, David Wiegand finds a more nuanced view of Prohibition, noting that the film captures "American politics, absolutist causes, the sociological and political empowerment of women, and the larger discussion of whether government can or should legislate human behavior."[29] The strength of the recovery movement among Americans might stimulate a reevaluation of Prohibition, which did reduce drinking and alcohol-related illnesses.[30] As Wiegand notes, "The temperance movement drew women toward political activism who might never have considered it in the past."[31] *The Wet Parade* may offer unexpected political and social resonance today.

In 1983 the Southern California ACLU celebrated its sixtieth anniversary with an outdoor reception to commemorate Liberty Hill and the events that launched its founding. They had announced that excerpts from *Singing Jailbirds* would be performed, but the master of ceremonies, Ned Beatty, decided that Sinclair's words were "too angry to be part of a lawn party on a beautiful afternoon."[32] Later that year, Dieter Herms argued for a reconsideration of Sinclair as a playwright, noting that *Singing Jailbirds* represents the beginnings of agitprop drama in America in the early twentieth century.[33] When Herms discovered the San Francisco Mime Troupe doing a similar kind of radical theater, he brought them to Germany to perform.[34]

In 1988 R. N. Mookerjee's book *Art for Social Justice: The Major Novels of Upton Sinclair* was published. Mookerjee noted with surprise the absence of any "detailed or critical examination of Sinclair's fiction."[35] Mookerjee argued that Sinclair's real affinity is with the mid-Victorian English reform novelists, like Charles Dickens.[36] That year the curator of the Museum of Modern Art, Eileen Bowser, wrote to Sol Lesser's son, Bud, that *Thunder Over Mexico* was thriving and that the museum regarded it as one of its greatest treasures.[37]

In 1988 the Upton Sinclair World Conference was held at the University of Bremen; that year also marked the official end of the *Upton Sinclair Quarterly* with an unsuccessful search for a new editor.[38] David Sinclair had died of lung cancer in 1987. He was survived by his wife, Jean Weidman, and daughter, Diana Sinclair, of Manhattan. Jean Weidman has since passed away, and Diana Sinclair's whereabouts are unknown.

A Man of His Time—and Ours

In 1990 Dieter Herms edited a unique collection of papers presented at the Upton Sinclair World Conference at Bremen. That year, Sachiko Nakada published a pamphlet in which she argues that Sinclair's novels changed the mentality of a whole generation of students in China, Japan, India, and Russia. Nakada concludes

Vol. VI Nos. 1 & 2   Spring - Summer 1982

The
UPTON SINCLAIR
QUARTERLY

28. *The Upton Sinclair Quarterly* represented the high point in Sinclair studies, published from 1977 to 1988. Courtesy of John Ahouse.

that it is "our responsibility today to gather Japanese information on Sinclair, buried and forgotten, and put our way of accepting him on record." She hopes that this might "help Sinclair come back in his colours in Japan, worthy of his past glorious popularity."[39]

In 1990 Nakada published a biography of Sinclair in Japanese, which has still not been translated into English. Sinclair's passionate following in Japan ignited an interest among Chinese readers, an influence that was recently examined by Hailin Zhou. Nakada notes that "Sinclair's literature was first brought to China through Chinese students who were members of the Creation Society and translated or referred to Japanese translations of Sinclair."[40]

It seemed as though Sinclair was indeed "coming back in his colours" for a while in the early 1990s. John Ahouse published a comprehensive bibliography of Upton Sinclair's work, and the University of California reissued *I, Candidate for Governor: And How I Got Licked* with an introduction by James Gregory. Greg Mitchell and Lyn Goldfarb created compelling new documentaries of the EPIC Campaign in print and film, introducing the dramatic story of the campaign to a generation hungry for models of engaged politics.[41]

Sinclair's pivotal role at Liberty Hill was recognized in 1998. *The Dispatcher*, the newspaper of the International Longshore and Warehouse Union, announced, "On May 9, 1998, the only state historic landmark celebrating the organizing efforts of maritime workers will be dedicated in San Pedro."[42] Retired longshoreman Art Almeida had founded the San Pedro Bay Historical Society in 1974, when he began to work toward the Liberty Hill Landmark application. Twenty years later, he finally received permission to locate the plaque from the Los Angeles Harbor Department. The site was declared as State Historic Landmark No. 1021 on March 20, 1997. Although the original waterfront bluffs had been leveled, Almeida found a stonemason to create a monument of rock and shells, now installed in front of the Los Angeles harbor workers' community center. At the dedication, I, along with other speakers, celebrated the fact that unlike many historic sites that commemorate the rich and powerful, this was a monument to the struggle of working people.

The house in Monrovia was put up for sale in 2006 and again in 2011. It has been in private ownership since Sinclair's death. The absence of an Upton Sinclair house has been a disadvantage for the ongoing study of his contributions to American life and thought. In an August 2001 series on American writers on C-Span, the recognition of Upton Sinclair was set outside a Chicago slaughterhouse, rather than a historic home or museum, and it entirely omitted his life in California. The row house in Baltimore on North Charles Street has been demolished.

But Sinclair's vision of California was resurrected in 2001, when Word for Word Theatre Company presented the first chapter of *Oil!* for audiences in San Francisco. The company commissioned a sculptor to create a giant musical car. The play debuted in the midst of California's energy crisis, complete with a power failure in the theater just before curtain. Karen D'Souza wrote, "When the realization strikes that this pilgrimage through the past is nearing an end, the theatergoer may experience the irresistible impulse to rush out and read the book from cover to cover."[43] The portrait of "oil men" had astonishing resonance, and viewers expressed amazement at Sinclair's prescient understanding of the importance of oil in the modern economy.[44]

In 2004 Heyday Books released my collection of Sinclair's writings about California. Shortly thereafter, I was contacted by Walter Hermann, whose father had traveled around Northern California during the EPIC Campaign. From the campaign bus he had screened *The Jungle*, onto which supporters had spliced a campaign ad. One of the five reels was missing, but I was able to view this magnificent film and find a home for it at the UCLA Film and Television Archive.

Upton Sinclair's intellectual heirs include Barbara Ehrenreich, who also worked in minimum-wage jobs to expose the conditions of the working poor; Mike Davis, who like Sinclair has crossed disciplines to explore the confluence of labor and ethnicity in Southern California in startling new ways; Alice Walker, who has produced powerful literary works intended to inspire readers to action; Michael Moore, who has excelled in the use of film to educate a mass audience; and Naomi Klein, who has led direct action on climate change. This merging of prolific work and political risk was a course that Sinclair pioneered. The recent release of Harry Belafonte's autobiography reminds us that he, like Sinclair, dedicated his life to the struggle for a better world, issue by issue, decade after decade.[45]

When Sinclair began his World's End series in 1940, the reviewer for *Time* magazine commented, "To the literary, the novels of Upton Sinclair are not literature. To historians they are not history. To propagandists they are not propaganda. But to millions of plain people they are all three of those things."[46] Scholars of popular culture might find his novels capable of captivating readers and affecting their political thinking.[47]

When a jury awarded the supermarket conglomerate Food Lion $5.5 million in damages to punish news reporters for going undercover in 1997 to document unsafe food preparation, the *San Francisco Examiner* editorialized that "undercover reporting is a proud tradition that dates back to Upton Sinclair. . . . Who will tell people the truth?"[48] Today, in the era of shock jocks and YouTube "exposés," as newspapers disappear, true investigative reporting is urgently needed and rarely found. In their introduction to *The Brass Check*, journalists Robert McChesney and Ben Scott note that now "the media are exceptionally concentrated, journalism is of dubious integrity."[49] The state of the mass media and public discourse is eerily similar to the one Sinclair documented a hundred years ago.

David Schwimmer has plans to adapt *The Jungle* as a new film.[50] This work may be more relevant than ever as Americans seek a better understanding of food safety.[51] Indeed, Sinclair's interest in the politics of food has influenced chefs like Alice Waters and Jamie Oliver.[52] These reformers seek to educate about food and health, trying to affect the menus of school cafeterias and reach underserved communities, believing as Sinclair did that lack of dietary knowledge is a denial of equality. The "slow food" movement, with its emphasis on locally grown organic produce, has largely reached only the more affluent, leaving too many without the information that Sinclair tried to impart.[53] Were he here, he would never have thought that the individual choice to buy organic was a substitute for government regulation to protect all consumers.

Sinclair's masculinity has been impugned by the labels of "prude" and "bluenose," labels that persist from his era into the present.[54] Stephan Ducat argues that since the nineteenth century, men allied with "feminine" social justice issues have been belittled.[55] Ingrid Kerkhoff hails Upton Sinclair as "one of the most interesting of American male feminist writers of the first half of the twentieth century."[56] This son of an alcoholic who marched with his mother in temperance and suffrage parades, this man who befriended rather than exploited the women in his life, created characters who exemplified his own choices. Sinclair's quintessential hero confounds the patriarchal imperative, allying himself with the powerless, the labor radicals, or the antifascist resistance.

The world of the twenty-first century is startlingly similar to that of Sinclair's early twentieth century, yet enormous new challenges have also emerged. Upton Sinclair was a visionary who believed we could solve our problems together. At a time of historic inequality, widespread joblessness, and increasing despair, we need Sinclair's faith in the ability of each individual to be awakened to injustice and moved to action. In this second decade of a century that does not include Upton Sinclair, his life and passions compel our attention.

Appendix A

UPTON SINCLAIR'S WOMEN FRIENDS

This book has attempted to demonstrate the centrality of female friendship in Upton Sinclair's life. Numerous names of American women activists appear throughout the text. However, a clearer documentation of Sinclair's friendships with women may be found by listing each of these women with one citation about them or by them. By so doing, I hope to introduce the reader to some extraordinary women who have been omitted from many American History courses and to provide evidence to those familiar with the history of American feminist radicalism that Sinclair was indeed part of this tradition. The women are listed in the order that Sinclair met them or discovered their work.

Charlotte Perkins Gilman
Ann J. Lane, *To Herland and Beyond: The Life and Work of Charlotte Perkins Gilman* (New York: Pantheon, 1995)

Jane Addams
Victoria Bissell Brown, *Jane Addams: Twenty Years at Hull-House* (New York: Bedford St. Martins, 1999)

Kate Richards O'Hare
Sally M. Miller, *From Prairie to Prison: The Life of Social Activist Kate Richards O'Hare* (Columbia MO: University of Missouri Press, 1993)

Margaret Sanger
Ellen Chesler, *Woman of Valor: Margaret Sanger and the Birth Control Movement in America* (New York: Simon and Schuster, 2007)

Appendix A

Edith Summers Kelly
Edith Summers Kelly, *Weeds*, with an afterword by Charlotte Margolis (New York: Feminist Press 1982)

Julia Ward Howe
Valerie H. Ziegler, *Diva Julia: The Public Romance and Private Agony of Julia Ward Howe* (Harrisburg PA: Trinity Press International, 2003)

Ella Reeve Bloor
Ella Reeve Bloor, *We are Many* (New York: International Publishers, 1940)

Inez Milholland
Linda J. Lumsden, *Inez: The Life and Times of Inez Milholland* (Bloomington: Indiana University Press, 2004)

Mary Austin
Helen McKnight Doyle, *Mary Austin: Woman of Genius* (New York: Gotham House, 1939)

Susan Glaspell
Barbara Ozieblo, *Susan Glaspell: A Critical Biography* (Chapel Hill: University of North Carolina Press, 2000)

Mary Beard
Nancy F. Cott, *A Woman Making History: Mary Ritter Beard through Her Letters* (Connecticut: Yale University Press, 1991)

Alice Stone Blackwell
Alice Stone Blackwell, *Lucy Stone: Pioneer of Woman's Rights* (Whitefish MT: Kessinger Publishing, 2010)

Miriam Allen deFord
"Throwback," in *New Eves: Science Fiction about the Extraordinary Women of Today and Tomorrow*, edited by Janrae Frank, Jean Stine, and Forrest J. Ackerman (Stamford CT: Longmeadow Press, 1984)

Agnes Smedley
Agnes Smedley, *Daughter of Earth*, with an afterword by Nancy Hoffman and foreword by Alice Walker (New York: Feminist Press, 1993)

Helen Keller
Dorothy Herrmann, *Helen Keller: A Life* (New York: Knopf, 1998)

Aline Barnsdall

Norman M. Karasick and Dorothy K. Karasick, *The Oilman's Daughter: A Biography of Aline Barnsdall* (Encino CA: Action Amer Productions, 1993)

Vera Brittain

Deborah Gorham, *Vera Brittain: A Feminist Life* (Toronto: University of Toronto Press, 2000)

Elizabeth Gurley Flynn

Helen C. Camp, *Iron in Her Soul: Elizabeth Gurley Flynn and the American Left* (Pullman: Washington State University, 1995)

Gertrude Atherton

Emily Wortis Leider, *California's Daughter: Gertrude Atherton and her Times* (Stanford CA: Stanford University Press, 1991)

Appendix B

Selected Works by Upton Sinclair

The following include recent annotated editions of Sinclair's work that I particularly recommend, along with other selected works by Upton Sinclair that have been discussed in this book.

Manassas. New York: Macmillan, 1904.

The Jungle. With illustrations by Charles Burns and introduction by Eric Schlosser. New York: Penguin Classics Deluxe Edition, 1906, 2006.

The Millennium: A Comedy of the Year 2000. Introduction by Carl Jensen. New York: Seven Stories Press, 1907, 2000.

Plays of Protest. New York: Mitchell and Kennerley, 1912.

The Cry for Justice. New York and Pasadena: Upton Sinclair, 1915.

King Coal: A Novel. New York: Macmillan, 1917.

Jimmie Higgins. New York: Boni and Liveright, 1919.

The Brass Check. Introduction by Robert McChesney and Ben Scott. Urbana: University of Illinois Press, 1920, 2003.

The Book of Life. Girard KS: Haldeman-Julius, 1921.

The Goslings. Pasadena: Upton Sinclair, 1921.

The Goose-Step: A Study of American Education. Pasadena: Upton Sinclair, 1922.

Singing Jailbirds. Pasadena: Upton Sinclair, 1924.

Oil! Introduction by Jules Tygiel. Berkeley: University of California Press, 1927, 1997.

Boston. Introduction by Howard Zinn. Cambridge MA: Robert Bentley, 1928, 1978).

Mental Radio. Charlottesville VA: Hampton Roads, 1930, 2001.

The Wet Parade. New York: Farrar and Rinehart, 1931.

I, Governor of California, and How I Ended Poverty: A True Story of the Future. New York: Farrar and Rinehart, 1933.

I, Candidate for Governor, and How I Got Licked. Introduction by James Gregory. Berkeley: University of California Press, 1935, 1994.

Co-Op. New York: Farrar and Rinehart, 1936.

The Gnomobile. New York: Grosset and Dunlap, 1936, 1965.

The Flivver King. Pasadena: Upton Sinclair, 1937.

Our Lady. Emmaus PA: Rodale Press, 1938.

World's End. New York: Viking, 1940.

The Enemy Had It Too. New York: Viking Press, 1950.

The Cup of Fury. New York: Channel Press, 1956.

My Lifetime in Letters. Columbia: University of Missouri Press, 1960.

The Autobiography of Upton Sinclair. New York: Harcourt Brace and World, 1962.

Coal War: A Sequel to "King Coal." Edited and with an introduction by John Graham. Boulder CO: Colorado Associated University Press, 1976.

Selected Bibliography

The following titles were especially helpful in my research for this book and are highly recommended.

Ahouse, John. *Upton Sinclair: A Descriptive Annotated Bibliography*. Los Angeles: Arundel Press, 1992.

Alpern, Sara, Joyce Antler, Elizabeth Perry, and Ingrid Scobie, eds. *The Challenge of Feminist Biography*. Urbana: University of Illinois, 1992.

Arthur, Anthony. *Radical Innocent: Upton Sinclair*. New York: Random House, 2006.

Bird, Stewart, Dan Georgakas, and Deborah Shaffer. *Solidarity Forever: An Oral History of the IWW*. Chicago: Lakeview, 1985.

Chaplin, Ralph. *Wobbly: The Rough and Tumble Story of an American Radical*. Chicago: University of Chicago, 1948.

Coodley, Lauren, ed. *Land of Orange Groves and Jails: Upton Sinclair's California*. Berkeley: Heyday, 2004.

Gifford, Carolyn De Swarte. *Writing Out My Heart: Selections from the Journal of Frances Willard, 1855–96*. Urbana: University of Illinois Press, 1995.

Dell, Floyd. *Upton Sinclair: A Study in Social Protest*. New York: Albert and Charles Boni, 1927.

Ducat, Stephan. *The Wimp Factor*. Boston: Beacon Press 2004.

Ehrenreich, Barbara, and Deirdre English. *Witches, Midwives, and Nurses: A History of Women Healers*. Brooklyn: Feminist Press, 1973.

Engs, Ruth Clifford. *Unseen Upton Sinclair*. Jefferson NC: McFarland, 2009.

Finney, Jack. *Time and Again*. New York: Orion, 1970.

Gamber, Wendy. *The Boardinghouse in Nineteenth-Century America*. Baltimore: Johns Hopkins University Press, 2007.

Herms, Dieter, ed. *Upton Sinclair: Literature and Social Reform*. Frankfurt: Peter Lang, 1990.

Mattson, Kevin. *Upton Sinclair and the Other American Century*. Hoboken NJ: John Wiley, 2006.

Mitchell, Greg. *The Campaign of the Century*. New York: Random House, 1992.

Mookerjee, R. N. *Art for Social Justice: The Major Novels of Upton Sinclair*. Metuchen NJ: Scarecrow Press, 1988.

Murphey, Kevin. *Political Manhood: Redbloods, Mollycoddles, and the Politics of Progressive Era Reform*. New York: Columbia University Press, 2008.

Nakada, Sachiko. *Japanese Empathy for Upton Sinclair*. Chiyoda-m Tokyo: Central Institute, 1990.

Renshaw, Patrick. *The Wobblies: The Story of Syndicalism in the United States*. New York: Ivan R. Dee, 1967, 1999.

Rotundo, Anthony. *American Manhood: Transformations in Masculinity from Revolution to the Modern Era*. New York: Basic Books, 1993.

Sinclair, Mary Craig. *Sonnets by M.C.S.* Pasadena: Upton Sinclair, 1925.

———. *Southern Belle*. With an afterword by Peggy Prenshaw. Jackson: University Press of Mississippi, 1957, 1999.

Yoder, Jon. *Upton Sinclair*. New York: Ungar Publishing, 1975.

Zinn, Howard. *A People's History of the United States*. New York: Harper Collins, 2003.

Notes

Preface

1. Howard Zinn, introduction to *Boston*, by Upton Sinclair (Cambridge MA: Robert Bentley, 1978), 6.

2. Dieter Herms, "An American Socialist: Upton Sinclair," *Upton Sinclair Centenary Journal* 1, no. 1 (September 1978): 52. Herms, born in 1937, must have come of age in Germany during the post-Nazi era.

3. Upton Sinclair, *The Autobiography of Upton Sinclair* (New York: Harcourt Brace and World, 1962), 327.

4. William Bloodworth, "From *The Jungle* to *The Fasting Cure*: Upton Sinclair on American Food," *Journal of American Culture* 2 (Fall 1979): 442.

5. Peggy Ann Brown, "Not Your Usual Boardinghouse Types: Upton Sinclair's Helicon Home Colony 1906–1907" (PhD diss., American University, 1993).

6. Cynthia J. Davis, *Charlotte Perkins Gilman: A Biography* (Stanford CA: Stanford University Press, 2010).

7. David Sinclair, interview by Muriel Freeman, "Upton Sinclair: Recalling a Muckraker," *New York Times*, December 17, 1978.

1. Southern Gentleman Drank, 1878–1892

Sinclair, *Autobiography*.

1. Fredrick Douglass, *Narrative of the Life of Frederick Douglass: An American Slave*, edited with an introduction by Deborah E. McDowell (New York: Oxford University Press, 2009).

2. Frederick Douglass, *Selected Speeches and Writings*, ed. Philip Foner and Yuvall Taylor (Chicago: Chicago Review Press, 2000), 580.

3. Christina Stead, *The Man Who Loved Children* (New York: Holt, Rinehart and Winston, 1965), 314. Stead was an Australian writer who once lived in Baltimore.

4. Howard Zinn, *A People's History of the United States* (New York: HarperCollins, 2003), 245.

5. Ironically, the *Constellation* became the flagship of the United States African Squadron from 1859 to 1861, interdicting three slave ships and releasing the imprisoned slaves.

6. *The Reminiscences of Upton Sinclair*, 1962, p. 2, the Columbia University Center for Oral History Collection (hereafter CUCOHC).

7. *Illustrated London News*, January 28, 1865.

8. *Fleetwood Chronicle*, June 9, 1865.

9. "When Liverpool was Dixie," accessed January 17, 2010, http://www.csa-dixie.com/liverpool_dixie/Lelia.htm.

10. Floyd Dell, *Upton Sinclair: A Study in Social Protest* (New York: Albert and Charles Boni, 1930), 21.

11. Upton Sinclair, *The Cup of Fury* (New York: Channel Press, 1956), 27.

12. *Reminiscences of Upton Sinclair*, 1962, p. 7, CUCOHC.

13. Sinclair, *Autobiography*, 3.

14. Wendy Gamber, *The Boardinghouse in Nineteenth-Century America* (Baltimore: Johns Hopkins University Press, 2007), 1.

15. Gamber, *Boardinghouse*, 78.

16. See Carlton Beals, *Cyclone Carry: The Story of Carry Nation* (Philadelphia: Chilton Company, 1962).

17. See W. J. Rorabaugh, *The Alcoholic Republic: An American Tradition* (New York: Oxford University Press 1979).

18. Jack Blocker, "Separate Paths: Suffragists and the Women's Temperance Crusade," *Signs* 10, no. 3 (Spring 1985): 467.

19. Blocker, "Separate Paths," 460.

20. See Ruth Borodin, *Frances Willard: A Biography* (Chapel Hill: University of North Carolina Press, 1986).

21. Frank Shivers, *Maryland Wits and Baltimore Bards: A Literary History* (Baltimore: Johns Hopkins University Press, 1985), 53.

22. *Reminiscences of Upton Sinclair*, 1962, p. 7, CUCOHC.

23. Dell, *Upton Sinclair*, 21.

24. Gamber, *Boardinghouse*, 21.

25. *Reminiscences of Upton Sinclair*, 1962, p. 14, CUCOHC.

26. Christina Hardyment, *Dream Babies: Three Centuries of Good Advice on Childcare* (New York: Harper and Row, 1983), 146.

27. Henry Adams, *The Education of Henry Adams* (Boston: Houghton Mifflin, 1918), 268.

28. Sinclair, *Autobiography*, 9.

29. *Reminiscences of Upton Sinclair*, 1962, p. 16, CUCOHC.

30. Terrapin (the name was derived from an Algonquian Indian word) were so plentiful in the 1700s that Maryland slaves protested the excessive use of this food source as their main protein. Late in the 1800s, the species was hunted almost to extinction for the famous Maryland dish of turtle soup.

31. Sinclair, *Autobiography*, 10.

32. Sinclair, *Autobiography*, 11.

33. Sinclair, *Cup of Fury*, 25.

34. See Helen Campbell, *Practical Motherhood* (London: Longman, 1910), for a discussion of the necessity for mothers to understand evolution and heredity as they affected baby care.

35. Sir Frances Galton, *Inquiry into the Human Faculty* (London: Macmillan, 1883).

36. Dell, *Upton Sinclair*, 23.

37. Kevin Mattson, *Upton Sinclair and the Other American Century* (Hoboken NJ: John Wiley, 2006), 22.

38. Sinclair, *Autobiography*, 15.

39. Upton Sinclair to Floyd Dell, July 1926, Upton Sinclair MSS, Lilly Library, Indiana University, Bloomington.

40. Sinclair, *Autobiography*, 12.

41. Anthony Arthur, *Radical Innocent: Upton Sinclair* (New York: Random House, 2006), 5.

42. Shivers, *Maryland Wits*, 215.

43. Alison Kibler, review of *Weird and Wonderful: The Dime Museum in America*, by Andrea Dennett, H-Net, Popular Culture Association/American Culture Association, May 1998.

44. The most notorious recruit was a teenage boy, born in Williamsburg, Brooklyn, in 1899 to Italian immigrant parents. His name was Alphonse Capone, later known as "Scarface" Al Capone.

45. Jack Finney, *Time and Again* (London: Orion, 1970), 126.

46. Gamber, *Boardinghouse*, 3.

47. Sinclair, *Autobiography*, 16-17.

48. Upton Sinclair, *Love's Pilgrimage* (New York: Mitchell and Kennerley, 1911), 14.

49. Sinclair, *Autobiography*, 16.

50. Albion W. Tourgee, "The Veteran and His Pipe," *Chicago Inter Ocean*, April 1885.

51. Sinclair, *Love's Pilgrimage*, 3-4.

52. Sinclair, *Autobiography*, 29.

53. Sinclair, *Autobiography*, 16.

54. Sinclair, *Autobiography*, 19.

55. Dell, *Upton Sinclair*, 37.

56. Upton Sinclair to Priscilla Sinclair, June 18, 1892, Upton Sinclair MSS, Lilly Library.

57. Upton Sinclair, *American Outpost* (New York: Farrar and Rinehart, 1932), 24.

2. Making Real Men of Our Boys, 1893–1904

Dell, *Upton Sinclair*.

1. Sinclair, *Autobiography*, 24.

2. See Robert Sobel's review of *City on a Hill: Testing the American Dream at City College*, by James Traub, *Electric News*, November 21, 1994.

3. Sinclair, *Autobiography*, 23.

4. In 2010 I polled students in an American history class about which nineteenth-century reform had the most relevance to them. An overwhelming majority picked alcoholism and the temperance movement.

5. Sinclair, *Autobiography*, 24.

6. Sinclair, *Autobiography*, 38.

7. Sinclair, *Love's Pilgrimage*, 17.

8. Sinclair, *Autobiography*, 31.

9. Anthony Rotundo, *American Manhood: Transformations in Masculinity from Revolution to the Modern Era* (New York: Basic Books, 1993), 1.

10. Rotundo, *American Manhood*, 6.

11. *Reminiscences of Upton Sinclair*, 1962, p. 98, CUCOHC.

12. Sinclair, *Autobiography*, 32.

13. Dell, *Upton Sinclair*, 39.

14. Dell, *Upton Sinclair*, 40.

15. Dell, *Upton Sinclair*, 34. A lodging house was a kind of boarding-house that did not provide meals.

16. Dell, *Upton Sinclair*, 41.

17. Christine Smallwood, "Talking with Tony Judt," *Nation*, May 17, 2010, 18.

18. William C. Hunt, *Twelfth Census of the United States: Taken in the Year 1900* (Washington: United States Census Office, 1902).

19. Sinclair, *Autobiography*, 36.

20. Upton Sinclair, "Confessions of a Young Author," *Independent*, November 20, 1902, 27.

21. Upton Sinclair to Priscilla Sinclair, c. 1894, Upton Sinclair MSS, Lilly Library.

22. Sinclair, *Autobiography*, 49.

23. Jane Addams, *Twenty Years at Hull-House* (New York: New American Library, 1961), 63.

24. *Reminiscences of Upton Sinclair*, 1962, p. 152 CUCOHC.

25. Sinclair, *Autobiography*, 58.

26. Sinclair, *Autobiography*, 59.

27. Upton Sinclair to Laura Stedman, April 12, 1899, Upton Sinclair MSS, Lilly Library.

28. Sinclair, *Autobiography*, 76.

29. Gamber, *Boardinghouse*, 21.

30. Jim Zwick, http://www.twainweb.net/jimzwick.html, brought Mark Twain's writings about the war to the attention of historians through his magnificent website.

31. Dieter Herms, "From West Point to Presidential Agent: 'Popular Literature' Elements in Upton Sinclair," *Upton Sinclair Quarterly* 4, no. 4 (December 1980): 13.

32. Herms, "From West Point to Presidential Agent," 18.

33. Herms, "From West Point to Presidential Agent," 17.

34. Kenneth Seib, "Upton Sinclair, Poet," *Upton Sinclair Quarterly* 5, no. 4 (December 1981). Published from the late seventies to the late eighties, the journal was the last scholarly publication devoted to Sinclair's life and work.

35. Sinclair, *Love's Pilgrimage*, 41.

36. Rotundo, *American Manhood*, 6.

37. Sinclair, *Autobiography*, 77.

38. Sinclair, *Autobiography*, 79.

39. Arthur, *Radical Innocent*, 14.

40. Upton Sinclair, "What Life Means to Me," *Cosmopolitan*, October 1906, 592.

41. *Reminiscences of Upton Sinclair*, 1962, p. 148, CUCOHC.

42. Meta Fuller, *Thyrsis and Corydon*, Upton Sinclair MSS, Lilly Library.

43. *Reminiscences of Upton Sinclair*, 1962, p. 22, CUCOHC.

44. *Reminiscences of Upton Sinclair*, 1962, p. 81, CUCOHC.

45. See Sinclair, *Love's Pilgrimage*.

46. Sinclair, *Autobiography*, 91.

47. Sinclair, *Autobiography*, 101.

48. Sinclair, *Autobiography*, 93.

49. Sinclair, *Autobiography*, 35.

50. Eric Foner, review of *Race and Reunion: The Civil War in American Memory*, by David W. Blight, *New York Times Book Review*, March 4, 2001.

51. Sinclair, *Autobiography*, 103.

52. Sinclair, *Love's Pilgrimage*, 304.

53. Arthur, *Radical Innocent*, 27.

54. Carrie Stout Chevalier, "Upton Sinclair Builds His Dream House," *Princeton Recollector*, March 1976, 8-9.

55. Chevalier, "Upton Sinclair Builds His Dream House."

56. Arthur, *Radical Innocent*, 34.

57. Sinclair, *Love's Pilgrimage*, 325.

58. Sinclair, *Love's Pilgrimage*, 326.

59. Sinclair, *Autobiography*, 96.

60. Sinclair, *Love's Pilgrimage*, 342.

61. Dell, *Upton Sinclair*, 51.

62. Dell, *Upton Sinclair*, 100.

63. Sinclair, *Autobiography*, 113.

64. Sinclair, *Autobiography*, 113.

65. Sinclair, *Autobiography*, 113. Sinclair had corresponded with London since reading his first novel, *The Sea Wolf*, in 1904.

66. Sinclair soon turned over the management of the ISS to Harry Laidler, who oversaw the organization through its long history until 1921.

67. Upton Sinclair, "The Interesting Career of Jack London," *World*, December l, 1916, 3.

68. James R. Barrett, *Work and Community in the Jungle: Chicago's Packing-House Workers, 1894–1922* (Champaign: University of Illinois Press, 1990).

69. Upton Sinclair, postscript, *The Journal of Arthur Stirling* (New York: Doubleday, Page and Company, 1906).

3. Good Health and How We Won It, 1905–1915

Percy Bysshe Shelley, *The masque of anarchy: A poem* (London: Edward Moxon, 1832).

1. Ernest Poole had written a fictional memoir of an immigrant stockyard worker, a character inspired by the thousands of men he had met working for the meatpackers union.

2. Ernest Poole, *The Bridge: My Own Story* (New York: Macmillan, 1940), 95-96.

3. Upton Sinclair, *Manassas* (New York: Macmillan, 1904), 57.

4. James D. Hart, *The Popular Book: A History of American Literary Taste* (New York: Oxford University Press, 1950), 205.

5. Arthur, *Radical Innocent*, 44.

6. See the chapter by Harper Leech and John Charles Carroll, "Portrait of a Beef Baron," in their book *Armour and His Times* (New York: Norton, 1938).

7. O. A. Mather, "Armour, A Leader in Vast Growth of Meat Packing," *Chicago Daily Tribune*, August 17, 1927.

8. "Death of Armour," *Time*, August 29, 1927.

9. Sinclair, *Autobiography*, 109.

10. See http://www.hullhouse.org/aboutus/history.html.

11. Sinclair, *Autobiography*, 110.

12. Sinclair, *Autobiography*, 110.

13. Sinclair, *Autobiography*, 109.

14. Sinclair, *Autobiography*, 112.

15. Arthur, *Radical Innocent*, 70.

16. Arthur, *Radical Innocent*, 69.

17. See the chapter by Frank Doubleday, "The Story of *The Jungle*," in his *The Memoirs of a Publisher* (New York: Doubleday, 1972), 158.

18. Doubleday, "The Story of *The Jungle*," 159.

19. Doubleday, "Story of *The Jungle*," 118.

20. Doubleday, "Story of *The Jungle*," 118. The Rough Riders were a group of American volunteers who went down to Cuba to fight against Spain and ended up dying in large numbers due to rotten canned meat.

21. Sinclair, *Autobiography*, 120. Ella Reeve Bloor was an activist in the suffrage movement during the 1880s and 1890s.

22. Theodore Roosevelt to Upton Sinclair, April 11, 1906, in Upton Sinclair's *My Lifetime in Letters* (Columbia: University of Missouri Press, 1960), 16.

23. Arthur, *Radical Innocent*, 78.

24. Upton Sinclair, *The Brass Check* (Pasadena: Upton Sinclair, 1920), 27.

25. *New York Times*, May 28, 1906.

26. Mattson, *Upton Sinclair and the Other American Century*, 66. Mattson cites "With Mother Bloor in *The Jungle*," *Time*, September 3, 1951, 8. See also Upton Sinclair, "*The Jungle*'s Aftermath," *Physical Culture* (April 1910): 355.

27. *New York Times*, May 29, 1906.

28. *New York Times*, May 29, 1906.

29. James Harvey Young, "Two Hoosiers, and Two Pure Food Laws of 1906," *Indiana Magazine of History* 88 (December 1992): 303-19.

30. Theodore Roosevelt, *Theodore Roosevelt: An Autobiography* (New York: Macmillan, 1913).

31. Theodore Roosevelt, "The College Man," address delivered at Harvard Union in 1907, from Kevin Murphy, *Political Manhood: Redbloods, Mollycoddles, and the Politics of Progressive Era Reform* (New York: Columbia University Press, 2008), 1.

32. Ronald Steel, "Theodore Roosevelt, Empire Builder," *New York Times*, April 21, 2010, 10.

33. See the chapter by Goldsworthy Lowes Dickenson, "Redbloods and Mollycoddles," in his book *Appearances: Notes of Travel East and West* (New York: Doubleday, 1914), 180.

34. Sinclair, *Autobiography*, 126.

35. Jon Yoder, *Upton Sinclair* (New York: Ungar, 1975), 44.

36. Sinclair, *Autobiography*, 124.

37. Sinclair, *Autobiography*, 124.

38. Sinclair, *Autobiography*, 115. In fact, the first thing he did do was buy a saddle horse for $125.

39. Upton Sinclair to Gaylord Wilshire, 1909, Upton Sinclair MSS, Lilly Library.

40. Carl Degler, introduction to *Women and Economics*, by Charlotte Perkins Gilman (New York: Harper Torchbooks, 1966), 7.

41. Upton Sinclair, *Industrial Republic* (New York: Doubleday, 1907), 262.

42. Jo Davidson, *Between Sittings: An Informal Autobiography* (New York: Dial Press, 1951), 30.

43. Lawrence Kaplan, "A Utopia During the Progressive Era," *American Studies International* 25 (Fall 1984): 63.

44. "Colony Customs," Upton Sinclair MSS, Lilly Library.

45. Kaplan, "Utopia During the Progressive Era," 69.

46. Sinclair, *Autobiography*, 129.

47. Sinclair, *Autobiography*, 135.

48. Kaplan, "Utopia During the Progressive Era," 71.

49. Sinclair, *Cup of Fury*, 26.

50. Sinclair, *Autobiography*, 135.

51. *Reminiscences of Upton Sinclair*, 1962, pp. 77-78, CUCOHC.

52. Sinclair, *American Outpost*, 208.

53. Brown, "Not Your Usual Boardinghouse Types," 6.

54. Kevin Starr, *Americans and the California Dream* (New York: Oxford University Press, 1973), 267.

55. In 1936, Sinclair gave a talk for the Western Writers Conference at the Scottish Rite Auditorium in San Francisco—"Four California Friends: A Talk by Upton Sinclair," *Epic News*, December 7, 1936.

56. Upton Sinclair, *Plays of Protest* (New York: Mitchell and Kennerley, 1912). Sinclair would again challenge John D. Rockefeller during the coal wars in Colorado five years later.

57. John Ahouse, "Meetings in the Mind: Sinclair's Experimental Theater," *Upton Sinclair Quarterly* 8, no. 2 (1984): 5-6. The play was originally published in *Wilshire's Magazine*, January 1910.

58. Upton Sinclair to Meta, n.d., Stone MSS, Lilly Library.

59. Upton Sinclair to Meta, n.d., Stone MSS, Lilly Library.

60. Franklin Walker, *The Seacoast of Bohemia* (Los Angeles: Book Club of California, 1966), quoted in *Upton Sinclair Quarterly* 4, no. 2 (June 1980): 4-5.

61. Barbara Ehrenreich and Deirdre English, *Witches, Midwives, and Nurses: A History of Women Healers* (Brooklyn: Feminist Press, 1973).

62. K. Patrick Ober, "The Pre-Flexnerian Reports: Mark Twain's Criticism of Medicine in the United States," *Annals of Internal Medicine* 126 (January 15, 1997): 157-63.

63. Sinclair, *Autobiography*, 125.

64. Upton Sinclair, *Good Health and How We Won It* (New York: Frederick Stokes, 1909), 3.

65. T. C. Boyle, *The Road to Wellville* (New York: Penguin, 1994).

66. Harry Kemp, *Tramping on Life: An Autobiographical Narrative* (New York: Boni and Liveright, 1922).

67. Sinclair, *Autobiography*, 160.

68. Mary Craig, *Southern Belle* (Jackson: University of Mississippi Press, 1999), 61.

69. Craig, *Southern Belle*, 63.

70. Sinclair, *Autobiography*, 163.

71. Sinclair, *Autobiography*, 164.

72. Sinclair, *Love's Pilgrimage*, 345.

73. Upton Sinclair, review of *The Visioning*, by Susan Glaspell, *New York Call*, December 3, 1911.

74. See Veronica Makowsky, *Susan Glaspell's Century of American Women: A Critical Interpretation of Her Work* (Oxford: Oxford University Press, 1993).

75. Brochure quoted in Mark Taylor, "Utopia by Taxation: Frank Stephens and the Single Tax Community of Arden, Delaware," *Pennsylvania Magazine of History and Biography* 126, no. 2 (2002): 315.

76. Sinclair, *Autobiography*, 165.

77. Frank Harris, *Contemporary Portraits: Third Series* (New York: Frank Harris, 1920), 15.

78. Sinclair, *Autobiography*, 170.

79. Sinclair, *Autobiography*, 171.

80. Sinclair, *Autobiography*, 171.

81. Milholland joined the Women's Trade Union League and the National Association for the Advancement of Colored People.

82. Mattson, *Upton Sinclair and the Other American Century*, 81.

83. Sinclair, *Autobiography*, 175.

84. Craig, *Southern Belle*, 77.

85. Sinclair, *Autobiography*, 176.

86. Craig, *Southern Belle*, 134.

87. Craig, *Southern Belle*, 145.

88. Sinclair, *Autobiography*, 193.

89. Margaret Sanger to Upton Sinclair, September 14, 1914, Upton Sinclair MSS, Lilly Library.

90. Ruth Clifford Engs, ed., *The Unseen Upton Sinclair* (Jefferson NC: McFarland, 2009), 41.

91. Engs, *Unseen Upton Sinclair*, 3.

92. Engs, *Unseen Upton Sinclair*, 149, quotes *Little Algernon*: fragments, Sinclair MSS, Lilly Library, 2-3.

93. Engs, *Unseen Upton Sinclair*, 105.

94. See also Mark Lause, *The Antebellum Crisis: America's First Bohemians* (Kent OH: Kent State University, 2009).

95. Sinclair, *Autobiography*, 182.

96. Craig, *Southern Belle*, 178.

97. Craig, *Southern Belle*, 151.

98. Ahouse, "Meetings in the Mind," 53.

99. Craig, *Southern Belle*, 149.

100. For more on this tent colony from an archeological perspective, see http://archaeology.about.com/cs/military/bb/ludlow.htm.

101. *Rocky Mountain News*, April 22, 1914.

102. *The Colorado Coal Miners Strike: Industrial Relations Final Report and Testimony* submitted to Congress by the Commission on Industrial Relations (Washington DC: August 23, 1912).

103. Craig, *Southern Belle*, 152.

104. Craig, *Southern Belle*, 155.

105. Craig, *Southern Belle*, 158.

106. Craig, *Southern Belle*, 161.

107. John Graham, introduction to *The Coal War: A Sequel to "King Coal"*, by Upton Sinclair (Boulder: Colorado Associated University Press, 1976), 66.

108. Craig, *Southern Belle*, 162.

109. Open letter, n.d., Upton Sinclair MSS, Lilly Library.

110. *Appeal to Reason*, July 18, 1914, 3.

111. Sinclair, *Autobiography*, 204.

112. Craig, *Southern Belle*, 169.

113. Steven J. Ross, "How Hollywood Became Hollywood," in *Metropolis in the Making*, ed. Sitton and Deverell (Berkeley: University of California, 2001), 255.

114. Upton Sinclair, "The Movies and Political Propaganda," in *The Movies on Trial: The Views and Opinions of Outstanding Personalities in ANENT Screen Entertainment Past and Present*, ed. William Pearlman (New York: Macmillan, 1936).

115. Philip Foner, "Upton Sinclair's *The Jungle*: The Movie," in *Upton Sinclair: Literature and Social Reform*, ed. Dieter Herms (Frankfurt: Peter Lang, 1990), 151.

116. Foner, "Upton Sinclair's *The Jungle*," 150.

117. *Motion Picture World*, May 13, 1911, 1082.

118. Foner, "Upton Sinclair's *The Jungle*," 151.

119. *Kinematograph and Lantern Weekly*, November 26, 1914, 24.

120. *Variety Film Review*, vol. 1 (New York and London: Garland, 1983).

121. Film Corporation Records and Sinclair Manuscripts, Upton Sinclair MSS, Lilly Library.

122. Foner, "Upton Sinclair's *The Jungle*," 156.

123. *Appeal to Reason*, June 12, 1914.

124. Hunter Kimborough, interviewed by Robert and Genevieve Hahn, c. 1975.

125. Sinclair, *Autobiography*, 204

126. Craig, *Southern Belle*, 179.

127. Kimborough, interview by Hahn, c. 1975.

128. Arthur, *Radical Innocent*, 159.

129. Arthur, *Radical Innocent*, 160.

130. Sinclair, *Autobiography*, 213.

131. Upton Sinclair to Kate Crane Gartz, July 18, 1927, Upton Sinclair MSS, Lilly Library.

132. Frank Harris, *Contemporary Portraits*, 30.

4. Singing Jailbirds, 1916–1927

Harrison Otis, *Los Angeles Times*, June 25, 1916.

1. Cedar Phillips, *Images of America: Early Pasadena* (Charleston SC: Arcadia, 2008), 7.

2. Craig, *Southern Belle*, 198.

3. Phillips, *Images of America*, 8.

4. See http://www.usc.edu/libraries/archives/la/historic/redcars/ for more on Los Angeles interurban history.

5. Craig, *Southern Belle*, 198.

6. Craig, *Southern Belle*, 198.

7. John Ahouse, "Irving Stone Recalls Upton Sinclair: An Interview," *Upton Sinclair Quarterly* 5 (September 1981): 8.

8. Upton Sinclair, "Our Office," *Upton Sinclair's*, February 19, 1919, 16.

9. *Reminiscences of Upton Sinclair*, 1962, pp. 98-99, CUCOHC.

10. In 1926 he was ranked eighth among local players.

11. This co-op was a forerunner of those he would describe in his novel of the 1930s, *Co-op*.

12. Judson Grenier, "Upton Sinclair: The Road to California," *Southern California Quarterly* 56, no. 4 (Winter 1974): 325.

13. Tim Doweling, *Inventor of the Disposable Culture: King Camp Gillette, 1855–1932* (London: Short Books, 2001), 14.

14. Richard Bak, *Henry and Edsel: The Creation of the Ford Empire* (New York: Wiley, 2003).

15. Samuel Crowther, "Henry Ford: Why I Favor Five Days' Work With Six Days' Pay," *World's Work* (October 1926): 613.

16. Steven Watts, *The People's Tycoon: Henry Ford and the American Century* (New York: Random House, 2006).

17. Craig, *Southern Belle*, 256.

18. Craig, *Southern Belle*, 256.

19. Mary Craig Sinclair, *Sonnets* (Pasadena: Upton Sinclair, 1925). Book 1 "Sisterhood," also includes a sonnet on suffrage.

20. Paul Jordan Smith, *The Road I Came* (Caldwell ID: Caxton, 1960), 36. Paul Jordan Smith was a journalist and editor; with Floyd Dell, he translated and edited Robert Burton's *Anatomy of Melancholy* (1927).

21. For more on Sinclair heroes, see Arun Pant, "The Little Narrow Circle of Consciousness: Pink Prototype in Upton Sinclair," in *Upton Sinclair: Literature and Social Reform*, ed. Dieter Herms (Frankfurt: Peter Lang, 1990).

22. Craig, *Southern Belle*, 233.

23. Craig, *Southern Belle*, 234.

24. Upton Sinclair, *Cry for Justice* (New York and Pasadena: Upton Sinclair, 1915), 2.

25. *Reminiscences of Upton Sinclair*, 1962, p. 138, CUCOHC.

26. George Mowry, *The California Progressives* (Chicago: Quadrangle Books, 1951), 48.

27. Margaret Sanger to Upton Sinclair, February 18, 1916, Upton Sinclair MSS, Lilly Library.

28. Andrew Lee, e-mail to author, January 7, 1997. Two years earlier, Dr. Grover Furr at Montclair State University had requested assistance in finding historical materials to supplement his use of *King Coal* in his course in "Literature of Social Protest in America." But *King Coal* was out of print, and Dr. Furr was unable to assign the book to his students.

29. George Brett to Upton Sinclair, May 9, 1916, Upton Sinclair MSS, Lilly Library.

30. Mary Craig to George Brett, May l, 1916, Upton Sinclair MSS, Lilly Library.

31. Peggy Whitman Prenshaw, afterword to *Southern Belle*, by Mary Craig, 416.

32. Graham, introduction to *The Coal War*, 77.

33. Upton Sinclair, *My Lifetime in Letters*, 109.

34. Sinclair, *My Lifetime in Letters*, 192.

35. Sinclair, *My Lifetime in Letters*, 57.

36. John Dewey, quoted in Michael E. McGerr, *A Fierce Discontent: The Rise and Fall of the Progressive Movement in America, 1870–1920* (New York: Free Press, 2003), 282.

37. N. J. Slabbert, "Promoting the Universe," *Chronicle of Higher Education*, June 20, 2010.

38. Upton Sinclair, speech in Los Angeles, March 10, 1918, Upton Sinclair MSS, Lilly Library.

39. Upton Sinclair, "Lincoln and Freedom," *Pearson's Magazine*, December 1919, 659.

40. Mattson, *Upton Sinclair and the Other American Century*, 103.

41. Sir Arthur Conan Doyle to Upton Sinclair, March 29, 1918, from Sinclair, *My Lifetime in Letters*, 164.

42. Nick Salvatore, *Eugene V. Debs: Citizen and Socialist* (Urbana: University of Illinois Press, 1982), 288.

43. *Upton Sinclair's Magazine*, September 1918, 5. In 1920 Sinclair published a pamphlet called *Debs and the Poets*, to which he wrote an introduction. Ruth Le Prade, ed. (Pasadena: Upton Sinclair, 1920).

44. Patrick Renshaw, *The Wobblies: The Story of Syndicalism in the United States* (Garden City NY: Doubleday, 1967), 188.

45. Ralph Chaplin, *Wobbly: The Rough and Tumble Story of an American Radical* (Chicago: University of Chicago Press, 1948), 254. The Nearings were antiwar activists who later wrote *Living the Good Life* about their sustainable lifestyle.

46. John Keegan, *The First World War* (New York: Vintage Press, 2000).

47. *Upton Sinclair's Magazine*, October 1918, 7.

48. Sinclair, "Lincoln and Freedom," 661.

49. Sinclair, *Appeal to Reason*, June 14, 1919, 4.

50. Upton Sinclair to Woodrow Wilson, February 3, 1917, Upton Sinclair MSS, Lilly Library.

51. Upton Sinclair, "Peace and Its Meaning," *Western Comrade* (March/April 1918): 37.

52. Upton Sinclair, *Appeal to Reason*, March 18, 1922, 1.

53. Mattson, *Upton Sinclair and the Other American Century*, 111.

54. Upton Sinclair, *Appeal to Reason*, May 15, 1920, 3.

55. Utz Riese, "Contribution to a Proletarian Aesthetic," in *Upton Sinclair: Literature and Social Reform*, ed. Dieter Herms (Frankfurt: Peter Lang, 1990), 17.

56. Gertrude Atherton to Upton Sinclair, October 21, 1918, from Sinclair, *My Lifetime in Letters*, 190.

57. Upton Sinclair, *Jimmie Higgins* (New York: Boni and Liveright,1919),265.

58. Leon Harris, *Upton Sinclair: American Rebel* (New York: Thomas Crowell, 1975), 172.

59. Sachiko Nakada, *Japanese Empathy for Upton Sinclair* (Chiyoda-m Tokyo: Central Institute, 1990), 77.

60. Sinclair, *Autobiography*, 220.

61. Riese, "Contribution to a Proletarian Aesthetic," 17.

62. Sir Conan Doyle to Upton Sinclair, July 25, 1929, from Sinclair, *My Lifetime in Letters*, 166.

63. Sir Conan Doyle to Upton Sinclair, July 25, 1929, from Sinclair, *My Lifetime in Letters*, 167.

64. Arthur, *Radical Innocent*, 177.

65. John Ahouse, *Upton Sinclair: A Descriptive Annotated Bibliography* (Los Angeles: Arundel Press, 1992), 47.

66. Sinclair, *My Lifetime in Letters*, 170.

67. Luther Burbank to Upton Sinclair, September 28, 1918, from Sinclair, *My Lifetime in Letters*, 170; he also thanked Craig for sending a volume of letters written by Kate Crane Gartz, *The Parlor Provocateur*, published by Mary Craig.

68. Luther Burbank to Upton Sinclair, November 10, 1918, from Sinclair, *My Lifetime in Letters*, 172.

69. David Sinclair, interview by Leon Harris, California, 1970, Leon Harris MSS, Lilly Library.

70. Sinclair, *Autobiography*, 222.

71. Blackwell's parents were Lucy Stone and Henry Blackwell, abolitionist and feminist agitators. As their only child, they took her with them during their fifty-year campaign of lecturing for women's rights.

72. Elizabeth Blackwell to Upton Sinclair, August 21, 1919, Upton Sinclair MSS, Lilly Library.

73. Elizabeth Blackwell to Upton Sinclair, August 21, 1919, Upton Sinclair MSS, Lilly Library.

74. Arthur, *Radical Innocent*, 180.

75. Sinclair, *Brass Check*, 221 and 39.

76. Max Eastman to Sinclair, November 30, 1919, from Sinclair, *My Lifetime in Letters*, 219.

77. Sinclair, *Autobiography*, 223.

78. Upton Sinclair, *Telling the World* (London: Cobham House, 1939), 192.

79. Upton Sinclair, "Experiments in Health," in *American Outpost* (New York: Farrar and Rinehart, 1932), 221.

80. Upton Sinclair, *The Book of Life* (Girard KS: Haldeman-Julius, 1921), 5.

81. Upton Sinclair, "My Life and Diet" (1924) in *Land of Orange Groves and Jails: Upton Sinclair's California*, ed. Lauren Coodley (Berkeley: Heyday, 2004), 14.

82. John Ahouse, "Upton Sinclair's Hollywood," in *Literary L.A.*, ed. Lionel Rolfe (Los Angeles: California Classics, 2002), 257.

83. Ross, "How Hollywood Became Hollywood," 266.

84. Upton Sinclair, "Big Business and Its Movies," in *Land of Orange Groves and Jails: Upton Sinclair's California*, ed. Lauren Coodley (Berkeley: Heyday, 2004), 97.

85. Mick LaSalle, *Complicated Women: Sex and Power in Pre-Code Hollywood* (New York: Thomas Dunne Books–St. Martin's Press, 2000).

86. Ahouse, "Irving Stone Recalls Upton Sinclair."

87. Upton Sinclair, *The Goose-Step: A Study of American Education* (Pasadena: Upton Sinclair, 1922), 45-46.

88. Sinclair, *The Goose-Step*, 301.

89. John Jay Chapman to Upton Sinclair, April 6, 1923, in Sinclair, *My Lifetime in Letters*, 289.

90. Delia Spencer Williams, interview by John Ahouse, in "An Interview with Delia Spencer Williams," *Upton Sinclair Quarterly* 4, no. 3 (September 1980): 6.

91. Jack Nelson, "Upton Sinclair and Educational Criticism," in *Upton Sinclair: Literature and Social Reform*, ed. Dieter Herms (Frankfurt: Peter Lang, 1990), 75.

92. Mike Davis, "Sunshine and the Open Shop," in *Metropolis in the Making: Los Angeles in the 1920s*, ed. Sitton and Deverell (Berkeley: University of California Press, 2001), 102.

93. *San Pedro Daily Times*, October 20, 1905.

94. Craig, *Southern Belle*, 280.

95. Dieter Herms, introduction to *Upton Sinclair: Literature and Social Reform*, ed. Dieter Herms (Frankfurt: Peter Lang, 1990), 6.

96. John Ahouse to Art Almeida, February 14, 1985. Her land was at 335 South Beacon Street.

97. Art Shields, *On the Battle Lines* (New York: International Publishers, 1986), reprinted in *The Shoreline* (March 1995): 34.

98. Shields, *On the Battle Lines*, 34.

99. Shields, *On the Battle Lines*, 34.

100. Hunter Kimbrough, "Cut Out That Constitution Stuff," from the *Haldeman-Julius Weekly* (1923), cited in "The Reluctant Activist: Upton

Sinclair's Reform Activities in California 1915-1930," by Martin Zanger (PhD diss. University of Michigan, 1971), 393.

101. Mary Craig Sinclair to John Hamilton, May 31, 1923, cited in Zanger, "Reluctant Activist," 394.

102. Craig, *Southern Belle*, 286.

103. See Art Almeida, "How San Pedro killed the Wobblies," *The Californians* (July/August 1984).

104. Louis Adamic, "Upton Sinclair on Liberty Hill," excerpt from *Open Forum* 4, no. 48 (November 26, 1927), reprinted in *Upton Sinclair Quarterly* 6, nos. 1, 2 (Spring 1982): 4.

105. Louis Adamic, "Upton Sinclair on Liberty Hill," 4.

106. Paul Irving, "Southern California ACLU Born on 4th and Beacon Streets," *Random Lengths*, April 4, 1991, 1.

107. Upton Sinclair, "Open Letter to Chief Oaks," *Nation*, June 6, 1923, 6.

108. Zanger, "Reluctant Activist," 406.

109. Upton Sinclair, postscript to *Singing Jailbirds* (Pasadena: Upton Sinclair, 1924); Upton Sinclair, *The Goslings* (Pasadena: Upton Sinclair, 1924).

110. Ella Reeve Bloor to Upton Sinclair, December 17, 1929, Upton Sinclair MSS, Lilly Library.

111. Dieter Herms, "An American Socialist: Upton Sinclair," *Upton Sinclair Centenary Journal* 1, no. 1 (1978): 52.

112. Sinclair, postscript to *Singing Jailbirds*; Sinclair, *Goslings*.

113. Miriam Allen deFord to Upton Sinclair, October 7, 1924. See also http://historymatters.gmu.edu/d/93/ for an interview with deFord by historian Sherna Gluck.

114. Upton Sinclair, "Singing Jailbirds," *New Republic*, n.d., 167.

115. Edith Summers Kelly to Upton Sinclair, September 13, 1923, Upton Sinclair MSS, Lilly Library.

116. Edith Summers Kelly to Upton Sinclair, October 8, 1923, Upton Sinclair MSS, Lilly Library.

117. Charlotte Margolis, afterword to *Weeds*, by Edith Summers Kelly (New York: Feminist Press, 1982), 354.

118. Edith Summers Kelly, "Helicon Hall" (manuscript posthumously edited by Mary Byrd David), 32.

119. Priscilla Sinclair, Scrapbook, 1911–1962, Upton Sinclair MSS, Lilly Library.

120. Craig, *Southern Belle*, 301.

121. Craig, *Southern Belle*, 301.

122. Roberta Nichols, "Idyll at Station B: The Sinclairs in Long Beach," *Upton Sinclair Quarterly* 4, no. 2 (June 1980): 6.

123. Upton Sinclair, "Letter to Readers," 1926, Upton Sinclair MSS, Lilly Library.

124. Nichols, "Idyll at Station B," 7.

125. Upton Sinclair, preface to *Oil!* (Berkeley: University of California, 1997).

126. R. N. Mookerjee, *Art For Social Justice: The Major Novels of Upton Sinclair* (Metuchen NJ: Scarecrow Press, 1988), 78.

127. Sinclair, *Oil!*, 17.

128. *Long Beach Press Telegram*, May 27, 1927, 1.

129. Ahouse, "Upton Sinclair's Hollywood," 61.

130. Floyd Dell to Upton Sinclair, 1926. Sinclair, *Lifetime in Letters*, 271.

131. Floyd Dell to Upton Sinclair, 1926. Sinclair, *Lifetime in Letters*, 271.

132. Dell, *Upton Sinclair*, 186.

133. Upton Sinclair, "Fiat Justitia! A Radical Seeks Justice in Denver," *New Leader*, August, 3, 1929, 4.

134. Sinclair, "Fiat Justitia!," 4.

135. Kinzo Satomura, "Reading Jimmy Higgins," *Bungei Sensen*, February 1927.

136. Upton Sinclair, *The Movies on Trial*, compiled and edited by William J. Perlman (New York: Macmillan, 1936).

5. How I Ran for Governor, 1928–1939

Albert Einstein, translated by John Ahouse from Einstein's inscription on a photograph from 1933, in Louis Hughes, "Einstein and Sinclair: Energy Equals" *Upton Sinclair Quarterly* 3, no. 3 (September 1979): 10.

1. Upton Sinclair to Kate Crane Gartz, August 5, 1927, Upton Sinclair MSS, Lilly Library.

2. Bartolomeo Vanzetti to Upton Sinclair, October 4, 1923, from Sinclair, *My Lifetime in Letters*, 287-88.

3. Zinn, introduction to *Boston*, by Upton Sinclair, 10.

4. Ingrid Kerkhoff, "Wives, Blueblood Ladies, and Rebel Girls: A Closer Look at Upton's Sinclair's Females," in *Upton Sinclair: Literature and Social Reform*, ed. Dieter Herms (Frankfurt: Peter Lang, 1990), 188.

5. Dennis Welland, "Upton Sinclair: The Centenary of an American Writer," *Bulletin of John Rylands* 61, no. 2 (Spring 1979), 491.

6. Lewis Joughin and Edmund Morgan, *The Legacy of Sacco and Vanzetti* (New York: Harcourt, Brace 1948).

7. Richard Burton to Upton Sinclair, April 22, 1929, Upton Sinclair MSS, Lilly Library.

8. Cited by Lionel Rolfe, "Upton Sinclair's Home at the Edge of Town," November 18, 2012, http://www.dabelly.com/columns/bohemian34.htm.

9. Upton Sinclair to Kate Crane Gartz, May 6, 1929, Upton Sinclair MSS, Lilly Library.

10. Upton Sinclair to Helen Keller, July 16, 1938, Upton Sinclair MSS, Lilly Library.

11. Ella Reeve Bloor to Upton Sinclair, August 23, 1930, Upton Sinclair MSS, Lilly Library.

12. Ella Reeve Bloor to Upton Sinclair, August 23, 1930, Upton Sinclair MSS, Lilly Library.

13. Upton Sinclair, "My Lifelong Love Affair," *Personal Romances*, 1937, 66.

14. Craig, *Southern Belle*, 224-25.

15. Nichols, "Idyll at Station B," 12.

16. Mattson, *Upton Sinclair and the Other American Century*, 151.

17. Upton Sinclair, *Mental Radio* (Charlottesville VA: Hampton Roads, 2001), 24.

18. Upton Sinclair to M. K. Ghandi, November 26, 1930, Upton Sinclair MSS, Lilly Library.

19. Upton Sinclair to M. K. Gandhi, November 26, 1930, Upton Sinclair MSS, Lilly Library.

20. M. K. Gandhi to Upton Sinclair, March 7, 1932, from Sinclair, *My Lifetime in Letters*, 361.

21. Slabbert, "Promoting the Universe."

22. Upton Sinclair to Albert Einstein, February 28, 1930, Upton Sinclair MSS, Lilly Library.

23. Upton Sinclair to Albert Einstein, June 2, 1930, Upton Sinclair MSS, Lilly Library.

24. Ahouse, *Bibliography*, 69.

25. Upton Sinclair to Albert Einstein, June 9, 1930, Upton Sinclair mss, Lilly Library.

26. Upton Sinclair to Albert Einstein, November 13, 1930, Upton Sinclair mss, Lilly Library.

27. Rolfe, "Upton Sinclair's Home at the Edge of Town."

28. Leon Harris, *Upton Sinclair: American Rebel*, 267.

29. Frederick Allen, *Since Yesterday: 1929–1939* (New York: Harper and Row, 1939), 28.

30. Upton Sinclair to M. K. Gandhi, July 2, 1931, Upton Sinclair mss, Lilly Library.

31. Denise Herd and Robin Room, "Alcohol Images in American Film, 1909–1960," *Drinking and Drug Practices Survivor* 18 (1982): 25.

32. Herd and Room, "Alcohol Images in American Film," 25.

33. Bige, review of *The Wet Parade*, *Variety*, April 24, 1932.

34. Sinclair, *Autobiography*, 44.

35. For an unusual analysis of the Sinclair-Mencken friendship, see Melville Kress, "Sinclair's Friend Mencken," *Upton Sinclair Quarterly* 5, no. 2 (June 1981): 10.

36. H. L. Mencken, *Nation*, September 23, 1931, 310.

37. Edith S. Kelly to Upton Sinclair, October 11, 1931, Upton Sinclair mss, Lilly Library.

38. Two years later, Irving Thalberg would be a major factor in defeating Sinclair's candidacy for governor of California.

39. Greg Mitchell, *The Campaign of the Century* (New York: Random House, 1992), 303.

40. William Boehnel, *New York World-Telegraph*, April 22, 1932.

41. Robin Room, "The Movies and the Wettening of America: The Media as Amplifiers of Cultural Change," *British Journal of Addiction* (1988): 83.

42. Richard Watts, *New York Herald-Tribune*, April 22, 1932.

43. Regina Crewe, *American*, April 24, 1932.

44. Robin Room, "A Reverence for Strong Drink," *British Journal of Alcohol and Alcoholism* 16 (1981): 540. See also M. Grant, "Drinking and Creativity: A review of the alcoholism literature," *British Journal of Alcohol and Alcoholism* 16 (1981): 88.

45. Allen, *Since Yesterday*, 117.

46. Mina Maxfield and Lena Eggleston, *The Wet Parade* (Washington DC: Board of Temperance, Prohibition, and Public Morals, 1932), and with a foreword by Upton Sinclair.

47. Upton Sinclair to Betty Sinclair, November 21, 1932, Upton Sinclair MSS, Lilly Library.

48. Upton Sinclair to David Sinclair, 1930, Upton Sinclair MSS, Lilly Library.

49. Edmund Wilson, "Lincoln Steffens and Upton Sinclair," *New Republic* 72 (September 1932): 174.

50. Upton Sinclair, "The Golden Scenario," *Los Angeles Magazine* 39 no. 12 (December 1994). It was finally published in 1994.

51. Max Knepper, *Sodom and Gomorrah: The Story of Hollywood* (Los Angeles: End Poverty League, 1935), with a preface by Upton Sinclair.

52. Mitchell, *Campaign of the Century*, 15.

53. Arthur, *Radical Innocent*, 228.

54. Harry Geduld and Ron Gottesman, eds., *Sergei Eisenstein and Upton Sinclair: The Making and Unmaking of "¡Qué viva México!"* (Bloomington: University of Indiana Press, 1970).

55. Mattson, *Upton Sinclair and the Other American Century*, 160.

56. Mary Beard to Upton Sinclair, February 22, 1931, Upton Sinclair MSS, Lilly Library.

57. Mary Beard to Upton Sinclair, February 22, 1931, Upton Sinclair MSS, Lilly Library.

58. Upton Sinclair to Albert Einstein, October, 12, 1931, Upton Sinclair MSS, Lilly Library.

59. Hunter Kimbrough to Upton Sinclair, October 9, 1931, Upton Sinclair MSS, Lilly Library.

60. Upton Sinclair to Sergei Eisenstein, August 28, 1931, Upton Sinclair MSS, Lilly Library.

61. Upton Sinclair, *Upton Sinclair Presents William Fox* (Los Angeles: Upton Sinclair, 1933), 9.

62. The Democratic delegation was led by Gilbert Stevenson, former owner of the Miramar Hotel.

63. Arthur, *Radical Innocent*, 250.

64. *New York Herald Tribune*, September 22, 1933.

65. *New York Herald Tribune*, September 22, 1933. *The Industrial Republic* (1907) was the book to which he referred.

66. Upton Sinclair to David Sinclair, November 1933, Upton Sinclair MSS, Lilly Library.

67. James Gregory, introduction to *I, Candidate for Governor, and How I Got Licked*, by Upton Sinclair (Berkeley: University of California, 1994), 15.

68. *Will Rogers' Weekly Articles*, vol. 6 (Sayre: Oklahoma State University Press, 1982).

69. *Los Angeles Examiner*, August 29, 1934.

70. Sinclair, *I, Candidate for Governor*, 77.

71. Mitchell, *Campaign of the Century*, 99.

72. Waldo Waldron, *Today*, October 6, 1934.

73. Mitchell, *Campaign of the Century*, 3.

74. Mitchell, *Campaign of the Century*, 4.

75. Carey McWilliams, "The Politics of Utopia" in *Fool's Paradise* (Berkeley: Heyday Books, 2001), 66.

76. Fay Blake and Morton Newman, "Upton Sinclair's EPIC Campaign: For Campaign Veterans, the 1934 Gubernatorial Race Lives On," *California History*, Fall 1984, 309.

77. Lorna Smith, "My Life was Changed by Upton Sinclair," *Upton Sinclair Centenary Journal* 1, no. 1 (September 1978): 3.

78. Upton Sinclair, *Depression Island* (Pasadena: Upton Sinclair, 1935). Sinclair also hoped to see it produced as a film.

79. Mitchell, *Campaign of the Century*, 16.

80. Betty Hanson, "Upton Sinclair: Political Campaigner," *Uppie Speaks* 2, no. 2 (March 1978): 5.

81. Smith, "My Life was Changed by Upton Sinclair," 4.

82. Robert Gottlieb and Irene Wolt, *Thinking Big: The Story of the Los Angeles Times, Its Publishers, and Their Influence on Southern California* (New York: G. P. Putnam Sons, 1977), 209.

83. Ed Ainsworth, "Remembering 'Uppie,'" *Saturday Review*, September 30, 1967, 32.

84. Donald Singer, "Hollywood, Hype and Hysteria," in *Upton Sinclair: Literature and Social Reform*, ed. Dieter Herms (Frankfurt: Peter Lang, 1990), 95.

85. Upton Sinclair, "The Future of EPIC," *Nation*, November 28, 1934, 616-17.

86. Hays was appointed in 1922; the goal of the MPAA was to renovate the image of the movie industry in the wake of the Roscoe "Fatty" Arbuckle rape and murder scandal, amid growing calls for federal censorship of the movies.

87. *Hollywood Reporter*, October 26, 1934.

88. "Film Stars Being Questioned in Los Angeles Registration Row; Refuse to Aid Merriam," *San Francisco Chronicle*, November 1, 1934.

89. Mitchell, *Campaign of the Century*, 483.

90. Aimee McPherson, quoted in *Bible Call Crusader*, November 7, 1934.

91. Donald Singer, "Hollywood, Hype and Hysteria," 99, citing *San Francisco Chronicle*, September 28, 1934.

92. *Los Angeles Times*, October 15, 1934.

93. For more on Aline Barnsdall, see Norman and Dorothy Karasick, *The Oilman's Daughter* (Encino CA: Charleston, 1993).

94. *Last Will and Testament*, pamphlet, n.d.

95. Frank Hoyt, "The Magic Sinclair Button," *Upton Sinclair Quarterly* 5, no. 2 (June 1981): 3-5.

96. *Osaka Asahi Shinbun*, October 5, 1934.

97. *Pasadena Post*, November 3, 1934.

98. Mitchell, *Campaign of the Century*, 565.

99. Upton Sinclair, *Autobiography*, 276.

100. David Sinclair, interviewed by Greg Mitchell, quoted in *Campaign of the Century*, 550.

101. *Los Angeles Herald*, November 7, 1934.

102. Mitchell, *Campaign of the Century*, 565.

103. Charles Larsen, "The EPIC Campaign of 1934," *Pacific Historical Review* (May 1958).

104. Theodore Dreiser, "The EPIC Sinclair," *Esquire* (December 1934).

105. Upton Sinclair, interview by Gottesman, 61.

106. EPIC *News*, November 12, 1934.

107. Mitchell, *Campaign of the Century*, 561.

108. Philip Dunne, interview by Greg Mitchell, quoted in *Campaign of the Century*, 561.

109. Carey McWilliams, "The Politics of Utopia," 66.

110. *Reminiscences of Upton Sinclair*, 1962, p. 61, CUCOHC.

111. Orman Kimbrough to Mary Craig, n.d., cited in Craig, *Southern Belle*, 364.

112. Craig, *Southern Belle*, 364.

113. In 1918, after John Merriam, Madison Grant, and Henry Fairfield Osborn viewed the widespread destruction of the forest in Humboldt County, they had organized the Save the Redwoods League.

114. *Reminiscences of Upton Sinclair*, 1962, p. 311, CUCOHC.

115. Julia Briggs, *A Woman of Passion: The Life of E. Nesbit 1858–1924* (New York: Penguin, 1989).

116. The Harry Potter series is a best-seller; children's authors are advised that boys will only read books with male protagonists.

117. See Alison Lurie, *Don't Tell the Grownups* (New York: Avon Books, 1990).

118. Kerkhoff, "Wives, Blueblood Ladies, and Rebel Girls," 190.

119. See http://www.waterfrontaction.org/history/history_signs/early_harbor.pdf.

120. Craig, *Southern Belle*, 363.

121. Upton Sinclair to Eleanor Roosevelt, January 5, 1937, Upton Sinclair MSS, Lilly Library.

122. Alice Stone Blackwell to Upton Sinclair, October 5, 1936, Upton Sinclair MSS, Lilly Library.

123. Kerkhoff, "Wives, Blueblood Ladies, and Rebel Girls," 190.

124. Kerkhoff, "Wives, Blueblood Ladies, and Rebel Girls," 176.

6. World's End, 1940–1949

Irving Stone, *Upton Sinclair Anthology* (Culver City: Murray and Gee, 1947).

1. Upton Sinclair to Alice Stone Blackwell, January 23, 1937, Upton Sinclair MSS, Lilly Library.

2. Alice Stone Blackwell to Upton Sinclair, February 21, 1937, Upton Sinclair MSS, Lilly Library.

3. Anna Strong to Upton Sinclair, February 26, 1937, Upton Sinclair MSS, Lilly Library.

4. Elizabeth Gurley Flynn to Upton Sinclair, April 30, 1939, Upton Sinclair MSS, Lilly Library.

5. Craig, *Southern Belle*, 376.

6. Upton Sinclair to Albert Einstein, August 20, 1937, Upton Sinclair MSS, Lilly Library.

7. Upton Sinclair to Albert Einstein, August 20, 1937, Upton Sinclair MSS, Lilly Library.

8. Upton Sinclair to Albert Einstein, September 17, 1937, Upton Sinclair MSS, Lilly Library. A few years later, David and Betty divorced. David, like his father, would have one child with his first wife followed by a successful second marriage.

9. Craig, *Southern Belle*, 379.

10. Victor Reuther in *Upton Sinclair: Forgotten Rebel*, 1978, produced by Norbert Bunge, directed by Michael Martin, ARD/WDR Berlin. It was translated by Ilka Hartman in 1996.

11. Vera Brittain to Upton Sinclair, October 17, 1937, Upton Sinclair MSS, Lilly Library.

12. Kerkhoff, "Wives, Blueblood Ladies, and Rebel Girls," 189.

13. *Reminiscences of Upton Sinclair*, 1962, p. 70, CUCOHC.

14. Upton Sinclair to William Dodd, March 23, 1938, Upton Sinclair MSS, Lilly Library.

15. *Reminiscences of Upton Sinclair*, 1962, p. 71, CUCOHC.

16. *Reminiscences of Upton Sinclair*, 1962, p. 71, CUCOHC. The story is echoed in the memoir of Charles Sorenson, Ford's right- and left-hand man; Charles E. Sorensen, with Samuel T. Williamson, *My Forty Years with Ford* (New York: Norton, 1956).

17. Upton Sinclair to David Randall, November 12, 1963, Upton Sinclair MSS, Lilly Library.

18. Ahouse, *Bibliography*, 92.

19. Helen Keller to Upton Sinclair, September 12, 1938, Upton Sinclair MSS, Lilly Library. By a strange coincidence, Helen Keller acquired a dog in Japan shortly after Sinclair got his dog, Duchess. Keller introduced the Akita breed to the United States.

20. Sinclair, *Autobiography*, 327.

21. Sally Parry, "Upton Sinclair's Lanny Budd: The Allies' Secret Weapon against the Third Reich," in *Germany and German Thought in American Literature and Cultural Criticism*, ed. Peter Freese (Essen: Verlag Die Blaue Eule, 1990).

22. Michael Riherd, "Upton Sinclair: Creating World's End" (PhD diss., University of Southern California, 1978), 7.

23. Upton Sinclair, cablegram to editor of *Pravda*, October 14, 1938, Upton Sinclair MSS, Lilly Library.

24. Leon Litwack, Winthrop Jordan, Richard Hofstadter, William Miller, and Daniel Aaron, *The United States Becoming a World Power* (Englewood NJ: Prentice Hall, 1987), 663.

25. Allen, *Since Yesterday*, 257.

26. Allen, *Since Yesterday*, 257.

27. James MacGregor Burns, *Roosevelt: The Lion and the Fox* (New York: Harcourt Brace, 1956), 387.

28. Williamson Murray and Allan R. Millett, *A War To Be Won: Fighting the Second World War* (Boston: Harvard University Press, 2001), 223.

29. Robert Dallek, *Franklin D. Roosevelt and American Foreign Policy, 1932–1945* (New York: Oxford University Press, 1995), 166.

30. William E. Leuchtenburg, ed., http://millercenter.org/president/fdroosevelt/essays/biography/3.

31. Parry, "Upton Sinclair's Lanny Budd," 257.

32. Parry, "Upton Sinclair's Lanny Budd," 192.

33. Ahouse, *Bibliography*, 89.

34. Herms, "An American Socialist: Upton Sinclair," 52.

35. Upton Sinclair, "World's End Impending," published 1940, reprinted in *O Shepherd, Speak!* (New York: Viking, 1949).

36. Upton Sinclair to Fulton Oursler, December 7, 1938. Oursler also grew up poor in Baltimore, Maryland.

37. Riherd, "Upton Sinclair: Creating World's End," 248.

38. Michael Riherd, interviewed by author, July 11, 1996.

39. Craig, *Southern Belle*.

40. Upton Sinclair to Elizabeth Gurley Flynn, August 6, 1941, Upton Sinclair MSS, Lilly Library.

41. Craig, *Southern Belle*, 380.

42. John Ahouse, e-mail to author, January 30, 1997.

43. Craig, *Southern Belle*, 381.

44. George Bernard Shaw to Upton Sinclair, December 12, 1941, from Sinclair, *My Lifetime in Letters*, 65.

45. Vera Brittain to Upton Sinclair, February 16, 1940, Upton Sinclair MSS, Lilly Library.

46. Upton Sinclair to Vera Brittain, February 19, 1940, Upton Sinclair MSS, Lilly Library.

47. Address by the President of the United States, *Declarations of a State of War with Japan, Germany, and Italy*, Senate Document No. 148 (December 8, 1941).

48. Arun Pant, "The Little Narrow Circle of Consciousness: Pink Prototype in Upton Sinclair," in *Upton Sinclair: Literature and Social Reform*, ed. Dieter Herms (Frankfurt: Peter Lang, 1990), 172.

49. Theodore Dreiser, quoted in Riherd, "Upton Sinclair: Creating World's End," 24.

50. *Time* 52, no. 10 (September 6, 1948): 90.

51. Abraham Blinderman, "Perspectives," in *Critics on Upton Sinclair*, ed. Abraham Blinderman (Coral Gables FL: University of Miami Press, 1975), 83.

52. Perry Miller, "Lanny Budd Rides Again," *New York Times*, August 20, 1948.

53. Germaine Warkentin, e-mail to author, January 27, 1997. Warkentin is a professor of English at the University of Toronto.

54. Robert Hahn, "A Personal Library: Its Establishing, Nurturing, and Projection," *Upton Sinclair Centenary Journal* 1, no. 1 (September 1978): 88.

55. John Ahouse, "Edward Allatt's Collection," *Upton Sinclair Quarterly* 8, no. 4 (Winter 1984–85): 11.

56. Jeffrey Youdelman, "In Search of Lanny Budd," *San Jose Studies* 6 (February 1980): 93.

57. Youdelman, "In Search of Lanny Budd," 88.

58. Lady Bird Johnson and Hugh Sidney to Leon Harris, in *Upton Sinclair: American Rebel*, 335.

59. Lady Bird Johnson and Hugh Sidney to Leon Harris, in *Upton Sinclair: American Rebel*, 335.

60. Helen Stauffer, ed., *Letters of Mari Sandoz* (Lincoln: University of Nebraska Press, 1992).

61. Gertrude Atherton to Upton Sinclair, May 6, 1943, Upton Sinclair MSS, Lilly Library. Sinclair actually wrote a prelude to a book entitled *Inside Hitler*, by Kurt Krueger (New York: Avalon, 1942). It was republished

as *I Was Hitler's Doctor* (New York: Biltmore, 1943) with a foreword by Sinclair. Upton Sinclair MSS, Lilly Library.

62. Gertrude Atherton to Upton Sinclair, May 6, 1943, Upton Sinclair MSS, Lilly Library.

63. Thomas Mann to Upton Sinclair, January 7, 1942, from Sinclair, *My Lifetime in Letters*, 378.

64. *Los Angeles Times*, February 25, 1942.

65. Craig, *Southern Belle*, 382.

66. Craig, *Southern Belle*, 384.

67. Upton Sinclair to David Sinclair, October 23, 1942, Upton Sinclair MSS, Lilly Library.

68. Craig, *Southern Belle*, 384.

69. Craig, *Southern Belle*, 385.

70. John Chamberlain, *New York Times*, n.d., cited in Leon Harris, *Upton Sinclair: American Rebel*, 334.

71. George Bernard Shaw to Upton Sinclair, December 12, 1941, from Sinclair, *My Lifetime in Letters*, 65.

72. Upton Sinclair, "My Ten Years Hard," *John O'London's Weekly*, September 30, 1949, 1.

73. Don Wolfe, "An Evening with Upton Sinclair," *Journal of Historical Studies* 1 (1967): 265.

74. Deborah Clark, "Historical Home Stands Proud Once Again," *Sierra Madre News*, May 2, 1996, 11.

75. John Stone to Ron Gottesman, June 1, 1965, Stone MSS, Upton Sinclair MSS, Lilly Library.

76. David Sinclair to Upton Sinclair, December 18, 1944, Upton Sinclair MSS, Lilly Library.

77. John Ahouse, e-mail to author, May 10, 2010.

78. Sally Parry, "Learning to Fight the Nazis: The Education of Upton Sinclair's Lanny Budd," in *Visions of War: World War II in Popular Culture and Literature*, eds. Paul Holsinger and Mary Anne Schofield (Bowling Green OH: Popular Press, 1992).

79. Sally Parry, e-mail to author, November 20, 2011.

80. Andrew Lee, e-mail to author, March 7, 1997.

81. Perry Miller, "Mr. Sinclair's Superman Carries On," *New York Times Book Review*, June 2, 1946.

82. Sinclair, *Autobiography*, 295.

83. Sinclair, *Autobiography*, 296.

84. Delia Spencer Williams, interviewed by John Ahouse, "An Interview with Delia Spencer Williams," *Upton Sinclair Quarterly* 4, no. 3 (September 1980): 6.

85. Upton Sinclair to Eleanor Roosevelt, November 10, 1944, Upton Sinclair MSS, Lilly Library.

86. Neil Vanderbilt to Upton Sinclair, April 15, 1945, from Sinclair, *My Lifetime in Letters*, 391.

87. Neil Vanderbilt to Upton Sinclair, April 15, 1945, from Sinclair, *My Lifetime in Letters*, 392.

88. Craig, *Southern Belle*, 387.

89. Upton Sinclair to Eleanor Roosevelt, April 13, 1945, Upton Sinclair MSS, Lilly Library.

90. Upton Sinclair, *One Clear Call* (New York: Viking Press, 1948), 9.

91. Helen Taubkin, letter to author, January 29, 1997.

92. Malvin Wald, interview with author, July 23, 1996. See also Charles Higham, *Trading With the Enemy* (New York, Delacorte Press, 1983) for a detailed account of Nazi-American wartime business relations.

93. Upton Sinclair to Eleanor Roosevelt, January 4, 1946, Upton Sinclair MSS, Lilly Library.

94. Upton Sinclair, *Limbo on the Loose* (Girard KS: Haldeman-Julius, 1948), 6. This was a reissue of *The Way Out: What Lies Ahead for America*.95. Sinclair, *Limbo on the Loose*, 7.

96. George Bernard Shaw to Sinclair, September 24, 1943, from Sinclair, *My Lifetime in Letters*, 69.

97. Upton Sinclair to David Sinclair, August 10, 1950, cited in Arthur, *Radical Innocent*, 315. David would later be hired by the AEC as a research scientist in aerosol physics.

98. Craig, *Southern Belle*, 384-85.

7. A Lifetime in Letters, 1950–1968

Margaret Sanger to Upton Sinclair, February 17, 1957, Upton Sinclair MSS, Lilly Library.

1. Mattson, *Upton Sinclair and the Other American Century*. See also, Edward L. Ayers, *The Promise of the New South: Life After Reconstruction* (New York: Oxford University Press, 1992), 227.

2. Upton Sinclair to Irving Flam, August 1, 1951, Upton Sinclair MSS, Lilly Library.

3. Upton Sinclair, "U.S. Can Claim Korea Victory Without Awaiting Unification," *Battle Creek Enquirer and News*, January 18, 1954, 6.

4. Upton Sinclair to Clinton Taft, October 18, 1949, Upton Sinclair MSS, Lilly Library.

5. Upton Sinclair to Lillian Muniz, December 7, 1949, Upton Sinclair MSS, Lilly Library.

6. Upton Sinclair, "Does Capitalism Mean Freedom? That's What Eastman Says Now," *New Leader*, May 2, 1955, 18.

7. Elaine Tyler May, "Anger and Security," *Chronicle of Higher Education*, July 11, 2010.

8. Upton Sinclair to Phyllis Bottome, September 16, 1946, Upton Sinclair MSS, Lilly Library.

9. May, "Anger and Security."

10. Kerkhoff, "Wives, Blueblood Ladies, and Rebel Girls," 191.

11. Upton Sinclair to Jacob Sonderling, April 21, 1950, Upton Sinclair MSS, Lilly Library.

12. Albert Einstein to Upton Sinclair, c. 1953, from Sinclair, *My Lifetime in Letters*, 359.

13. F. S. Saunders, *USA: The Cultural Cold War: The CIA and the World of Arts and Letters* (New York: The New Press, 2000).

14. Mattson, *Upton Sinclair and the Other American Century*, 234.

15. Upton Sinclair to Allan Mordell, October 18, 1949, Upton Sinclair MSS, Lilly Library.

16. Granville Hicks, "Warmakers and Peacemakers," *New Republic* 102 (June 1940): 863.

17. Upton Sinclair to Carl Jung, August 3, 1955, Upton Sinclair MSS, Lilly Library.

18. Wolfe, "Evening With Upton Sinclair," 265.

19. Graham Berry, "Upton Sinclair near 78, and Still Crusading," *Los Angeles Times*, August 26, 1956, 6.

20. Sinclair, *Autobiography*, 253.

21. The American Medical Association declared that alcoholism was an illness in 1956.

22. Sinclair, *Cup of Fury*, 2.

23. Joel Silver, "Upton Sinclair," *Bookman's Weekly* 99, no. 6 (February 10, 1997): 374.

24. Mary Craig to David Randall, June 26, 1958, Upton Sinclair MSS, Lilly Library.

25. See http://libraries.claremont.edu/.

26. John Ahouse, e-mail to author, August 4, 1996.

27. Arthur, *Radical Innocent*, 313.

28. Jill Kerr Conway, *Written by Herself: Autobiographies of American Women* (1992); *Written by Herself: Women's Memoirs from Britain, Africa, Asia, and the United States* (1996); and *In Her Own Words: Women's Memoirs from Australia, New Zealand, Canada, and the United States* (1999).

29. *Time*, November 18, 1957.

30. Bruce Bliven, *New Republic*, December 23, 1957.

31. Mary Craig to Hunter Kimbrough, June 1955, collection of Hunter Kimbrough, courtesy of Peggy Prenshaw.

32. Letter from Mary Craig to Hunter Kimbrough, October 30, 1956.

33. Letter from Mary Craig to Hunter Kimbrough, October 30, 1956.

34. Ron Gottesman, interviews by Anthony Arthur, April 2003 and May 2004, in Arthur, *Radical Innocent*, 318, 319.

35. Upton Sinclair to Bertha Klausner, August 31, 1961, Upton Sinclair MSS, Lilly Library.

36. Sinclair, *My Lifetime in Letters*, 8.

37. Upton Sinclair, letter, *New Republic*, May 2, 1960, 24.

38. Sinclair, *Autobiography*, 318.

39. Miriam Allen deFord Shipley to Upton Sinclair, April 27, 1961, Upton Sinclair MSS, Lilly Library. She was at that time the widow of Maynard Shipley.

40. Obituary of Mary Craig Sinclair, *Jackson Clarion-Ledger*, April 1961.

41. Upton Sinclair to Mrs. Giffen, September 14, 1961, Upton Sinclair MSS, Lilly Library.

42. Richard Armour, "Matchmaker: An Interview," with John Ahouse, *Upton Sinclair Quarterly* (Spring 1982): 11.

43. Richard Armour, "Matchmaker," 12.

44. Arthur, *Radical Innocent*, 319.

45. Lorna Smith to Leon Harris, July 14, 1970, Leon Harris MSS.

46. Upton Sinclair, interview by Mike Wallace, November 25, 1963, Upton Sinclair MSS, Lilly Library.

47. Ainsworth, "Remembering 'Uppie,'" 32.

48. Ainsworth, "Remembering 'Uppie,'" 32.

49. Anthony Fellow, "Friendship under Glass: The Story of *L.A. Times* Hatchet Man and Upton Sinclair," *Upton Sinclair Quarterly*, II, no. 7 (August 1978): 3.

50. Ainsworth, "Remembering 'Uppie,'" 33.

51. Howard Fast, review, *Saturday Review*, December 1, 1962, 34. Fast had been a victim of HUAC, jailed in 1950, and then black-listed.

52. Renate von Bardeleben, "Upton Sinclair and the Art of Autobiography," in *Upton Sinclair: Literature and Reform*, ed. Dieter Herms (Frankfurt: Peter Lang, 1990), 118.

53. Ahouse, *Bibliography*, 11.

54. Ahouse, "Edward Allatt's Collection," 11.

55. The film is in the possession of Lauren Coodley as a videotape, courtesy of Edward Allatt. Filmography from Allatt, February 15, 1996.

56. Ron Gottesman, interviews by Anthony Arthur, in *Radical Innocent*, 319.

57. Ron Gottesman, interviews by Anthony Arthur, in *Radical Innocent*, 319.

58. Upton Sinclair to David Sinclair, March 15, 1963, Upton Sinclair MSS, Lilly Library.

59. Upton Sinclair to David Sinclair, December, 23, 1964, Upton Sinclair MSS, Lilly Library.

60. Upton Sinclair to David Sinclair, November 30, 1963 and April 18, 1963, Upton Sinclair MSS, Lilly Library.

61. "Upton Sinclair Speaks to Three Groups," *Indiana Daily Student*, October 19, 1963.

62. Arthur, *Radical Innocent*, 321.

63. Arthur and Lila Weinberg, "A Saintly Glow," *Washington Post*, October 19, 1964.

64. Weinberg, "Saintly Glow."

65. Sinclair, *My Lifetime in Letters*, 24.

66. Weinberg, "Saintly Glow."

67. Smith, "My Life was Changed by Upton Sinclair," 1.

68. Mario Savio, December 3, 1964, quoted in D. L. Goines, *The Free Speech Movement: Coming of Age in the 1960s* (Berkeley: Ten Speed, 1993), 122.

69. Weinberg, "Saintly Glow."

70. Weinberg, "Saintly Glow."

71. Upton Sinclair, *The Enemy Had It Too* (New York: Viking Press, 1950), 79.

72. Tony Schwartz's "daisy" ad showed a little girl picking the petals off a daisy until a nuclear bomb exploded in the background. It was one of the first examples of negative political ads on television.

73. Weinberg, "Saintly Glow." Two months before the election, Sinclair's first wife, Meta Fuller Sinclair Stone, died in Florida where she had been president of the Poetry League.

74. Bill Moyers, "How Wall Street Occupied America," *Nation*, November 2, 2011.

75. Mattson, *Upton Sinclair and the Other American Century*, 240.

76. Buffalo speech, clippings from David Sinclair, Upton Sinclair MSS, Lilly Library.

77. David Sinclair to David Randall, October 12, 1968, Upton Sinclair MSS, Lilly Library.

78. John Dorsey, "Upton Sinclair Relives His Baltimore Childhood," *Baltimore Sun*, October 10, 1965.

8. Afterword, 1969–2011

Laura Restrepo, *No Place for Heroes* (New York: Nan A. Talese/Doubleday, 2010).

1. Ryo Namikawa, "Literary Work of Upton Sinclair," *Eigo Seinen*, February 1969, cited in Sachiko Nakada, *Japanese Empathy for Upton Sinclair*, 78.

2. See Peter Monaghan, "A Scholar Takes a Literary Tour—and Wonders Why," *Chronicle of Higher Education*, October 19, 2011, for a discussion of the significance of writers' homes.

3. John Ahouse, e-mail to author, December 9, 1996. Harris had previously written for magazines including *Good Housekeeping*, and *Cosmopolitan*.

4. Hunter Kimbrough, interview by Robert Hahn, July 1992. Lauren Coodley collection. When interviewed, Hunter Kimbrough referred to Harris as "a damn liar."

5. H. Wentworth and S. Flexner, eds., *Dictionary of American Slang* (New York: Thomas Crowell, 1975), 329.

6. David Sinclair to Irving Stone, April 18, 1982, courtesy of John Ahouse.

7. Ahouse, "Irving Stone Recalls Upton Sinclair."

8. David Sinclair to Irving Stone, April 18, 1982, courtesy of John Ahouse.

9. Yoder, *Upton Sinclair*, 3.

10. Graham, introduction to *The Coal War*.

11. It was published by Robert Hahn and edited by Louis Hughes, and later by John Ahouse.

12. Muriel Freeman, "Upton Sinclair: Recalling a Muckraker," *New York Times*, December 17, 1978.

13. Freeman noted that Upton Sinclair's son continued to work, even at age seventy-seven, as an experimental physicist with the Department of Energy.

14. Letter from David Sinclair to Robert Hahn, October 31, 1978, in *Uppie Speaks* 2 (Fall 1978): [3].

15. Smith, "My Life Was Changed by Upton Sinclair," 1.

16. Smith, "My Life Was Changed by Upton Sinclair," 2. Robert Hahn wrote her obituary, "Lorna Smith, 1897–1981," *Upton Sinclair Quarterly* 4, no. 4 (December 1980): 3.

17. Robert Hahn, "Die Drei Deutschen," *Uppie Speaks* 2, no. 7 (August 1978): 6. The same issue mentions that Katherine Ainsworth had become one of California's best-known regional authors.

18. Marion Schulze, "German Reception of Upton Sinclair: A Bibliography," in *Upton Sinclair: Literature and Reform*, ed. Dieter Herms (Frankfurt: Peter Lang, 1990), 249.

19. The translation was done orally, for the purpose of this research.

20. Erich Fried, *Upton Sinclair: A Forgotten Rebel*, produced by Norbert Bunge, directed by Michael Martin, ARD/WDR (Berlin, 1978).

21. Dieter Herms, *Upton Sinclair: Amerikanischer Radikaler* (Frankfurt-am-Main: Maerz/Zweitausendeins, 1978).

22. Riherd, "Upton Sinclair: Creating World's End."

23. Ahouse, "Edward Allatt's Collection," 11.

24. Ahouse explains that additional funding arrived from David and Jean Sinclair, from Sinclair's close friend of later years, Sol Lesser, and from Lesser's grandson Stephen.

25. Andre Muraire, "Dear Diary: The Unpublished Zillions," *Upton Sinclair Quarterly* 5, no. 1 (March 1981): 4.

26. Robert and Genevieve Hahn, interview by John Ahouse, *Upton Sinclair Quarterly* 4, no. 1 (March 1980): 12.

27. Robin Room, e-mail to author, November 8, 1996.

28. Pacific Film Archive Program Notes, February 9, 1982.

29. David Wiegand, "'Prohibition' Review: When the Country Went Dry," *San Francisco Chronicle*, October 1, 2011.

30. David Oshinsky, "Temperance to Excess," *New York Times*, May 23, 2010, 20.

31. Wiegand, "'Prohibition' Review."

32. John Ahouse, "ACLU Honors Founder Sinclair," *Upton Sinclair Quarterly* 7, no. 1 (Spring 1983): 3.

33. Dieter Herms, "The Novelist and Dramatist: A Note on Upton Sinclair's Plays," *Upton Sinclair Quarterly* 7, nos. 2-3 (Summer/Fall 1983). Herms focuses his essay on his favorites from the twenty-nine published scripts: *John D*, *Singing Jailbirds*, and *Oil!*

34. According to Mime Troupe member Bruce Bawer, Herms personally guaranteed audiences and brought them to an enthusiastic German public four times during the 1980s and showed Bawer his library of Upton Sinclair's publications.

35. Mookerjee, *Art for Social Justice*, 2. Writers of sentimental fiction consciously participated in political controversies; works by Elizabeth Gaskell and others were political tools of cultural significance.

36. Mookerjee cites Walter Rideout, *The Radical Novel in the United States* (Cambridge MA: Harvard University Press, 1956), 54.

37. Eileen Bowser to Bud Lesser, in Bud Lesser, "The Rescue of *Qué viva México!*," *Upton Sinclair Quarterly* 12, nos. 1–2 (Fall 1988): 4.

38. In all, there had been forty issues published.

39. Nakada, *Japanese Empathy for Upton Sinclair*, 3.

40. Hailin Zhou, "Upton Sinclair, Guo Moruo, and Creation Society: A Route through Japan," *Chinese Cross Currents*, November 17, 2012, http://www.riccimac.org/ccc/eng/ccc74/artsandletters/article 2.

41. Lyn Goldfarb's film, *We Have a Plan*, was screened on PBS as part of The Great Depression series.

42. Lauren Coodley, "Liberty Hill Becomes a State Historic Landmark," *Dispatcher*, March 1998, 7.

43. Karen D'Souza, *San Jose Mercury News*, January 13, 2001.

44. Scholars Gray Brechin, Jules Tygiel, and Lauren Coodley moderated audience discussions after each performance.

45. Adam Bradley, "How Harry Belafonte Changed America," review of *My Song*, October 29, 2011, http://bnreview.barnesandnoble.com.

46. *Time*, June 24, 1940, 92.

47. Welland, "Upton Sinclair: The Centenary of an American Writer."

48. James Finfrock, "Killing the Messenger," *San Francisco Examiner*, January 26, 1997.

49. Robert McChesney and Ben Scott, introduction to *The Brass Check* (Urbana: University of Illinois Press, 2003), 31.

50. Sean O'Connell, "David Schwimmer Wants to Adapt Upton Sinclair's *The Jungle*," July 6, 2011, www.cinemablend.com/new/David-Schwimmer-Wants-To-Adapt-Upton-Sinclair-s-The-Jungle-25565.html.

51. "Ongoing Listeria Outbreak Illustrates the High Stakes of Food Safety Regulation," Office of Management and Budget Watch, October 12, 2011, http://www.omb.org, and Bob Egelko, "Supreme Court Favors Federal Slaughterhouse Laws," *San Francisco Chronicle*, November 10, 2011.

52. See www.jamieoliver.com/campaigns/jamies-food-revolution and www.chezpanissefoundation.org/publications.

53. See John Robbins, *Diet for New America* (Walpole NH: Stillpoint Publishing, 1987), and Frances Moore Lappe and Anna Lappe, *Hope's Edge* (New York: Jeremy Tarcher, 2002).

54. Merriam-Webster's defines "bluenose" as "a person who advocates a rigorous moral code." Synonyms: prude, moralist, Mrs. Grundy, nice nelly, puritan. See http://www.merriam-webster.com/dictionary/bluenose.

55. Stephan Ducat, interview by Lakshmi Chaudhry, October 29, 2006, http://www.alternet.org/media/20343.

56. Kerkhoff, "Wives, Blue Blood Ladies, and Rebel Girls," 192.

Index